Paralegal Handbook
California Criminal Defense Edition

The Staff of
Bakersfield Paralegal

with commentary and sample pleadings by
Roger Lampkin

Bakersfield Paralegal
1412 17th Street, Ste. 351
Bakersfield, CA 93301
(661)873-4423

Attorney Roger Lampkin
1234 L Street
Bakersfield, CA 93301
(661)633-1234

A portion of the royalties from this book
will be donated to indigent defendants and charities assisting the accused.

ISBN: 978-1-950418-00-8

TABLE OF CONTENTS

→ • • Ω • • ←

Practical Tip:
Learn how to properly use every computer program and every webpage used by your office. The day will come when something is due immediately and the only person who knows software is out of the office. You can save the day by learning how to use legal research software, how to format appellate briefs, how to electronically file documents, how to use spreadsheets, how to use forms software, how to play multiple audio and video formats, how to copy different types of computer media, and how to use the other software the office depends on before an emergency arises.

ACKNOWLEDGMENTS

Special thanks Roger Lampkin for providing some of the pleadings in this book and for reviewing and commenting on other pleadings in this book.

Many of the pleadings in this book are simplified versions of pleadings filed in the various California Courts. Others were created based on specific statutes or case law, and others were taken from ideas discussed by members of the legal community. Most of the pleadings have been filed in many different forms by many different attorneys in many different cases. As such, the original source of some of the pleadings is unknown and full credit to the original authors cannot be given.

In addition to the commentator, tips, pleadings, and ideas have been gleaned from many fine attorneys.

Would you like to be included in a future book? Send your favorite tips, motions, quotes, pointers, and ideas to Admin@661Justice.com.

→••Ω••←

"Your Honor, may I have a moment to call my paralegal?"

A. INTRODUCTION

1. What does a Criminal Defense Paralegal do?

A Criminal Defense Paralegal works under the direction of an attorney or attorneys to help criminal defendants with their cases.

The American Bar Association (ABA) defines a paralegal as "a person, qualified by education, training or work experience who is employed or retained by a lawyer, law office, corporation, governmental agency or other entity and who performs specifically delegated substantive legal work for which a lawyer is responsible."

California Business and Professions Code §6450 gives a similar definition and goes on to explain the duties of a paralegal:

> Tasks performed by a paralegal include, but are not limited to, case planning, development, and management; legal research; interviewing clients; fact gathering and retrieving information; drafting and analyzing legal documents; collecting, compiling, and utilizing technical information to make an independent decision and recommendation to the supervising attorney; and representing clients before a state or federal administrative agency if that representation is permitted by statute, court rule, or administrative rule or regulation.

In practice, a Criminal Defense Paralegal will often have many responsibilities beyond those described above, especially when working for a solo practitioner. Paralegals generally have responsibilities that may include most of the following:

a. **Interview clients.** Collect basic client information (name, address, phone, etc.) and basic facts about the case.

b. **Interview witnesses.** Obtain written or recorded statements related to the client's case.

c. **Obtain discovery.** Work with the prosecution to obtain copies of the discovery (evidence). This might include copying files,

scanning documents, or copying computer disks at the District
Attorney's office.

d. **Legal Research.** Find statutory and case law related to issues in
the client's cases.

e. **Witness Research.** Conduct criminal record checks on witnesses,
search social media for information on witnesses, etc.

f. **Jury Research.** Conduct research on potential jurors.

g. **Prepare Documents.** Type and format motions, writs, appeals,
subpoenas, and other pleadings and documents.

h. **Office Management.** Calendar cases, answer phones, manage
office files, coordinate services (phone, internet, etc.), and
otherwise handle the day-to-day business of a law firm.

i. **Interact with Legal Professionals.** Serve papers on the
prosecution and other law firms, file papers with the clerk, etc.

j. **Witness Coordination.** Serve subpoenas, arrange for witness
transportation, arrange witness appearance times, etc.

k. **Inmate Services.** Arrange for clothes for inmates to wear during
trial, deliver documents to inmates, collect DNA samples from
inmates, and schedule visits for other legal professionals.

l. **Transcription.** Listen to and type transcripts of 911 calls, witness
interviews, jail calls, and other audio files.

m. **Conduct Administrative Hearings.** Represent clients before
administrative law judges in Department of Motor Vehicle
hearings, Labor Board hearings, Worker Compensation hearings,
and other such administrative hearings when the law specifically
allows them to do so.

n. **Suggest Strategy to the Attorney.** Suggest which motions to file,
which witnesses to call, what evidence to use, and how the attorney
can best help the client.

2. What does a Criminal Defense Paralegal not do?

More important than knowing what a Criminal Defense Paralegal does is knowing what a Criminal Defense Paralegal does NOT do. A paralegal is a support person to an attorney. The attorney is in charge of the cases, and the attorney is the person who will use his knowledge, education, experience, and skill to control the case. All legal work performed by the paralegal will be under the supervision of an attorney, which means that there are many things a paralegal can NOT do.

A paralegal cannot practice law; however, the term "practice law" is not defined in any California statute, so there are some ambiguities in what constitutes the practice of law.

The California Supreme Court has provided some guidance "[A]s the term is generally understood, the practice of the law is the doing and performing services in a court of justice in any matter depending therein throughout its various stages and in conformity with the adopted rules of procedure. But in a larger sense, it includes legal advice and counsel and the preparation of legal instruments and contracts by which legal rights are secured although such matter may or may not be depending in a court." (*People v. Merchants Protective Corp.* (1922) 189 Cal. 531, 535)

However, the California Supreme Court has also expressed difficulty in determining whether some acts do or do not constitute the practice of law:

> "It must be conceded that ascertaining whether a particular activity falls within this general definition may be a formidable endeavor. In close cases, the courts have determined that the resolution of legal questions for another by advice and action is practicing law if difficult or doubtful legal questions are involved which, to safeguard the public, reasonably demand the application of a trained legal mind. Less perplexing is the determination of whether participation on behalf of another in hearings and proceedings before a board or commission constitutes the practice of law. The cases uniformly hold that the character of the act, and not the place where it is performed, is the decisive element, and if the application of legal knowledge and technique is required, the activity constitutes the practice of law, even if conducted before an administrative board or commission." (*Baron v. City of Los Angeles* (1970) 2 Cal. 3rd 535; internal citations omitted)

Attorney Roger Lampkin provided the following list of suggestions:

a. **Do NOT be ambiguous in introductions.** When meeting a new client, introduce yourself with your position and clarification of your role, such as "I'm Maria, a paralegal at the firm. I assist Mr. Lampkin."

b. **Do NOT be ambiguous on the phone.** At the earliest appropriate opportunity during a phone call, explain your role. Callers to a law firm often immediately begin soliciting legal advice, such as, "my car was rear-ended, and the airbag broke my nose, how much do you think my case is worth?" Answering such questions might be the practice of law. A bad option is to answer with something like, "we got $100,000 for someone with a similar case." A good option would be to reply with something like, "the attorney would have to talk to you and evaluate the case. I'm his paralegal. May I set an appointment for you?"

c. **Do NOT be ambiguous on the paper.** If you have a business card, it should contain your title as should any other paper seen by clients that contains your name.

d. **Do NOT appear in court.** While this appears obvious, it is at times problematic. Judges become accustomed to seeing people who regularly frequent the courtroom, so a judge may address a paralegal with a simple question, "we are at the end of the calendar. Could you stand-in for Mr. Lampkin just to put his continuance on the record?" It is common for attorneys to stand-in for one another on uncontested matters. For the sake of efficiency, judges often grab the nearest attorney to stand-in for an absent attorney because the stand-in does little more than stand. The stand-in needs no knowledge of the case or even of the proceedings. He simply stands while the court puts some matter on the record. Logically, anyone or anything can stand-in, even a puppy, because the stand-in does nothing. Legally, only an attorney can stand-in. Don't fall into the trap of appearing in court, even as a stand-in.

e. **Do NOT set fees.** An attorney, not a paralegal, must set fees for legal services. If the attorney provides the paralegal with a specific fee schedule (e.g., $5,000 deposit on all family law cases; $6,000 retainer for a retainer on a first time DUI with no accident), the paralegal can inform the client of the fees. Otherwise, the client must get a fee quote from the attorney.

f. **Do NOT solicit clients.** It would be natural for a paralegal to wish to help his employer find new clients; it would be illegal for the paralegal to hang out at the hospital emergency room to tell accident victims to retain the attorney. The attorney should first give approval before the Criminal Defense Paralegal makes any attempts to help the attorney find clients.

g. **Do NOT give legal opinions.** An extremely common question posed to paralegals is, "do I have a good case?" A good answer would be, "let's ask the attorney." It is extremely common for clients to ask paralegals for legal opinions. Be polite, but avoid the answer, no matter how obvious. It may be obvious that the search of a defendant's home was illegal, but that is for an attorney to argue and the judge to decide. The paralegal should only share his legal opinions with his supervising attorney – not the clients.

h. **Do NOT gossip about cases.** Some criminal cases are extremely exciting. In some of the more sensational cases, the media often gets the facts wrong. It is tempting to tell friends and family members the true facts. Don't do it. Keep anything you learn about a client to yourself.

i. **Do NOT accept undisclosed gratuities.** A good criminal defense paralegal has a valuable commodity – access to defendants. Some people may try to capitalize on this commodity by offering the paralegal improper gratuities. A bail bondsman, attorney, or expert witness may offer gratuities to paralegals who help them find clients. Such gratuities are usually, but not always, unethical. Anytime anyone other than your employer offers you any form of gratuity, inform your supervising attorney and get clarification as to whether or not you can accept it.

j. **Do NOT have undisclosed conflicts of interest.** If you are related to the defendant, you previously helped a witness in the case, the defendant harmed someone you love, you would in any way benefit from the defendant being convicted, or you hate the defendant just because of the accusations against him, you probably have a conflict of interests. If you are in any way hesitant about giving your full efforts to the defense of the accused, tell your supervising attorney. Your supervising attorney will decide whether the conflict is significant enough to warrant your removal from the case.

3. Additional help

Electronic versions of the pleadings in this book are available at BakersfieldParalegal.com and at 661Justice.com.

Consider obtaining copies of other books published by Legal Research Services, such as *Handbook for the Accused*, *California Criminal Defense Motions in Limine*, or *Passing Time While Doing Time*.

Visit some of the web pages maintained by Legal Research Services including:

- BakersfieldParalegal.com – Bakersfield Paralegal's home page
- 661Justice.com – Legal Research Services' home page
- TheMentorCompany.com – Get help publishing your own book
- ProPerKits.com – Free legal forms and information
- KernSeminars.com – Free legal help seminars
- AttorneyScreening.com – Network of attorney screening sites
- RogerLampkin.com – Attorney Roger Lampkin
- BakersfieldDivorce.com – Divorce and family law services
- KernEviction.com – Eviction services
- BakersfieldService.com – Process service throughout California

B. CONTACT CAVEATS

A Criminal Defense Paralegal will have many contacts with defendants, defendant family members, witnesses, investigators, experts, and other people. The following suggestions are offered about how to conduct yourself during such contacts. Review these suggestions with your supervisor to ensure that the suggestions conform to your firm's policies.

1. Be polite

Be polite and respectful to everyone who comes in contact with you.

Dan Derty is accused of raping a dozen babies. He made videos of everything he did, and he made a full confession. He also pushed an old lady into oncoming traffic as she crossed the street, and he laughed about it. When he calls from the jail to talk to his attorney, it is tempting, frankly nearly irresistible, to tell him how you feel about his case and your wishes for his future. Don't do it. The clients who call and visit are <u>clients</u>, not enemies. They, and their family and friends who may call about them, should be treated with respect. You may not respect them, and you may be shocked by the accusations against them, but you should respect the process and understand that clients are always presumed innocent until proven guilty. Try to keep this in mind when speaking with clients, potential clients, and anyone else who calls or comes to the office.

2. Avoid predictions

In the world of criminal defense, the converse to the problem of being rude is often the problem of being too encouraging because it can border on predicting a case outcome.

Amy's husband, a chronic alcoholic and methamphetamine addict, came home from his date with a hooker and decided to beat her to death. Fortunately, Amy, a volunteer at the homeless center and a youth minister, had a gun that was left to her by her father, a Medal of Honor recipient, so she was able to defend herself with the unfortunate result of accidentally killing her evil husband. Unfortunately, the police arrested her for murder, and you work for her attorney. It is tempting to tell her things like "we'll get you off" or "these charges will never stick."

Don't do it. Amy is a client, not a friend. The true facts leading to the death of her husband may never be fully known, and it is not your job to judge the facts that are known to you. Your job is to serve as her paralegal. Don't share your opinion of her case with her, her family, or her friends. Let the attorney be the one who gives her an opinion of her chances at trial.

3. Give a positive answer

People will often call a law firm and request information that you should not give, such as the attorney's private number, or cannot give, such as how a judge will rule. It is best to give a positive answer to such questions when possible. A positive answer is less confrontational and tends to put an end to the matter.

If asked a question like, "Where is Mr. Green?" don't answer with something like, "I don't know" or "he's in the restroom." It is better to answer with something like, "I will try to track him down and give him your message" or "let me try to take message with enough details that he can be prepared when he calls you back." If you answer, "I don't know," the person may lose some faith in your abilities, the firm's calendaring system, or your firm's dedication to the case. If you answer with Mr. Green's location, the caller may decide to show up at that location and interrupt whatever Mr. Green is doing. By answering that you "will try" and offering to take a message you are not committing to finding Mr. Green at any specific time, and you are not committing Mr. Green to take any immediate action. Naturally, you will want to let the caller know if Mr. Green is on vacation, in trial, or otherwise unavailable to return calls in a timely manner.

If asked, "What is Mr. Green's cell number?" it is better to answer, "I will ask him to get that to you the next time I speak with him" instead of answering, "I'm not allowed to give that." The first answer does not imply that you have the number, but it does indicate that you will try to help the caller get the desired information.

If asked, "Why is this case taking so long?" it is better to answer, "Mr. Green likes to be fully prepared. I'll ask him to talk to you about it," instead of answering, "I have no idea," "Mr. Green has a lot of cases," "Mr. Green is a very busy man," "The courts are really backed up," or "It is always like this." "I have no idea" makes it seem like the firm doesn't know what they are doing. "Mr. Green has a lot of cases" and "Mr. Green is a very busy man" implies that Mr. Green does not have adequate time to represent this client properly. "The courts are really backed up" and "It is always like this" implies a lack of control over the process.

Try to ensure that your answers are positive, convey a desire to help, avoid disclosing matters that should not be disclosed, and defer substantive answers to the attorney.

4. Avoid promises

Often, defendants will ask that an attorney, investigator, or another member of the defense team visit them in jail. More often, defendants will request copies of discovery. Defendants may ask that certain witnesses be interviewed, certain motions be filed, or certain defenses be pursued. When these defendants ask you to cause these things to happen, it is tempting to respond to such seemingly reasonable requests with answers like, "the attorney will visit you this week" or "I'll have the discovery delivered to you." Don't fall for this trap. The correct answer to almost every request is, "I'll pass your message along and express your concerns."

5. Protect your personal information

Some firms use the full names of employees on advertising, web pages, and business cards, and some paralegals have been known to correspond with defendants, become friends on social media, or otherwise share personal information with defendants. This can lead to problems.

The names have changed to protect the paralegals, but the following paraphrase interactions between paralegals and clients are the reason we warn against disclosing too much personal information.

Karen and Kevin

While in custody, Keven telephoned his attorney's office, and Karen answered the phone using her full name. Her name is unique enough that Kevin's sister was able to find Karen's Facebook page and share information from it with Kevin, including that Karen's husband worked on an offshore rig. During a later phone call, Keven commented that Karen must get lonely with her husband away from home so often. Fortunately, Karen deleted her Facebook account, refused to accept calls from Kevin, stopped letting clients know her full name, and learned from her mistake.

Elaine and John

Elaine chatted with John, an inmate. John was very friendly and handsome, and there was no danger of him ever meeting with Elaine because he was serving a life sentence, so Elaine agreed to write to him in prison. Things went well for a while, and they each wrote about one letter a week, but then Elaine started getting letters from other inmates that John had told about Elaine. Some of the letters asked Elaine for help with legal forms, help looking up cases, and other matters related to paralegal work. Being a kind person, she often replied and tried to help. Soon she was corresponding with a dozen inmates, and then some began asking her to perform tasks that can only be performed by an attorney. Others asked her to put money on their books, and some asked her to buy books for them.

Things got worse. Elaine got a call from the sister of an inmate she had written to.

The sister asked to use Elaine's address as the inmate's parole address because the sister lived next to a school, and he was not allowed to parole there. Then a former inmate showed up at her door seeking a handout. He wasn't even someone she had written to, but he had heard about how helpful she was. Elaine moved to a different apartment but forwarded her mail, so some inmates found her again. Even though she stopped responding, it was more than a year before the letters stopped.

6. Be skeptical about sad stories

In-custody defendants will often have compelling, sad stories that are used to convince law firm employees to do their bidding. These stories may sometimes be true but are often simply scams, such as the following.

Withdrawal will kill me.

When paralegal Paul visited Sally at the jail just days after her arrest, she looked terrible. She was shaking and in obvious pain. Sally explained that she used to be a heroin addict, but she abandoned that lifestyle, so she is now on prescription Suboxone. She has been going through withdrawals because the jail won't give her the required medicine until she sees a doctor.

Paul saw her again the next day, and she looked even worse. Sally explained that she had diarrhea and vomiting and that without her medicine, she would die but she couldn't get an appointment with the jail doctor for two weeks. She would be dead by then. Sally had a way to save her life – Sally's sister would give Paul enough of Sally's medicine to keep her alive until she could see the doctor.

This sad story has been repeated many times, and even attorneys have fallen prey to it. A Bakersfield attorney succumbed to similar pressure from an inmate, but his attempt to do a good deed led to his arrest, conviction, and disbarment.

Grandma is dying.

Paralegal Paula saw that Defendant Dan was crying as he waited for their conference in the private meeting room. When guards finally opened the door to let her in, Dan explained that his grandmother was in the hospital dying. Dan couldn't call her there even though he had money on his books because the hospital wouldn't take his calls. If only he could borrow Paula's phone for a minute or two, he could say his last good-byes to grandma. Paula succumbed, and Dan made the call, but not to grandma. He called a friend who was scheduled to surrender and go into custody. The friend agreed to bring certain items to Dan by hiding the items in his body. Grandma was healthy and happy that Dan was in custody instead of stealing from her.

Oops, too many zeros.

Defendant Donny told Paralegal Paul that he needed money on his books, but the jail only allows a maximum of $200 total. Donny's mother isn't in town to put money on his books, so Donny had asked her to mail a money order to Paul so he could cash it and put the money on his books. Mom even added $20 as a gift to thank Paul for his efforts.

Unfortunately, Donny's mother doesn't hear very well, and she isn't very good with technology, so instead of ordering a money order for $220, she ordered one for $2,200. Paul received the money order for $2,200.

Paul is honest, and he would never take advantage of such an error, so he asks Donny what to do. Donny apologizes for the error and suggests that Paul put $200 on Donny's books, keep $200 for his efforts, and send a check for the balance, $1,800 back to mom so she will have enough money to pay her rent, buy food, and buy her medication. Without the money that was sent in error, she will probably be homeless, starving, and in constant pain because she doesn't have her medication.

Paul agrees, so Donny's girlfriend (posing as his mother) gets $1,800, Donny gets $200 on his books, and Paul has been scammed out of a total of $2,000. The money order is a forgery. Paul's hopes of getting an easy $200 led to a $2,000 loss.

Money in the works.

Other common stories involve money in the works (defendant is the beneficiary of a trust, defendant is getting money from an insurance settlement, defendant is set to inherit millions, defendant has a winning lottery ticket, etc.), don't fall for it. If a defendant has money to give someone, let him give it to the attorney and the attorney will decide what to do with it.

Help with bail and get extra money.

Defendant David is a welder for a high-tech company that is working on the Mars shuttle for Elon Musk. There are few such qualified welders in the world, so David is paid $400 an hour for his efforts.

His bail is only $50,000, and he can easily pay the $1,000 deposit. Unfortunately, all his assets are tied up in offshore accounts, so he needs a cosigner for his bail.

If only you, a trusted paralegal, will help him, he will give you an extra $2,000 for your troubles. The total bail premium, $4,000, is nothing compared to his extraordinary hourly rate. He'll have the premium paid off in less than two days. It is petty cash to him when he is working, but he can't work if he is in jail. If you just sign where requested, he will be out of custody, and you will be $2,000 richer - if only it were all true.

David isn't actually a great welder, but he has seen someone weld - once. He has also heard of the Mars shuttle, but with a sixth-grade education, he doesn't know what all the fuss is about. His family did come up with the $1,000 deposit for his bail, but he needs to trick someone into agreeing to pay the remainder of his $50,000 bail. An agreement to cosign on bail is usually an agreement to pay all fees owed, including the full bail amount if the defendant fails to appear in court. If you sign for David's bail, he plans to visit his sister in Yemen and let you worry about how you will come up with the $50,000 he tricked you into paying.

Under this scenario, you'll probably only be required to pay $49,000. $50,000 would be too much.

7. Get consent before disclosing information

Defendant Dave appears to be in big trouble. He is accused of harming his children. Fortunately, his wife appears to be sympathetic, so she calls to ask about his defense. She explains how desperate she is to help the defendant, her loving husband, and she will do anything to help him. Unfortunately, she really wants him to burn in hell, so she only called so she can use any information she gained against him.

Do not discuss a client's matter with anyone outside the defense team without the express consent of the defendant's attorney.

8. Always have pen and paper close at hand.

Always carry pen and paper with you. Keep 3" x 5" cards, post-it notes, phone message pads, a notebook, or even pieces of folded up copy paper in your purse or pocket at all times along with a few pens.

When answering the phone, immediately jot down the name of the caller and the number shown on caller id. When speaking with anyone about a case, take notes. When attending a hearing, take notes. Take notes. Take more notes. Faded ink is better than a faded memory.

9. Remember who you don't work for

Many people who recognize you as a Criminal Defense Paralegal will, without expectation of giving you any compensation for your efforts, attempt to give tasks to do for their benefit. You don't work for these people. You don't have to do their bidding – you shouldn't do their bidding.

Defendants and defendant family members will demand that you make copies of discovery for them. Investigators and experts will make similar demands. Your family and friends will pepper you with legal questions and requests for you to complete pleadings and forms for them.

Don't let clients and their family take advantage of your time. When clients want you to do something for them, simply defer to your boss, the attorney.

When investigators and experts ask you to make copies, fetch coffee, bring items to them, or do anything else, defer to the attorney with comments like, "I have a list of things Mr. Smith has given me to do, shall I ask him if I can add your request to the list?"

Often you will be asked to give legal opinions on subjects that you know nothing about, such as "do I have to register my boat under the Treaty of Victorovna if I take it from an American port to a Mexican port because I registered the boat under the Venezuelan flag after registering my tax certificate in Portugal and my sailor's license in Chile?" Such bizarre questions are easy to answer if you remember who you work for. The answer is, "I'm a paralegal, but let me see if I can get you an appointment with the attorney so you can get a better answer than I could ever give..." Such an answer often forestalls further inquiries, but the odds of terminating the conversation can be greatly increased by mentioning money, "...Mr. Jones sometimes gives a discount off of his normal consultation fee, so you may want to ask him if you qualify for one of the discounts."

10. Don't get attached

It is a sad fact that most of those who are accused will be convicted. The majority of those convicted are guilty, but many are clearly innocent. This means that many of the defendants you work with will be sent to prison; some will be killed in prison, and some will take their own lives to avoid prison. Keep your relationships with clients cordial and professional but distant.

C. IMPORTANT TERMS

The exact meaning of certain legal terms may be important for a paralegal to know in relation to a case, but such would be a rare occurrence. Most of the time a paralegal doesn't need a deep understanding of a legal term – an understanding of current usage is enough. A good legal dictionary, such as *Black's Law Dictionary*, will have an exhaustive list of legal terms and is probably sitting, gathering dust, on a shelf in the office of an attorney you work with. While Black's is authoritative, respected, and exhaustive, it is rarely necessary for a paralegal to resort to such a tome. Rather, there is a small set of critical legal terms a paralegal should understand, and the paralegal should be available to find definitions for other terms using free online resources.

A list of essential legal terms criminal defense paralegals should understand is below, but definitions of other terms can be quickly found using one of the many free online dictionaries, such as:

- Lectric Law Library - lectlaw.com/def.htm
- Duhaime - duhaime.org
- FindLaw Legal Dictionary - dictionary.findlaw.com
- Nolo's Dictionary of Law Terms and Legal Definitions - nolo.com/dictionary
- The People's Law Dictionary - dictionary.law.com
- The Free Dictionary - legal-dictionary.thefreedictionary.com

The explanations below are greatly simplified. Some of the terms have wide use in a legal setting, but the explanations provided are limited to their application in criminal proceedings.

Accessory

Someone who helps another person commit a crime or hide the fact that a crime has been committed. An accessory is usually not physically present during the crime.

Example: John murders Mary and later tells Amy what he did. To help John, Amy takes the murder weapon from John and throws it into the canal. Amy is an Accessory to the murder.

Accomplice

Someone who helps a person commit a crime. An accomplice is guilty the same as if he personally committed the offense.

Example: John tells Amy that he wants to murder Mary. Amy drives John to Mary's house, but she stays in the car while he does the deed. Mary is an Accomplice to the murder of Mary.

Appeal

An appeal is a review of a case by a higher court. Felony convictions in Superior Court are reviewed by the Court of Appeal. Misdemeanor convictions in Superior Court may be reviewed by the Appellate Division of the Superior Court or by the Court of Appeal. An appeal can only be taken from a final order of the court. Interim orders, such as rulings on motions, are generally not appealable (see Writ). Final orders include rulings such as:

- Verdict after court or jury trial (*Penal Code §1237(a)*)
- Ruling on a contested violation of probation (*Penal Code §1237(b)*)
- Denial of a motion to suppress evidence, but only after the defendant is otherwise convicted (*Penal Code §1538.5(m)*)
- An improper sentence after a valid plea (*Rules of Court, rule 8.304(b)*)
- An improper calculation of custody credits, but only if "the defendant first presents the claim in the trial court at the time of sentencing, or if the error is not discovered until after sentencing [and] the defendant first makes a motion for correction of the record in the trial court" (*Penal Code §1237.1*)
- A plea bargain, but only if "The defendant has filed with the trial court a written statement, executed under oath or penalty of perjury showing reasonable constitutional, jurisdictional, or other grounds going to the legality of the proceedings. [and] The trial court has executed and filed a certificate of probable cause for such appeal with the clerk of the court." (*Penal Code §1237.5*)

Acquittal

A finding that the defendant is not guilty.

Advance

To move a matter forward in time. For example, advance a trial from January 24 to January 13. (see Continuance; see Trail)

Arbuckle Waiver

If a defendant enters a plea, the judge who takes the plea must be the sentencing judge unless the defendant waives that right. The waiver of the right to have the plea judge be the sentencing judge is called an Arbuckle Waiver.

Arraignment

An arraignment is the proceeding where a defendant is advised of the charges against him, and he enters a plea to the charges. If the defendant is already represented by an attorney, reading of the charges will usually be waived.

The most common pleas are "guilty," "not guilty," and "no contest." A defendant may also demurrer to the charges or enter a plea of not guilty by reason of insanity. A "no contest" plea is treated the same as a "guilty" plea for most purposes.

The arraignment often involves other matters, such as:
- The court may ask the defendant if he can afford an attorney, and the court will appoint an attorney for the defendant.
- The Public Defender or other assigned attorney may declare a conflict and request that a different attorney be assigned to the defendant.
- The court may play a video recording explaining defendants' rights and the court process.
- The court may set or change bail.
- The court may set future court dates.
- Defendant or his attorney may request discovery from the court or from the District Attorney, and discovery may be provided.

Bench Trial

A trial by the judge alone without a jury.

Boykin/Tahl Advisement

Before a defendant enters a plea of guilty or no contest, the court is required to ensure that the plea is knowing and voluntary. The court must (1) advise defendant of his constitutional rights to a jury trial, to confront witnesses against him, and against self-incrimination, and (2) obtain defendant's waivers of those rights.

These rules were established in the cases of *Boykin v. Alabama* (1969) 395

U.S. 238, 243-244 (Boykin) and *In re Tahl* (1969) 1 Cal. 3rd 122, 130-133 (Tahl).

A failure to give these admonishments and obtain waivers may still be harmless if the record shows the plea was voluntary and intelligent under the totality of the circumstances, but most courts orally give the Boykin/Tahl Advisement along with other advisements or the court may require the defendant to complete and sign a form containing the advisements.

Brady Material

Evidence that is favorable to the defendant's case, either helpful in defending the charges or helpful in reducing punishment.

Cervantes Motion

A request for "judicial determination of the appropriateness, the amount, if any, and the terms of payment of restitution" as described in *People v. Cervantes* (1984) 154 Cal. App. 3rd 353.

Circumstantial Evidence

Evidence that requires an inference. This is generally all evidence other than eyewitness testimony regarding the actual crime. Circumstantial evidence is admissible and is often the only evidence available in a criminal case.

Examples: fingerprints, DNA, a witness who sees the defendant near the crime scene.

Complaint

A Complaint is the initial charging document. It contains a list of the charges and enhancements against the defendant. (See "Information")

Concurrent Sentence

Sentences for different crimes are served at the same time. Example, a two-year sentence concurrent with a four-year sentence would only require the defendant to serve the four-year sentence.

Consecutive Sentence

Sentences for different crimes are served one after another. Example, a two-year sentence consecutive to a four-year sentence would require the defendant to serve the four-year sentence then serve the two-year sentence.

Continuance

A continuance is a request for more time. It is a request that the court move a hearing to a later date. (see Advance; see Trail)

Conference

Conferences are generally for two purposes – negotiate a settlement and/or set dates for additional hearings. Conferences go by many names, such as Preliminary Hearing Setting Conference, Pre-Preliminary Hearing, Status Conference, Readiness Conference, or Trial Setting Conference.

Corpus Delicti

Tangible evidence that a crime has been committed, such as a dead body. The Corpus delicti rule requires that before a defendant's confession may be used against him at trial, there must be some evidence that a crime was committed.

Cruz Waiver

A Cruz Waiver, from the case of *People v. Cruz* (1988) 44 Cal. 3rd 1247, allows a defendant to be released from jail pending sentencing based on his promise to appear for sentencing. The waiver is made after a defendant enters into a plea bargain. If the defendant fails to appear for sentencing, he may receive a sentence greater than the one agreed to in the plea bargain. The maximum allowable sentence for the charges pled to may be imposed, even if that sentence is greater than that allowed by the original plea bargain.

Deferred Entry of Judgment

The defendant enters a plea but is not sentenced until a future date. If the defendant meets certain requirements by that date (complete a drug program, complete anger management classes, etc.) the case will be dismissed or the sentence reduced depending on the terms of the original plea bargain.

Demurrer

A demurrer is a document claiming that the allegations in the document charging defendant (the Complaint, Indictment, or Information) does not properly allege a crime or that the court is otherwise without authority to proceed. A demur is the objection in the demurrer. The demur claims that the charging document is not sufficient to establish that defendant's conduct criminal, adequately described, and committed within the jurisdiction of the court.

The demur is the actual objection, and the demurrer is the pleading containing the demur.

Discovery

The evidence concerning a case is called discovery.

Duces Tecum
See "Subpoena"

e.g.

Abbreviation for the Latin phrase exempli gratia, meaning "for example." It is used to introduce examples, as in "Dave had many animals (e.g. chickens, goats, and sheep)."

Enhancement

A fact that if proven will increase the punishment for a crime. Common enhancements are personal use of a firearm, infliction of great bodily injury, or that the crime was committed for the benefit of a gang.

et seq.

Abbreviation for the Latin phrase et sequens, meaning "and the following." "*Penal Code §290*, et seq." refers to *Penal Code §290* and the sections following it.

Ex Parte

A communication between one party and the court without involvement of the other party. As examples, police obtain an ex parte search warrant from the court – the defendant has no say in the matter. The defense obtains an ex parte order appointing a private investigator to assist with the case – the prosecution has no say in the matter.

Ex Post Facto

Latin phrase meaning "after the fact." It is used to describe an act that was not criminal at the time it was committed, but became a crime at a later date, the punishment for the crime was increased, or the standard of proof was decreased. Examples:

Dave was arrested for DUI on December 31, 2020. On January 1, 2021, the legislature lowered the blood alcohol limit from .08 to .06. If Dave was tried under the .06 standard, it would be easier for the state to obtain a conviction. This would be an ex post facto law.

Dan legally buys his prescriptions from Canada, but before the prescriptions arrive, a new law is passed making it illegal to purchase prescriptions from out of the country. If Dan were charged, he could argue that the law is ex post facto because he did not commit any crime when he placed the order – the conduct was criminalized after he committed the act required for the crime.

Exculpatory

Evidence that helps the defendant is exculpatory. Evidence that tends to harm the defendant is inculpatory.

Extant

Something extant is in existence and available as in, "The witness to the incident is extant." The witness is readily available. This term is often used in the negative, such as "The document is not extant" meaning that the document is currently missing.

Grand Jury

A group of people appointed to hear evidence and determine if there is probable cause to believe that a crime has been committed and that the defendant has committed the crime. They meet secretly and have evidence presented to them by the District Attorney. Most cases in California are prosecuted using a Preliminary Hearing in front of a judge, but some cases still go before a Grand Jury.

Habeas Corpus

A Writ of Habeas Corpus, commonly referred to as simply Habeas Corpus, is an order to bring a person to court so that the court may determine whether it is proper to hold the person in custody. The document used to request the Writ is a Petition for Writ of Habeas Corpus, commonly called a Habeas Petition. There is rarely a reason to file a Habeas Petition until a defendant has been convicted and had his conviction reviewed on appeal.

Harvey Waiver

When sentencing a defendant, the judge is only allowed to consider the charges the defendant is actually convicted of. The judge cannot give any consideration to charges that have been dismissed. A Harvey Waiver abandons this rule and allows the judge to consider dismissed charges when deciding on an appropriate sentence or restitution.

i.e.

Abbreviation for the Latin phrase id est, meaning "that is." The term is used to clarify an existing statement or idea and can be used as a substitute for "in other words," "namely," "specifically," or "that is to say." "Dave was at his mother's house, i.e. his alibi was established."

Ibid.

Short for "ibidem" in Latin, meaning "the same place." Used to indicate that the citation being referenced is the same as the last citation referenced and at exactly the same place. For example, *People v. Jones* is cited in one paragraph and again in the next paragraph without any other citations in between you can reference the second use of the citation as "*Jones, supra*" or simply as "ibid." (see Id.)

Id.

Short for "idem" in Latin, meaning "the same." Used to indicate that the citation being referenced is the same as the last citation. For example, People v. Jones is cited in one paragraph of a pleading and again in the next paragraph without any other citations in between. The second reference to People v. Jones may be written as "Jones, supra" or simply as "id." (See Ibid.)

Impeach

To discredit or show that a witness is incorrect. Impeachment may be done by showing the witness has reason to lie, such as asking, "the defendant is your brother, isn't he?" Impeachment may also be done by showing the witness suffered from a physical disability that prevented him from observing or remembering events accurately, such as questioning the witness about his state of intoxication, his poor vision, or a mental disability that prevents him from remembering. Impeachment may also be done by showing that the witness suffers from felony convictions or other crimes of moral turpitude.

In Limine

A motion made in front of the trial judge shortly before the start of evidence in a trial.

Indictment

A document listing the charges against a defendant following a grand jury hearing.

Information

The charging document filed by the prosecution after a preliminary hearing. A defendant is initially charged using a Complaint. If the judge presiding over the preliminary hearing rules that there is sufficient evidence to believe that the defendant is guilty, the prosecution will be allowed to file an Information listing the charges against the defendant.

Infra

Latin for "below." This is used to reference a subject or citation that will be discussed later in the document, such as "This case is similar to *People v. Smith*, infra, in that the defendant was not present." The citation for *People v. Smith* will be given later in the document, such as "*People v. Smith* (2010) 15 Cal 50."

Infra is also used to indicate an argument that will follow in the document, such as "Defendant's prolonged detention, infra, led to an illegal search." The prolonged detention will be discussed later in the document.

Practice tip: if you use "infra," make sure whatever is to follow actually follows. It is not uncommon to see documents that use infra to reference a future citation that never comes.

Inter Alia

Latin for "among other things." It is commonly used in sentences, such as, "Defendant is charged with, inter alia, first degree burglary." The defendant is charged with first degree burglary and other charges. This wording usually infers that the defendant's most serious charge is first degree burglary.

Judicial Notice

A rule of evidence allowing a fact to be introduced as evidence if it can be readily determined and cannot reasonably be disputed. As examples:

- Chester Avenue in downtown Bakersfield runs North and South until Garces Circle.
- A person born in 1802 is no longer living.
- On January 1, 2021 at 10:00 p.m. in Bakersfield, California, the sun had already set.
- The Complaint in Kern County Superior Court case number BF123456A was filed on May 23, 2008.

Limine
See "In Limine"

Low Term
See "Sentencing"

Mandamus
See "Petition"

Mandate
See "Petition"

Malice
See "Mental State"

Marsden Motion

A Marsden Motion is a request to replace the defendant's appointed attorney with a different attorney. Unless there are unusual circumstances, it is usually a bad idea for a defendant to bring a Marsden Motion.

Mental State

It is not enough that a defendant committed an act; he must also have a certain mental state before he can be convicted of a crime. The common mental states are General Intent, Specific Intent, and Malice.

For General Intent, the prosecution must prove that the defendant acted willfully. For Specific Intent the prosecution must prove that the defendant acted willfully and with the specific intent that the crime be committed. For Malice, the prosecution must prove that the defendant acted deliberately with conscious disregard for life.

Mid Term
See "Sentencing"

Motion

A Motion is a request that the court issue an order. As examples, "defendant moves that the Court continue the Trial date" means the defendant requests that the judge set a new date for the trial. "Defendant moves the Court for a discovery order," means the defendant requests that the judge order the District Attorney to give the defendant evidence concerning the case. The attorney "moves" the court to take some action. This process is known as a "motion."

Move
See "Motion"

Nolo Contendere
See "No Contest"

No Contest

A plea in which the Defendant does not admit guilt but consents to the court entering a finding of guilt.

Nunc pro tunc

Latin for "now for then." This is used to indicate that a correction being made will be made effective on an earlier date. For example, a defendant enters a plea and is sentenced to four years. The court later realizes that the maximum sentence is three years. The court corrects the sentence to reflect that the sentence is three years, nunc pro tunc to the date of sentencing.

The record will not reflect that the defendant's sentence was reduced from four years to three years; it will show that his sentence as of the date of the original sentencing was for three years.

Objection

A complaint to the court that something is being done wrong. As examples, if the prosecution vouches for a witness, the defense may state, "Objection – vouching." If the defense begins to argue with a witness, the prosecution may state, "Objection – argumentative."

When an objection is made, the court will rule either "overruled" or "sustained." Overruled means the court does not find the complaint valid. Sustained means that the court does find the complaint valid.

Own Recognizance

The release of the defendant from jail without paying bail based on the defendant's promise to appear in court when required.

Party

Party refers to the plaintiff and the defendant in a case. In a California criminal matter, the "People of the State of California" are the plaintiff, and they are represented by the District Attorney. The "People of the State of California" are a Party, and the defendant is a Party.

With few exceptions, only the attorney for a Party may file motions or other pleadings in a case. For example, the alleged victim is not a Party. The alleged victim cannot dismiss the case or even bring motions because he is not a Party.

Passim

Used in an index, table of cases, or similar list of citations to indicate that a citation appears so many times in a document that it is not practical to list each page where the citation appears. For example, a document has a citation to *People v. Marvin* on three pages and a citation to *People v. Paul* on thirty pages, so the index shows:

People v. Marvin (2019) 99 Cal 5th 888..........5, 23, 122
People v. Paul (2021) 1 Cal 5th 17...................passim

Petition

A Petition, like a motion, is a request that the court issue an order. Petitions are often ruled on without a hearing and are often not directed to the trial court, but instead are directed to a reviewing court. The party "petitions" the court to take some action, and the court issues a "writ" to cause the action to happen. Examples:

- Petition for Writ of Habeas Corpus – see "Habeas Corpus."
- Petition for Writ of Mandamus or Petition for Writ of Mandate is a petition asking a higher court to order the trial court to do something, such as mandate that the trial court grant a motion.
- Petition for Writ of Prohibition is a petition asking a higher court to order the trial court to stop doing something, such as prohibit the trial court from prosecuting the defendant.
- Petition to Dismiss is a request that the court dismiss a misdemeanor or a low-level felony after the defendant has completed their sentence.
- Petition to Seal is a request to seal an arrest record that did not result in a conviction.

Pitchess Motion

Motion to view officer personnel records. (See sample on page 229). The procedure is now set by statute in *Code of Civil Procedure §1005(b)*

Preliminary Examination

A formal examination to establish whether the prosecution has enough evidence to establish that a crime has been committed and that it was the defendant who committed the crime. Most hearsay is allowed, and the prosecution does not have to prove their case beyond a reasonable doubt. The prosecution only needs to convince a judge that the allegations in the Complaint are probably true. Sometimes called a Preliminary Hearing.

Preliminary Hearing Setting Conference
See "Conference"

Pre-Preliminary Hearing
See "Conference"

Pretrial Conference
See "Conference"

Prior

A prior conviction. The term usually refers to a prior conviction that can be used to give a defendant a longer sentence, such as a "strike" or a prior involving a prison term.

Pro Per

Short for "propria persona" which is Latin for "proper person." This means the person represents himself in court. (see Pro Se)

Pro Se

Latin for "for himself." This means the person represents himself in court. (see Pro Per)

Prohibition
See "Petition"

Redact
Mark out or make something unreadable.

Readiness
See "Conference"

Removal

An order directed to a warden or sheriff requiring a prisoner to be removed from that person's custody and taken to court to be a witness.

Romero Motion

A request that the court dismiss sentencing enhancements and give the defendant a lesser sentence.

Sentencing

Entry of an order giving the punishment the defendant will receive. California uses a three-level sentence structure for felonies. A felony prison sentence will be expressed as three levels, such as 2,3,5 - the lower term, the middle term, and the upper term. If the defendant receives the lower term, he will be sentenced to two years plus any enhancements for prior "strike" offenses, prior prison terms, gang enhancements, gun enhancements, etc.

Sic

Used to indicate an error is in the original quote. For example, a document has the following text: "Defendants has the right to an attorney." The word "has" is clearly the wrong word, but you want to give the quote without making it look like you made an error, so you write the quote as: "Defendants [sic] has the right to an attorney."

Side Bar

To have a conversation with the judge outside the presence of the jury while the jury is still in the room.

Status Conference
See "Conference"

Strike

Strike is generally given one of two meanings:
1. Erase, such as "strike Count One," meaning the defendant will no longer be charged with count one.
2. A serious or violent felony, such as "defendant suffers a strike for a robbery," meaning that defendant was previously convicted of robbery and that conviction will be used to enhance his current sentence if he is convicted.

Sua Sponte

An action taken by the court or other authority without being requested to do so. As an example, a judge realizes that trial has been scheduled beyond the last date allowable without violating a defendant's right to speedy trial, so the judge sua sponte advances the trial date.

Subpoena

An order telling a person that they must come to court to testify or produce evidence.

Suppress

To forbid the use of evidence. Example: the defendant's house was searched without permission and without a warrant. If the court suppresses what was found, the prosecution cannot use or referred to at trial.

Supra

Latin for "above." This can refer to a case that has already been cited or an argument that has already been made.

Supra is commonly used to indicate that the full citation for a case has already been given in the document. For example, the first time a case is cited, multiple citations may be given for the same case, such as "*Miranda v. Arizona* (1966) 384 U.S. 436; 86 S. Ct. 1602; 16 L. Ed. 2nd 694; 10 A.L.R. 3rd 974." Any of these citations may be used to look up the case: "384 U.S. 436" or "86 S. Ct. 1602" or "16 L. Ed. 2nd 694" or "10 A.L.R.3rd 974" can be used to find the case. When the case is again cited in the document, it can be cited as "*Miranda, supra*." Because of the use of computers for legal research, it is now common to only cite to one source for a given case, such as "*Miranda v. Arizona* (1966) 384 U.S. 436" with future citations in the same document still being, "*Miranda*, supra."

If it is unclear what name will be used for later references in the document, a parenthetical reference can be made to clear up the ambiguity, such as "*Adams v. Smith* (2020) Cal 5th 17 (Smith)." Later citations to the case will be made as "*Smith*, supra" as indicated by the word in parenthesis.

Supra is also used to indicate an argument that has already been made, such as "The illegal search, supra, followed Defendant's prolonged detention." The illegal search has already been discussed earlier in the document.

Practice tip: for well-known cases, such as *Miranda*, *Pitchess*, and *Marsden*, use only "supra" for all citations after the case has been cited once, but for other cases, include a full citation if there is great separation between locations were the case is cited along with "supra" to note that the case has been cited before, such as "Adams v. Smith (2020) 1 Cal 5th 17, supra."

This allows a reader to look up the case without having to search the document for the first time the case was cited.

Time Waiver

A defendant has the right to a speedy trial. A time waiver is an agreement that a certain amount of time will not be counted towards the time within which the case must be brought to trial.

Trail

To trail is to have a limited continuance so that a matter can be heard at a later time or date.

For example, a suppression hearing is scheduled for 10:00 a.m. but the judge has many other hearings to conduct, and he doesn't want everyone involved to have to wait in the courtroom while he hears other matters so he "trails" the suppression hearing until 1:30 p.m. At 1:30 p.m. the judge is still busy, so he "trails" the hearing until 8:30 a.m. the next morning.

To "trail" is to have a short continuance until some condition is met, such as trailing while waiting for a witness to be available, trailing while waiting for a courtroom to be available, or trailing a misdemeanor case until a defendant's felony case is resolved.

Trial

The formal presentation of evidence against a defendant. This is when the trier of fact (usually a jury in a criminal case) hears evidence and decides whether the defendant is guilty or that guilt has not been proven.

Trial Setting Conference
See "Conference"

Trier of Fact

The person or group of persons who decide whether the defendant is guilty or not guilty. The trier of fact may be the jury, but some defendants opt for a court trial (also known as a bench trial) where the judge alone is the trier of fact.

Upper Term
See "Sentencing"

Voir Dire

Questioning of prospective jurors or experts regarding their eligibility to participate in a case.

Waiver

To give up a right. A defendant who enters a time waiver gives up the right to a speedy trial within the limits of the waiver, e.g. a twenty-day waiver gives the prosecution twenty more days to bring the case to trial. A waiver of personal appearance allows an attorney to attend court proceedings without the defendant present, and a waiver of right to counsel allows the defendant to represent himself. When accepting a defendant's plea, the court will require a specific waiver of all of the defendant's rights associated with trial.

West Plea

A plea entered so the defendant can get the benefits of a specific plea bargain, but not admit the conduct that the pled-to charge alleges. The plea is sometimes used for a defendant who claims actual innocence but enters a plea to avoid the dangers of trial. Named after the case of *People v. West* (1970) 3 Cal. 3rd 595.

Wobbler

A charge that can be filed as a felony or a misdemeanor.

Writ
See "Petition"

$$\rightarrow \bullet\bullet \Omega \bullet\bullet \leftarrow$$

Isn't it about time to catch up on scanning?

We have eight-foot ceilings.

D. OFFICE ORGANIZATION

A Criminal Defense Paralegal should help the attorney be where he is supposed to be, when he is supposed to be there. and with everything readily at hand that he needs to do his job. To do this, the paralegal should become proficient at office organization.

1. Maintain a calendaring system

It is essential that a law firm maintain a calendar system. Calendaring systems and procedures can vary dramatically from firm to firm. Some attorneys maintain a paper calendar, some use electronic calendars, such as Outlook, Google Calendar, Time Matters, or eLawSoftwares, and some attorneys maintain both paper and electronic calendars. Check with your supervisor or office manager for exact procedures for your firm, but the following is a general description of the procedure.

Procedure

Criminal calendaring is the procedure of keeping track of court dates to help ensure that the attorneys, defendants, witnesses, and support personnel are in the right place at the right time.

Calendar dates are generally obtained from one or more of three sources:

- From an attorney's list. Upon receiving court dates, some attorneys will keep a list of future dates. This procedure, which is highly recommended, makes it easy to update calendar. Add each date from the list to the calendar or calendars. A typical list might look like this:

    Jones, John – Jan. 15 Readiness – Jan. 25 Trial
    Adams, Abraham – Feb. 2 Conf. – Feb. 7 Prelim.
    Smith, Mary – June 5 Pretrial
    Roe, Ruth – March 2 Sentencing

- In court. During court proceedings the judge, or sometimes the clerk, will announce coming court dates and order the defendant back to court on those days. If the Criminal Defense Paralegal attends proceedings with the attorney, the paralegal should record any dates given and add them to the calendar or calendars.

- From minute orders. Some courts give attorneys and/or defendants a minute order, note, or other document notifying them of future court dates to be added to the calendar or calendars.

- From an official web page or list. Some courts and other government agencies have an official list of cases or a web page to look up cases. Calendars can be updated using such pages and lists but use such web pages with caution because they often do not contain a full list of court dates. Take for example the Tulare County Sheriff's web page, which has a single entry labeled "CourtDate – CourtTime" followed by a date, but no time is listed. The information provided does not contain a time, and it only shows the next court date. The Kern County Superior Court web page has an apt disclaimer:

  > Notes: 1. Not all case information is available via the Internet. To obtain additional case information, visit Court Records. 2. Calendars for each court may periodically change as court schedules are modified by court personnel. Persons viewing the court calendar assume full responsibility for appearing at the proper date and time and at the proper court irrespective of the information contained herein.

- From an attorney's calendar. Copying dates from one calendar to another is probably the worst system, but it is, unfortunately, in common practice. When a Criminal Defense Paralegal receives an attorney's calendar to use for updates, the paralegal must compare each future date on the master calendar (the one obtained from the attorney) to each date on other calendars to be updated and then updating those calendars. This requires the paralegal to look at all future dates on the calendar to conform each calendar to the master.

If you are given authority to establish a calendaring system, we offer the following suggestions for doing so.

First, use a paper calendar. Technology is great but it is more prone to errors and unexpected outages. Sometimes the electricity goes off. Sometimes Wi-Fi goes down, and sometimes computers, tablets, and phones just lock up unexpectedly. Sometimes phones are even dropped. Any of these events can cause an electronic calendaring system to fail.

Even though paper calendaring systems can fail due to an unexpected coffee spill, the loss of a pen, or other such events, recovery time is generally fast. Even a stained page is usually readable, and pens are easily borrowed. A dropped paper calendar will probably suffer little damage, but a dropped phone, tablet, or laptop may become unusable.

Second, use the "initial system" to ensure all paper calendars are updated. The "initial system" is not mentioned above, or anywhere else we could find, because we invented and named it. However, it is such an obvious system that someone else has surely invented the same system in the past.

A law office may have multiple paper calendars that need to be updated by multiple different people. Electronic calendars should automatically update when one person updates their own portion of the calendar, but paper calendars must be updated manually. The "initial system" is designed to ensure that each of these calendars is updated. To use the system, any person having an item (date, time, and event) to add to the calendar adds the item to a master list along with their own initials. The master list can be on a pad of paper, a whiteboard, or some other media in a common area.

Each person maintaining a calendar checks this master list and adds all new items to his or her calendar and then initials the item on the master list. The last person to update a calendar deletes or strikes out the item on the master list. If five calendars are being updated, a person seeing a calendar item with four sets of initials next to it will know that he is the last person whose calendar needs the entry, so he will update the calendar and remove the item from the master list.

Third, use an electronic calendar. Use an electronic calendar, such as Google Calendar, which is free, to share dates across multiple devices. A good electronic calendar should be able to install and automatically update on personal computers, Android devices, and Apple devices. This way, updates on any one device will be reflected on all other devices.

Felony Calendar Entries

With few exceptions, the defendant must be present for all felony proceedings. Calendar entries should be made for all proceedings, and out-of-custody clients should be notified of the proceedings. Court proceedings in Felony cases generally proceed as follows:

1. Arraignment on the Complaint
2. Conference (may be called Pre-Preliminary Hearing, Preliminary

Hearing Setting Conference, Scheduling Conference, etc. This step may repeat many times.)
3. Preliminary Hearing
4. Arraignment on the Information
5. Pretrial Motions (this step may repeat many times)
6. Readiness Conference (this step may repeat many times)
7. Trial
8. Sentencing

Misdemeanor Calendar Entries

For some misdemeanor proceedings, the attorney may be allowed to appear without the defendant being present. All proceedings should therefore be calendared and clients should be notified of the proceedings, but ask the attorney which clients he wants present at which proceedings. Court proceedings in Misdemeanor cases generally proceed as follows:
1. Arraignment on the Complaint
2. Pretrial Motions (this step may repeat many times)
3. Pretrial Conference (this step may repeat many times)
4. Trial
5. Sentencing

2. Put all client matters in files

Every paper, disk, pleading, photograph, or other such item associated with a client should be placed in a client file. This seems obvious, but unfortunately papers are often left out for an attorney or other person to read before going into a file. Such papers can eventually form a mound of confusion. The remedy is to place all such papers in a client file. If the attorney needs to review the papers, suggest the following options.

a. For short documents, make a copy and mark it "temp copy." The original goes in the client file and the temp copy goes to the attorney, who can read and dispose of it.

b. For longer documents, copy the first page and mark it "temp copy, first of ____ pages" with the ____ replaced by the number of pages. Place the original in the client file and give the temp copy to the attorney to use as a reminder to read the remainder of the document.

c. For odd items, such as CDs, DVDs, Blu-ray, flash drives, and color photos, describe the item in a memo, place the original item in the client file along with the memo, and give the attorney a copy of the memo.

3. Only open one file at a time

Your firm may have dozens or even hundreds of active cases at any given time. It is essential that documents from one case do not accidentally get into the file for another case. To prevent this from happening, only open one file at a time on any given surface. If you have a desk, only open one file on the desk. If you have a separate return on the desk, only open one file on the return. If you are fortunate enough to also have a worktable, you can have three files open at the same time; however, don't let papers from one case stray too close to papers from another.

4. Pull tomorrow's files today

A good calendaring system lets the Criminal Defense Paralegal know which cases are coming up for hearing, and a good filing system makes it easy to find files for those cases. At least a day before a case comes for hearing, pull each case file, let the attorney know which files have been pulled, and ask if anything needs to be done before hearing. Typical things that can be done to help cases go more smoothly include:

a. Call out-of-custody defendants to remind them about court
b. Call investigators, witnesses, and others associated with a case to remind them about court
c. Arrange for transportation for witnesses, defendants, or others
d. Set out exhibits

5. Get the full message

"This is Dave," the caller says. "Please, ask attorney Adam to return my call." The paralegal diligently takes down the message on a pad, "Dave called. Please, return his call."

Such a message may raise more questions than it answers:
1. Dave who?
2. When did the call come in?
3. Which case does it concern?
4. Is Dave an existing client?
5. How can Dave be contacted?
6. Why did I hire this paralegal?

When taking a phone message, get at least the following information:

1. Caller's first and last name or a sufficient description of the caller, such as "Mary, the mother of John Jones" or "James from Taft Copy Works."
2. Date and time of the call. This helps prevent wasted time when the caller and the person being called have already spoken after the message was taken.
3. Case. Is this a new case or an existing one? Which case does this concern?
4. Subject matter. What does the caller want? What is the goal of the call? Is this a sales call? For example, "He wants to talk to you about his alibi," "She wants to discuss her son's case," or "He needs more funds."
5. Phone number. Even if the caller is well-known to the attorney, get a phone number.

6. Use a directory structure

When writing a quick memo, note, or pleading, it is tempting to save the document on the computer desktop or in the computer's default location, the documents directory. Don't do it. Computer files should be organized into directories by client name, case number, or some other system that allows anyone using the computer to quickly find the files, such as in the following example:

```
C:\Firm\Criminal\Adams Joe BF123456A
C:\Firm\Criminal\Brown Amy BF345434A
C:\Firm\Criminal\Brown Sam BF432321A
C:\Firm\Criminal\Cantrell David BF432321A
...
```

Hopefully, the firm you work for already has such a system, but if not, you greatly improve the workflow by establishing such a system. The system can be refined with additional subdirectories, such as in the following example:

```
C:\Firm\Criminal\Adams Joe BF123456A\Correspondence
C:\Firm\Criminal\Adams Joe BF123456A\Discovery
C:\Firm\Criminal\Adams Joe BF123456A\Pleadings
...
```

Further subdirectories to the subdirectories can be used to refine the organization even better, such as in the following example:

```
C:\Firm\Criminal\Adams Joe BF123456A\Discovery\Photos
C:\Firm\Criminal\Adams Joe BF123456A\Discovery\Reports
C:\Firm\Criminal\Adams Joe BF123456A\Discovery\Gang
C:\Firm\Criminal\Adams Joe BF123456A\Discovery\Lab
...
```

The more organized the computer files are, the easier it will be to find important documents at a later date. Further, if the documents are kept on a common server or cloud system, such as Dropbox, Google Backup and Sync, or Microsoft OneDrive, the firm will not be dependent on any one person to find computer files.

7. Put everything in a file

As noted above, client matters go in client files, but offices often become cluttered with other items that appear to have no place. Flyers for upcoming training events, inquiry letters from potential clients, bills, messenger service news, new case summaries, and many other papers flow into a law firm, but such documents usually have no particular home in the office – give them a home. Start a file for training events; start a file for inquiry letters. If it is a document that you wish to keep, give the document a home.

8. Scan when you can

Criminal case files may contain hundreds or thousands of pages. Often, copies of these pages must be shared with multiple members of the defense team, such as investigators, gang experts, DNA experts, fingerprint experts, paralegals, secretaries, mental health professionals, and other experts. Multiple copies can be made for members of the defense team, or all case documents can be scanned one time and then shared with other members of the defense team as needed. The added benefit of scanning documents is that, generally speaking, those documents can be destroyed once the case ends.

Naturally, original documents should be preserved, but most documents found in the files of criminal defense firms are copies of discovery held by the prosecution, copies of pleadings filed with the court, and copies of expert witness reports. All such documents should be scanned and saved on the computer.

Other documents in the case file usually include notes from members of the defense team, which can also be scanned, and copies of documents that the firm received in electronic format and printed for convenience sake, which need not be scanned. It is rare to find a document in a criminal defense file that cannot be converted to an electronic format. Any document that can be preserved electronically should be preserved electronically.

9. Swiftly shred superfluous sheets

At the conclusion of a case, a criminal defense case file will often contain multiple superfluous items. For example, during trial preparation a firm will often prepare extra copies of motions in limine to be serviced on the prosecution and all codefendants along with an original to be filed with the court. It is generally not necessary to preserve the original or the many copies because the motions, which were probably typed by the Criminal Defense Paralegal, are still on the computer in electronic format.

Neither is it required to preserve paper copies of any documents that have been scanned. Portions of the file that are preserved in electronic format should be removed and shredded unless firm policy dictates otherwise.

10. Data disks deserve duplication

If consistent with the law firm's policies, electronic data, including that provided in discovery and scanned documents as discussed above, should be copied to electronic media and then removed from the firm's computers as needed to make room for additional electronic files. At least two copies should be made of each case file, and the copies should be stored at different locations, such as one copy at the firm and one copy at the attorney's home. A list of archived files should also be kept at both locations with entries by disk and by client.

The first list should be a chronological list of disks with a full list of all case files contained on that disk, such as "Disk 1 – Baker, Adam; Chance, Mike; Fields, Doug; Jones, John; King, Arnold…"

The second list should be an alphabetical list of all past clients with the number of the disk where the client's files are archived, such as "Aardvark, Adam – Disk 17; Abrams, Dave – Disk 12; Abba, Ruth – Disk 32…"

Using such a system will allow the paralegal, or anyone else with access to the disks, to quickly determine what is contained on a given disk and quickly find the files of any particular client.

These backup disks should be created using current technology, such as Blu-ray, but should be copied to new media types as technology changes. Otherwise, it may become extremely difficult to recover files from old archives. Imagine being asked to recover files from computer media that was in common use in the past, such as 8" floppy disks, 5-1/4" minifloppy disks, or even 3-1/2" compact floppy disks. Upgrade to new technology before the older technology becomes completely obsolete. This means copying old client files to new computer media.

E. BAIL

1. Introduction and duties

Often a defendant will be in custody, and it will be the defendant's family and friends who retain the attorney. The defendant's loved ones usually want to get him out of custody as quickly as possible. The attorney may, therefore, ask the Criminal Defense Paralegal to help the family arrange for bail.

Bail can be as small as a promise to appear; it can be as high as several million dollars, or bail can be denied completely for a defendant facing very serious charges or a defendant who has previously failed to appear.

Bail is the court's security that a defendant will appear at future court dates. However, the future of bail is uncertain because in late 2018 the governor signed a bill that effectively abolished cash bail in favor of a system that allows judges to decide on a case-by-case basis who goes home and stays in jail while waiting for trial. The bill was set to go into effect in late 2019, but implementation has been blocked by a voter referendum on the November 2020 ballot. In March 2021, the California Supreme Court decided the matter of *In re Humphrey* (2021) 11 Cal 5th 135, which held that much of the existing bail system is unconstitutional. More changes to the bail system are, therefore, expected in the near future.

A Criminal Defense Paralegal may help with bail in several ways:

a. **Prepare a motion to set or reduce bail.** See sections in this book "Pleadings before trial" and "Sample pleadings before trial."

b. **Find a bail bond company.** Unfortunately, this is not as simple as looking up bail bond companies on the Internet. Not all bond companies are the same. When helping find a bond company, consider the following:

Percentage Rate. Some bond companies charge ten percent of the bail amount, but others may charge eight or even seven percent. This can make a huge difference. For example, a $50,000 bail bond would cost $5,000 at 10% but would only cost $3,500 for a bond that charges 7%. By helping find a low-rate bond company you help the family save money, which helps ensure they will have enough money to pay the cost of defense.

Payment Plan. A bond company may require the entire premium to be paid upfront or may allow the premium to be made in payments. For example, a $50,000 bail bond at 10% with the full premium due before release would require the family to come up with $5,000 up front; a bond company that charges 7% with the full premium due before release would require the family to come up with $3,500 up front, but a bond company that only requires 1% down would only require the family to come up with $500 before the defendant is released. When only part of the premium is to be paid up front, the amount and timing of payments should also be considered. High monthly payments may make it impossible for the defendant to keep up. Payments are still due even if the case is dismissed or otherwise finished.

Interest. Some bond companies charge interest on amounts due; others do not. To help the family make a more informed decision, learn how each bond company being considered charges interest.

Fees. Bond companies may charge writing fees, document fees, recording fees, resumption fees, or any number of other fees that are meant to add profit to the bond company without granting any real benefit to the family. Inquire about such fees so the family can make a more informed decision.

Collateral. Bond companies may require some form of collateral, such as the title to a vehicle or a lien on a house. If collateral will be required, inform the family.

Cosigners. Bond companies may require one or more cosigners. Find out what the cosigner requirements are by asking the bond company questions like:

What are the qualifications of a cosigner?

How many cosigners are required?

How do you notify cosigners of default or late payments?

c. **Arrange Interviews.** A Criminal Defense Paralegal may need to arrange for a representative from a bail bond company to meet with a defendant's family, arrange for a notary to meet defendant at jail to sign documents, or arrange for other meetings to facilitate the posting of bail and the release of the defendant.

d. **Collect Documentation.** Whether for a judge deciding the proper amount of bail or a representative from a bond company is deciding if a defendant and his family are a good credit risk, a Criminal Defense Paralegal may be asked to collect and organize documentation related to a defendant's flight risk. This may require the paralegal to:

Draft letters of recommendation as dictated or summarized by family and friends and obtain their signatures.

Collect documents related to a defendant's employment record.

Collect documents showing that a defendant has multiple ties to the community, such as home ownership, family members in the area, or attendance at a local church.

e. **Answer bail questions.** Even though a Criminal Defense Paralegal cannot give legal advice, the paralegal can and should answer basic bail questions, such those in the following sections.

As a Criminal Defense Paralegal, you should not recommend a bond company, but should collect information about bond companies to help defendants and their families make an informed decision.

2. Common bail questions

a. What is the procedure for bailing someone out of jail?

Generally, a bail bond company will be contacted to begin the bail procedure. During the initial consultation, most companies will ask for information about the defendant and the persons assisting with bail to determine the risk involved in the bond and begin the approval process.

Once the bail bond is approved, the customer will need to sign basic bail bond documents including an application, Indemnity Agreement, and receipt. After the paperwork is finalized and payment has been made, a licensed bondsman will post the bail bond at the jail and the defendant will be released.

The time it takes to actually release a defendant depends on the city and county in which the defendant is located, but in most cases, defendants are released within two to four hours after the bond is posted.

b. What is an indemnitor/cosigner?

An indemnitor or cosigner is the person who agrees to be financially responsible for the defendant and the full amount of the bond if the defendant fails to appear in court. An indemnitor is also responsible for all costs incurred for a defendant missing a court appearance. If there is more than one indemnitor who has signed for the release of a defendant, each is jointly responsible for all expenses, which means funds will be collected from each indemnitor until all expenses are fully paid.

c. What is collateral?

Collateral is something of value that is used to secure a debt or ensure payment. Sometimes a bail bond company will receive collateral in order to ensure that the defendant appears in court. Most bail bond collateral is in the form of real estate or cash, but some take jewelry, title to vehicles, or other forms of collateral. A bail bond company must return collateral at the resolution of the case.

d. Is collateral always required?

No, some bond companies negotiate no collateral bail bonds. These are called signature bonds.

e. If collateral is required, when is it returned?

When the defendant's case has been completed and all financial obligations are satisfied, collateral is returned to the individual who pledged it.

f. What is the responsibility of someone who bails another person out of jail?

When a person bails someone out of jail, he or she is called the bail bond indemnitor. He takes full responsibility for the defendant to show up in court as required. Most issues with appearance in court are easily resolved and rarely escalate beyond a simple phone call.

g. What happens if the defendant fails to appear in court?

If the failure to appear in court was a simple mistake, then the bail bond company or an attorney can usually arrange for the defendant to return to court (see Recall Warrant in the sections on pleadings before trial). Courts generally understand that people get sick, traffic or car problems arise, and other unforeseen circumstances occur. This is most commonly the situation and is easily remedied.

"Yes, as a paralegal assigned to your case, our conversations are confidential, and I appreciate your efforts to help me understand all the facts of your case, but when I said, "start from the beginning," I was hoping for something a little closer in time than your third birthday party and what you did with the cake you hid in your pocket. However, I am glad your sinuses finally cleared up."

F. DISCOVERY

1. Duty to Disclose

Discovery is the pretrial exchange of evidence between the prosecution and defense. The stated goal of pretrial discovery in criminal cases is:

(a) To promote the ascertainment of truth in trials by requiring timely pretrial discovery.
(b) To save court time by requiring that discovery be conducted informally between and among the parties before judicial enforcement is requested.
(c) To save court time in trial and avoid the necessity for frequent interruptions and postponements.
(d) To protect victims and witnesses from danger, harassment, and undue delay of the proceedings.
(Penal Code §1054)

The Prosecution (District Attorney, Police, and everyone else prosecuting the case) has a duty to provide the Defense with the following:

(a) The names and addresses of persons the prosecutor intends to call as witnesses at trial.
(b) Statements of all defendants.
(c) All relevant real evidence seized or obtained as a part of the investigation of the offenses charged.
(d) The existence of a felony conviction of any material witness whose credibility is likely to be critical to the outcome of the trial.
(e) Any exculpatory evidence.
(f) Relevant written or recorded statements of witnesses or reports of the statements of witnesses whom the prosecutor intends to call at the trial, including any reports or statements of experts made in conjunction with the case, including the results of physical or mental examinations, scientific tests, experiments, or comparisons which the prosecutor intends to offer in evidence at the trial.

2. Duty to Prevent Disclosure

Statutory law provides many protections to restrict the disclosure of information that could be used to harm a victim or witness, and multiple laws, both state and federal, prohibit disclosure of medical records.

The main restrictions on disclosure applicable to criminal cases are found in *Penal Code §§964* and *1054.2*, but *Penal Code §528* et. seq. further restricts disclosure of personal identifying information if that information is to be used for an unlawful purpose.

Penal Code §1054.2 prohibits an attorney from disclosing "the address or telephone number of a victim or witness…" in a criminal case. When a defendant is acting as his own attorney, the burden falls on the court "to protect the address and telephone number of a victim or witness…"

Penal Code §964 places a burden on "the district attorney and the courts… to protect confidential personal information regarding any witness or victim [which] includes, but is not limited to, an address, telephone number, driver's license or California Identification Card number, social security number, date of birth, place of employment, employee identification number, mother's maiden name, demand deposit account number, savings or checking account number, or credit card number." However, by inference the defense should also take steps to protect this information from disclosure.

Penal Code §530.55 lists specific items of information that should be kept private, including "…taxpayer identification number… state or federal driver's license, or identification number, social security number, place of employment…[and] information contained in a birth [] certificate…"

In accordance with these statues, you should prevent disclosure of the following information concerning all victims and witnesses:

1. Address
2. Phone number
3. Date of birth
4. Place of employment (and by implication, school attended)
5. Employee identification number
6. Mother's maiden name
7. Demand deposit account number
8. Credit card number
9. Health insurance number
10. Taxpayer identification number
11. School identification number
12. State or federal driver's license, or identification number
13. Social security number
14. Professional or occupational number
15. Savings account number
16. Checking account number

17. PIN (personal identification number)
18. Password
19. Alien registration number
20. Government passport number
21. Any information contained in a birth or death certificate

To "disclose" means to reveal something that was previously unknown, so it is proper to discuss information that is already known to the person, public information, or information that is logically required for defense of a case.

For example, if a crime is alleged to have taken place at Taco, Inc., it would be unreasonable to withhold the location of the alleged crime from a defendant because it happens to be the employment place of all or most of the witnesses. Likewise, if a defendant is accused of sending harassing text messages, the phone number that allegedly received the messages should be made available to the defendant. Nonetheless, before providing anyone outside the law firm with any information from the list shown above, obtain authorization from the defendant's attorney.

Only provide discovery to defendants when specifically authorized to do so by the defense attorney. When providing copies of discovery to a defendant, examine each page of the discovery to determine whether the page contains any of the items from the list provided above. If the page contains only items from the list along with names, the entire page can be withheld. If the page contains some items from the list, those items should be blacked out using a black felt pen, redaction software, or some other method that prevents the information from being seen, even if held up to the light. This may mean blacking out the information on a copy of a page and then making a copy of the copy to ensure that the redaction is unreadable.

G. PREPARING DOCUMENTS

A Criminal Defense Paralegal will generally be responsible for preparing and formatting three general categories of documents: Judicial Council Forms, Free Form Pleadings, and Letters. Included in letters are memos, reports, and other such documents that do not have strict formatting rules. Freeform pleadings include motions, petitions, memoranda of points and authorities, trial briefs, oppositions to prosecution motions, and other documents. It is essential for a Criminal Defense Paralegal to know how to craft and format free-form pleadings.

1. Greater Grammar

Readers of this book probably know basic grammar and sentence structure – such basic knowledge is required for paralegals - but some writing blunders are so prevalent, by attorneys and paralegals alike, that we offer suggestions to help you avoid them. In doing so we are confident that readers will find many grammatical errors in this book, and we welcome your suggestions as to how such errors should be corrected and avoided.

Often an attorney will give a Criminal Defense Paralegal a document template (such as the sample motions included in this book) along with dictation, a short note, a transcript, or simply verbal instructions as to how to complete the document. The Criminal Defense Paralegal will, therefore, be primarily responsible for writing the document. The following ten grammar guidelines are provided to help ensure that such documents are easy to read, unambiguous, and written in a dignified style.

1. Complete the thought
2. Complete the comparison
3. Clarify modifiers
4. Prevent puzzling pronouns
5. Use the Oxford comma
6. Use a dependent clause comma
7. Don't comma splice
8. Know your homophones
9. Beware of Possessives
10. Use paired commas
11. Use active voice
12. Don't yell
13. Avoid abundant allegations
14. Limit long legalese
15. Mind your malaprops
16. Check your numbers

Complete the Thought

Ensure that documents contain enough facts to complete thoughts essential or beneficial to the document. Consider the following example of a poorly worded statement prepared for an alibi witness.

> I am David's sister. Mary is my sister-in-law. I was with David that night at my house so I know he could not have done what Mary said he did.

In the following revision there are multiple additions meant to help ensure the reader knows who the speaker is and what the speaker actually knows. Without the revisions, it is unclear where David and Mary were, what time they were together, what day they were together, who else was present, etc.

> I, Emily Smith, declare:
>
> I am David Smith's sister. Mary Smith is David's wife and my sister-in-law. I was with David from about 5:00 p.m. until about 10:00 p.m. on January 1, 2019, at my house, 1234 L Street, Bakersfield, CA 93301. Mary was not present at any time on that night, but Joe Jones (661-555-1212), Jane Jones (559-555-1212), and James Jones (310-555-1212) were present the entire time. I can be reached at 213-555-1212.
>
> I declare under penalty of perjury under the laws of the State of California that the foregoing is true and correct and this declaration was executed on March 1, 2022, at Bakersfield, California.

The second document, in the form of a declaration, gives information as to how to contact the declarant and additional witnesses, and it clearly states the details of the alibi defense.

Complete the Comparison

Ensure that any comparison lists all items being compared. For example:

> Mr. Davis is both taller and stronger, so the jury should be instructed on the theory of defense of others.

Mr. Davis is taller and stronger than who? Such sentences can often be corrected by adding the word "than" and the words that naturally follow it, such as the following:

> Mr. Davis is both taller and stronger <u>than Defendant's wife</u>, so the jury should be instructed on the theory of defense of others.

> Mr. Davis is both taller and stronger <u>than Mrs. Smith</u>, so the jury should be instructed on the theory of defense of others.

> Mr. Davis is both taller and stronger <u>than the person he was fighting</u>, so the jury should be instructed on the theory of defense of others.

Clarify Modifiers

A modifying word must be clearly connected to the word being modified. Modifiers should be as close as possible to the word being modified. Otherwise, clarity is lost. This error, commonly called a Dangling Modifier, often happens when a sentence starts with a modifier contained in a dependent clause, such as the following:

After becoming exhausted, the officer caught up to Mr. Jones.

Who became exhausted, the officer or Mr. Jones? To fix the problem, change the sentence structure to include the modified word in the same clause as the modifier:

After Mr. Jones became exhausted, the officer caught up to him.

The error also arises when the word being modified is omitted, such as in the following example, which is also an example of poor use of passive voice:

Hoping to gain a favorable sentence, evidence of past good deeds will be offered.

This sentence can also be corrected in multiple ways.

Hoping to gain a favorable sentence, Defendant will offer evidence of his past good deeds.

Defendant will offer evidence of his past good deeds in hopes of gaining a favorable sentence.

Consider the following additional examples:

Incorrect: After considering the statement in mitigation, the sentence should be reduced.

Correct: The Court should consider the statement in mitigation and reduce Defendant's sentence.

Correct: After considering the statement in mitigation, the Court should reduce the sentence.

Incorrect: The identification having failed, the second suspect was released.

Correct: The identification of the second suspect by Mr. Jones failed, so the second suspect was released.

Correct: Mr. Jones identification of the second failed, so that suspect was released.

Prevent Puzzling Pronouns

Pronouns make documents easier to read, and the lack of pronouns can make a document frustrating to read. Consider the following example.

David got in the car and started the car before David saw the cat. The cat was behind the car, so the car would have hit the cat if David had not seen the cat.

Use of pronouns makes the sentence less harsh on the ears.

David got in the car and started it before he saw the cat. It was behind the car, so the car would have hit it if he had not seen it.

Consider the following example of confusing pronouns adapted from a preliminary hearing.

Q: What did you see?
A: I saw Dave and Mike.
Q: What did they do; if anything?
A: He hit him with the bottle, and he tried to grab the knife.
Q: What happened then?
A: He ran away and threw it in the bushes.

This exchange raises more questions than it answers. Who used a bottle to hit whom? Who had the knife, and who tried to grab it? Who ran away, and what was thrown in the bushes?

Also consider the following example: When Sasha untied the dog, she was very happy.

Who was happy, Sasha or the dog?

Take care to ensure that your pronouns are unambiguous. If there is any ambiguity, don't use a pronoun to replace a noun.

Use the Oxford Comma

The Oxford comma is a comma used before the conjunction in a list of three or more items. Consider the following examples.

Correct: I ate dinner with Dave, my boss, and the Duke of Earl.

This sentence means that the speaker ate dinner with three people:
1. Dave
2. His boss
3. Duke of Earl

Incorrect: I ate dinner with Dave, my boss and the Duke of Earl.

The sentence now means that the speaker ate dinner with Dave, who happens to be his boss and is also the Duke of Earl.

Correct: My heroes are my children, Superman, and Laura Croft.

The speaker's heroes are:
1. His children
2. Superman
3. Laura Croft

Incorrect: My heroes are my children, Superman and Laura Croft.

The sentence now means that the speaker's heroes are his children, and his children are Superman and Laura Croft.

Use a Dependent Clause Comma

Add a dependent clause to the start of an independent clause using a comma. An independent clause can stand alone as a complete sentence. A dependent clause would be an incomplete sentence if it stood alone. A dependent clause can be tacked on to the start of an independent clause using a comma; however, usually punctuation is not required to add a dependent clause to the end of an independent clause, such as in the following examples:

Because he was late to work, Mr. Jones was speeding at the time of the collision.

Mr. Jones was speeding at the time of the collision because he was late to work.

"Because he was late to work" is a dependent clause – it cannot stand on its own as a sentence. "Mr. Jones was speeding at the time of the collision" is an independent clause – it can stand as a complete sentence on its own. The two can be joined using a comma if the dependent clause is first or joined without punctuation if the dependent clause is last. Examine the following examples in which the independent clause is underlined:

Every time Mr. Jones came to the house, <u>defendant was in fear.</u>
<u>Defendant was in fear</u> every time Mr. Jones came to the house.

Due to the stab wounds, <u>the victim died.</u>
<u>The victim died</u> due to the stab wounds. (A better sentence would be "The victim died because of the stab wounds" or "The victim died from the stab wounds.")

Until the victim was transported to the hospital, <u>no one knew his name.</u>
<u>No one knew his name</u> until the victim was transported to the hospital.

After the alleged victim was shown a picture of the defendant, <u>she was able to identify him in a live lineup.</u>
<u>The alleged victim was able to identify the defendant in a live lineup</u> after she was shown a picture of him.

Don't Comma Splice

Two independent clauses can stand alone as separate sentences; they can be joined with just semicolon; they can be joined with a comma-conjunction combination, or they can be joined by a semicolon-transition-comma combination. Independent clauses should not be joined using a comma alone. If two independent clauses are joined with a comma, the error is called a comma splice.

Incorrect: Dave left the house, he went to the store.

Correct:　Dave left the house. He went to the store.
　　　　　Dave left the house; he went to the store.
　　　　　Dave left the house, so he went to the store.
　　　　　Dave left the house; moreover, he went to the store.

Comma-conjunction combinations may include:

> And – Dave left the house, and he went to the store.
> But – Amy bought a taco, but she did not eat it.
> Or – Juan was hungry, or he may have just been tired.
> Nor – Mary did not want to go, nor did she want to stay.
> Yet – Joe was not shot, yet he was still injured.
> So – Jane was tired, so she went to bed.

Each of the above examples can also be written as two independent sentences:

> Dave left the house. He went to the store.
> Amy bought a taco. She did not eat it.
> Juan was hungry. He may have just been tired.
> Mary did not want to go. She did not want to stay.
> Joe was not shot. He was still injured.
> Jane was tired. She went to bed.

Note that removal of "nor" generally requires addition of the word "not" for clarity.

The independent clauses can also be joined with just a semicolon:

> Dave left the house; he went to the store.
> Amy bought a taco; she did not eat it.
> Juan was hungry; he may have just been tired.
> Mary did not want to go; she did not want to stay.
> Joe was not shot; he was still injured.
> Jane was tired; she went to bed.

Again, removal of the conjunction "nor" requires addition of "not" to clarify. The independent clauses in the examples above can also be joined using a semicolon-transition-comma combination. Such transitions are generally referred to as conjunctive adverbs, and some authors have called conjunctive adverbs harsh names, such as a "sad travesty and pretension," but they are in common use. Conjunctive adverbs using the semicolon-transition-comma combination can be used to join the independent clauses in the examples above:

> Dave left the house; subsequently, he went to the store.
> Amy bought a taco; however, did not eat it.
> Juan was hungry; on the other hand, he may have just been tired.

Mary did not want to go; in contrast, she did not want to stay.
Joe was not shot; nonetheless, he was still injured.
Jane was tired; consequently, he went to bed.

When independent clauses are connected in this way, the transition describes a relationship between the two clauses, such as in the following examples of transitions:

Moreover	Also	Equally important
Furthermore	In addition to	Besides
First	Second	Again
Further	Finally	Immediately
Next	Likewise	Similarly
In fact	As a result	Consequently
In the same way	In a like sense	To this end
With this in mind	Thus	With this purpose in mind
Therefore	Otherwise	Specifically
Especially	In particular	To explain
Namely	Including	For example
In other words	In particular	Specifically
On the contrary	Nevertheless	Notwithstanding this fact
In spite of this	In contrast	On one hand
Rather	Conversely	On the other hand
At the same time	Still	While this may be true

Consider these examples using transitions:

Dave was injured; equally important, he was sad.
Dave was injured; while this may be true, he was sad.
Dave was injured; therefore, he was sad.
Dave was injured; with this in mind, he was sad.
Dave was injured; notwithstanding this fact, he was sad.

Mary wanted food; with this purpose in mind, she went to the store.
Mary wanted food; therefore, she went to the store.
Mary wanted food; as a result, she went to the store.
Mary wanted food; still, she went to the store.
Mary wanted food; immediately, she went to the store.

Mark was mortally stabbed that night; therefore, he died.
Mark was mortally stabbed that night; subsequently, he died.
Mark was mortally stabbed that night; in other words, he died.
Mark was mortally stabbed that night; in the same way, he died.

Know Your Homophones

Speech-to-text systems combined with autocorrect have made words that sound similar even more of a problem today than in the past. While errors such as "discover emotion" in place of "discovery motion" are easier to catch, homophones present more of a problem. Carefully check documents to ensure these homophones are used correctly.

It's and Its
It's is short for "it is" or "it has" as in, "It has [it's] been hours since I ate." Its is possessive as in, "The cat lost its ball."

Tip: Replace its or it's with "it is." If the sentence sounds right, the correct word is probably it's.

You're and Your
You're is short for "you are" as in, "You are [you're] waiting to eat also." Your is possessive as in, "Your food is on the table."

Who's and Whose
Who's is short for "who is" or "who has" as in, "Who is [who's] ready?" Whose is possessive as in, "Whose food is this?"

They're, Their and There
They're is short for "they are" as in, "They are [they're] ready to go." Their is possessive as in, "Their food is ready." There denotes a location as in, "The food is there."

Note: There're is a similar sounding word meaning "there are" as in, "There are [there're] three cars in the lot."

Affect and Effect
Affect is a verb as in, "The use of a gun will affect the jury's decision." Effect is a noun as in, "The effect alcohol had on her inhibited her ability to drive."

Than and Then
While not truly homophones, than and then are commonly confused. Than compares things as in, "He is taller than I am." Then relates to time as in, "He shot the gun then fled on foot."

To, Too, and Two
To denotes direction as in, "Throw the ball to me."

Too denotes excess as in, "You threw it too hard."
Two is a number as in, "The two of us play catch."

<u>Accept and Except</u>
Accept denotes agreement, as in "We accept the prosecution's theory."
Except denotes exclusion, as in "We like the schedule, except for Tuesday."

Beware of Possessives

Speech-to-text also has difficulty handling possessives, so phrases like "Defendant's motion to suppress" may become "Defendants motion to suppress" and "Mr. Jones's admission" may become "Mr. Jones admission." These errors should be sought out and corrected.

Use Paired Commas

An aside is a short thought that is not required to make a complete sentence, but has been added for clarity, explanation, or to give more information. Use paired commas to insert asides, such as in the following examples:

Correct: Defendant, a thirty-year-old man, was married to Jane.

Incorrect: Defendant a thirty-year-old man was married to Jane.

"Defendant was married to Jane" is a complete sentence. The fact that he is "a thirty-year-old man" is an aside that should be set out with commas. The following are examples of paired commas:

Correct: The defendant and his girlfriend, Ms. Jones, went to the store.

Incorrect: The defendant and his girlfriend Ms. Jones went to the store.

Correct: The first suspect armed himself with a firearm, the revolver that was later found in the alley, before he fled the scene.

Incorrect: The first suspect armed himself with a firearm the revolver that was later found in the alley before he fled the scene.

Use Active Voice – It is usually best to avoid the use of passive voice sentences in legal writing, but this is not a firm rule. Active voice is when a noun takes action on another noun, such as "Dave shot the gun." Dave (a noun) took action (shot) another noun (the gun).

Passive voice reverses the order, so the noun being acted on is first, such as "the gun was shot by Dave." Revise passive voice sentences into active voice sentences, such as in the following examples.

Passive: The car was driven by Defendant.
Active: Defendant drove the car.

Passive: Mr. Smith was shot by the gunman three times.
Active: The gunman shot Mr. Smith three times.

Passive: The bullet was removed by Dr. Smith.
Active: Dr. Smith removed the bullet.

Don't yell – It is tempting to yell when arguing a point, but doing so will probably only have a negative impact on the reader. Yelling with the written word comes in several forms: exclamation points, capitalization, excessive use of bold or underlining, rhetorical questions, and use of hyperbole. Consider the following:

Incorrect:

> Defendant was not present at the crime scene!!!

> Defendant WAS NOT PRESENT at the crime scene.

> Defendant **was not present** at the crime scene!

> Defendant, who is unequivocally innocent and is being falsely accused of a crime he clearly did not and could not have committed, was not present at the crime scene.

> The <u>completely innocent</u> Defendant, a man wrongfully arrested and charged, was not even anywhere close to where the crime was committed, so why are we even here?

Correct:

> Defendant was not present at the crime scene.

Avoid abundant allegations – Generally, it is best to avoid making admissions on behalf of a defendant. Instead, pleadings usually refer to allegations made by the prosecution. This can lead to burdensome language, such as in the following example.

> Defendant allegedly entered the car and allegedly drove away. The police chased the car that was allegedly driven by Defendant before he allegedly crashed into a parked car before allegedly fleeing on foot. After he allegedly entered a house to avoid capture, officers apprehended him as he allegedly hid in the shower.

This paragraph can be revised to remove most instances of "allegedly."

> The Prosecution alleges as follows. Defendant entered the car and drove away. The police chased the car driven by Defendant before he crashed into a parked car and fled on foot. He entered a house to avoid capture, but officers apprehended him as he hid in the shower.

Avoid Adverbs – An adverb, such as honestly, innocently, justifiably, and aggressively, may be used to modify a verb, but doing so will generally add little value to the writing. Instead, and adverb will often interject unneeded argument. Unlike an adjective, which is often neutral, an adverb will often add unneeded argument.

Example: The first victim's actions were clearly provocative and overly aggressive.

This sentence is bad for multiple reasons. The adverbs "clearly" and "overly" add nothing but argument to the sentence, but the sentence admits that there was a victim, and the word "first" fails to clearly identify the person being discussed.

Limit long legalese – Legalese should be avoided. When possible, use plain language.

Incorrect:

> The perpetrator of the particular individual felony alleged herein, subsequently alleged to be one Mr. Clarence Green (hereinafter, "Mr. Green"), defendant herein, who stands as the accused, was described by one Ms. Sara Smith, in her initial contact with law

enforcement agents during their interview with her as a witness, as a person with which she previously kept company with during an amorous relationship traversing a period of approximately one year, more or less, prior to the incident described herein and relating to the present charges alleged against Mr. Green.

Correct:

Officers interviewed Sara Smith, who reported that she dated Defendant for approximately one year prior to the incident leading to his arrest.

Mind your malaprops – Some legal terminology is commonly misused, misspoken, or simply messed up. For entertainment purposes, some cases and other legal authorities containing malaprops are included. Beware of the following:

Correct: Corroborating evidence
Incorrect: Collaborating evidence
Misused in *Edgefield v. Audubon Nature Institute, Inc.* (2018) 318 So. 3rd 65
Memory aid: double r in corroborating evidence

Correct: Due diligence
Incorrect: Do diligence
Misused in *Trovare Capital Group, LLC v. Simkins Industries, Inc.* (2011) 646 F.3rd 994
Memory aid: diligence is owed, so the debt is due.

Correct: Elicit a response
Incorrect: Illicit a response
Misused in *State v. Ferguson* (2011) 804 N.W. 2nd 586
Memory aid: elicit a response from the dealer of illicit drugs

Correct: Ensure a fair trial
Incorrect: Insure a fair trial
Incorrect: Assure a fair trial
Misused in *Scalia v. International Longshore and Warehouse Union* (N.D. California 2020) 337 F.R.D. 281)
Memory aid: ensure is make certain; assure is to promise, and insure is to buy protection from risk

Correct: Ex parte
Incorrect: Ex party

Misused in *Wardley Development v. Superior Court* (1989) 213 Cal.App.3rd 391
Memory aid: no party at an ex parte because there are not enough guests

Correct: Flesh out
Incorrect: Flush out
Misused in *Cabe v. Superior Court* (1998) 63 Cal.App.4th 732
Memory aid: flesh out the argument that people should flush out the pipes

Correct: Moot point
Incorrect: Mute point
Misused in *Bates v. Duby* (2003) 2003 WL 21921169 (unreported case)
Memory aid: mute is silent; moot is unsettled

Correct: Pass muster
Incorrect: Pass mustard
Misused in *In re Vansickel* (2004) 309 B.R. 189
Memory aid: mustard is a condiment; muster is an inspection

Correct: Peremptory challenge
Incorrect: Preemptory challenge
Misused in *People v. Baker* (2021) 10 Cal.5th 1044
Memory aid: No double e in peremptory

Correct: Proscribes the conduct
Incorrect: Prescribes the conduct
Misused in *Commonwealth v. Howard* (2021) 257 A.3rd 1217
Memory aid: laws proscribe; doctors prescribe

Correct: Regardless
Incorrect Irregardless
Misused in *Driskill v. State* (2021) 626 S.W.3rd 212
Memory aid: irregardless is always wrong

Correct: Tenet of construction (also tenet of the Constitution, tenet of the church, tenet of the penal code, etc.)
Incorrect: Tenant of construction
Misused in *Nichols v. CitiGroup Global Markets, Inc.* (N.D. Alabama 2004) 364 F.Supp.2nd 1330
Memory aid: tenet is a belief; tenant is an occupant

Check your numbers – Often additional arguments, authorities, discovery requests, or other numbered items will be added to pleadings resulting in misnumbered paragraphs. For example, this section of the book purports to contain "ten grammar guidelines," but the list presented has sixteen entries. Check documents for consistency in numbering and for number parallelism. Consider the following errors.

Deleted paragraphs:

> First, the court should consider the defendant's age and immaturity…
> Second, the court should consider the defendant's lack of criminal history…
> Fourth, the court should consider the intent of Proposition 57….

Inserted paragraphs:

> Defendant requests production of the following items:
> 1. All offense reports related to this matter…
> 2. All RAP sheets for any defendant or witness…
> 2. All evidence that any defendant or witness was a member of a gang, associated with a gang, or an affiliate of a gang…
> 3. All video and/or audio recordings of the events leading to the defendant's arrest.

Non-parallel paragraphs:
> One, the defendants were not apprehended at the scene…
> Second, the lineup was overly suggestive and only had two other suspects…

Such errors are easily seen when on the same page, but pleadings and numbering systems usually span multiple pages, so any numbering system should be checked for consistency prior to finalization of the pleadings.

2. Magic Incantations

There are no magic incantations necessary to invoke the law, but some paralegals and attorneys get caught up with long statements and Latin phrases when their use is unnecessary and confusing.

Take for example, the following from an actual notice of motion:

> PLEASE TAKE NOTICE that on May 30, 2001 at 8:30 a.m. or as soon thereafter as the matter can be heard in the above-entitled court located at 1415 Truxtun Avenue, Bakersfield, California, 93301, in the County of Kern, the defendant will

move for an order to withdrawing her guilty plea to the offense charged in Counts 5 and 6 of the information, to wit, a violation of Health and Safety Code section 11377(a) and Vehicle Code 23152(a), namely Possession of a Controlled Substance and Driving Under the Influence, and enter pleas of not guilty to those offenses.

This could be shortened to something like:

PLEASE TAKE NOTICE that on the date noted above, the defendant will move to withdrawing her guilty plea.

The court should not deny the motion just because the pleading does not contain the address of the courthouse in the text of the pleading – the prosecution knows where the courthouse is, and the branch or division is indicated in the heading. Similarly, it goes without saying that the case may not be heard at exactly 8:30 a.m., so there is no need to write, "or as soon thereafter as the matter can be heard." Include the extra language if the attorney requests it but omit extra fluff when possible.

The same notice of motion also included the following:

The motion will be based on this Notice of Motion, on the attached memorandum of points and authorities and filed herewith and such supplemental memorandum of points and authorities that may be hereafter filed with the court or stated orally at the conclusion of the hearing, on the attached declaration of defendant, on the attached transcript of the take of defendant's plea, on all papers and records on file in this action and on such oral and documentary evidence as may be presented at the time of the motion or filed in pleadings subsequent to hearing of the motion.

It is difficult to imagine a judge denying a motion because the defense failed to ask the judge to consider "all papers and records on file in this action" or the "oral and documentary evidence as may be presented at the time of the motion." The judge is always expected to consider the pleadings and argument.

Similarly, there is no magic incantation needed to invoke a declaration. Some attorneys prefer, "I, John Smith, do declare under pain and penalty of perjury" but it is equally effective in most courts to simply begin an attorney's declaration with, "I declare." Courts generally assume that the attorney, as an officer of the court, is attempting to be truthful in a declaration.

Most pleadings include a summary of legal authority, but this can be entitled "Memorandum of Points and Authorities," "Points and Authorities," "Points, Authorities, and Argument," "Memorandum of Points and Authorities in Support of Defendant's Motion to Compel Discovery," or anything similar. As noted in the Maxims of Jurisprudence, "The law respects form less than substance." (*Civil Code §3528*)

Res ipsa loquitur, ipso facto, in loco parentis, nolle prosequi… this sounds like a wizard trying to summon creatures from another realm, yet sometimes such phrases sneak into places where they are not needed. Instead of writing something like, "Defendant entered a nolo contendere plea in this case in exchange for nolle prosequi in case 98765," write "Defendant pled no contest in exchange for an agreement to dismiss case 98765."

Avoid all but the most common Latin words and phrases. Avoid wordy introductions and wordy declarations. Pay more attention to meaning than to form.

When preparing pleadings, don't try to use some specific magic language found in this or any other book. Read the pleading templates and mold the facts of the case you are working on.

3. Pleading Rules

The California Rules of Court (CRC) contain the rules for formatting pleadings. Title Two of the CRC contains Trial Court Rules (Rules 2.1 - 2.1100), which includes the rules for formatting documents that are to be filed in the trial court. Title Eight of the CRC contains Appellate Rules (Rules 8.1 - 8.1125), which contain entirely different formatting rules. Further, local rules may require additional formatting or electronic filing.

The following summary is for pleadings filed in the Superior Court based on Title Two of the CRC as it generally applies to criminal matters.

- Printing must only be on one side of the paper (*Rule 2.102*).
- Font size must be at least 12 points (*Rule 2.104*).
- Font must be Courier, Times New Roman, or Arial (*Rule 2.105*).
- The left margin of each page must be at least one inch from the left edge and the right margin at least 1/2 inch from the right edge

(*Rule 2.107*).

- The lines on each page must be one and one-half spaced or double-spaced and numbered consecutively (*Rule 2.108*).
- Quotations and footnotes may be single-spaced (*Rule 2.108*).
- Line numbers must be placed at the left margin and separated from the text by a vertical column of space at least 1/5 inch wide or a single or double vertical line. Each line number must be aligned with a line of type, or the line numbers must be evenly spaced vertically on the page. Line numbers must be consecutively numbered, beginning with the number 1 on each page. There must be at least three line numbers for every vertical inch on the page (*Rule 2.108*).
- Each page must be numbered consecutively at the bottom. The page numbering must begin with the first page and use only Arabic numerals (e.g., 1, 2, 3). The page number may be suppressed and need not appear on the first page (*Rule 2.109*).
- Except for exhibits, each page must have a footer in the bottom margin, placed below the page number and divided from the rest of the document page by a printed line. The footer must contain the title of the paper (examples: "Motion to Suppress," "Reply to Motion for Discovery") or some clear and concise abbreviation. (*Rule 2.110*)
- The title of the paper in the footer must be in at least 10-point font (*Rule 2.110*).
- The first page of each paper has special formatting rules as follows (*Rule 2.110*):
    o In the space commencing one inch from the top of the page with line 1, to the left of the center of the page, the page must have the name, address, telephone number, fax number, e-mail address, and State Bar number of the attorney. (Tip: the first page also needs to identify the person represented by the attorney, such as "Attorney for Defendant, John Jones." This information is usually on or about line 5)
    o In the first 2 inches of space between lines 1 and 7 to the right of the center of the page, a blank space for the use of the clerk.
    o On line 8, at or below 3 1/3 inches from the top of the page, the title of the court.
    o Below the title of the court, in the space to the left of the center of the page, the title of the case.
    o To the right of and opposite the title, the number of the

case.
  o Below the number of the case, the nature of the paper
  o Below the nature of the paper, the date, place, and time of any anticipated hearing on the paper followed by the trial and readiness dates, if those dates have been set. (note: this requirement is found in other rules).

- Pages should be stapled on the top left (*Rule 2.113*).
- Each paper must be two-hole punched, centered 2½ inches apart and 5/8 inch from the top of the paper (*Rule 2.115*).

It may seem that there are many rules, but that is only because there are many rules. It would be difficult to create pleading paper from scratch that satisfies of these rules. Fortunately, almost every law firm has a few already formatted documents; however, many firms use documents that are close to correct, but not quite correct, and sometimes clerks reject documents for being close but wrong. A formatted pleading template is available at BakersfieldParalegal.com. It has the added feature of inserting the current date and the document name in the margin. This comes in handy when multiple versions of a document are created or when trying to locate a file to use as a template.

A better option is to obtain a collection of formatted templates for standard pleadings. These are also available at BakersfieldParalegal.com, 661Justice.com, and through multiple other sources.

4. Filing Pleadings

Generally, pleadings are filed by delivering them to the proper court clerk. This usually means preparing and serving the pleadings as described above, attaching a proof of service, and delivering the pleadings to either the court's felony counter or the court's misdemeanor counter. However, there are many exceptions to this general rule, and exceptions vary from court to court.

- Ex parte requests for funds are not served on any party. Some courts require that such requests are submitted to a specific judge, courtroom, clerk, or other person. Check your local rules.

- Requests for funds in capital cases are delivered directly to the capital clerk. Each court has a designated capital clerk.

- Some courts require that an ex parte request for order shortening time be served on all interested parties. Most courts have specific rules for orders shortening time, such as that such motions are filed before 11:00 a.m. or that such motions are delivered to a specific department.

- Most courts require that in addition to serving opposing counsel (the District Attorney in most cases) pleadings also be served on all codefendants.

- Most courts require that Pitchess motions be served on the police agency, the agency's attorney, and the prosecutor before being filed.

List any local filing rules here:

_____

_____

_____

_____

_____

_____

_____

_____

_____

_____

_____

_____

_____

5. Word Processing Tips

It is not enough for a paralegal to be able to type quickly; a paralegal should learn to use symbol shortcuts, autocorrect, keyboard shortcuts, and standard pleadings to more quickly and efficiently prepare pleadings.

Symbol Shortcuts

One of the most used symbols in law is the section symbol, such as its use in *Penal Code §17*. To insert the section symbol using Microsoft Word can take multiple steps:
   a.   Choose the "Insert" menu
   b.   Select "Symbol"
   c.   Select "More Symbols"
   d.   Select "Special Characters"
   e.   Select "Section"
   f.   Select "Insert"

These steps can be shortened to a few simple keystrokes, such as Alt-C. To define Alt-C to make the § symbol, instead of choosing "Insert" at step "f." choose "Shortcut Key" and assign the § symbol to Alt-C or any other convenient key combination.

List any special shortcuts used by you or your employer here:

_____

_____

_____

_____

_____

_____

_____

_____

_____

Autocorrect Shortcuts

Autocorrect can be your friend or your enemy.

Autocorrect may be your enemy if it changes (c) to © at the wrong time. It is, therefore, helpful to prevent the word processing software from making undesired corrections. Criminal pleadings often include (c) such as in *Penal Code §1054.1(c)* but it is rare for criminal pleadings to require the © symbol. However, Microsoft Word will attempt to "correct" *Penal Code §1054.1(c)* to *Penal Code §1054.1©* and it will attempt to "correct" *Penal Code §1054.1(e)* to *Penal Code §1054.1€*. To prevent these "corrections" from happening, follow these steps:

    a. Choose the "Insert" menu
    b. Select "Symbol"
    c. Select "More Symbols"
    d. Select "AutoCorrect"
    e. Select "(c)"
    f. Select "Delete"
    g. Select "(e)"
    h. Select "Delete"

Autocorrect can also be your friend by typing common names, locations, and phrases. For example, a "ql" can be defined as ROGER LAMPKIN, an attorney who assisted with this book.

Similarly, autocorrect can be used to change "qd" it to a standard declaration:

> I declare under penalty of perjury that the foregoing is true and correct, except those matters alleged on information and belief, and I believe those matters to be true.

The letter "q" is helpful as the first letter of most predefined Auto Correct phrases because it is almost always followed by the letter "u." This minimizes the danger that autocorrect will type something undesirable, and "q" provides its own pneumonic, as in "qd" standing for "quick declaration," and "qr" stands for "quick report," which expands to:

> I have completed my review of the initial discovery in this matter and report the following findings:

To create such timesaving Auto Corrections, follow these steps:

a. Choose the "Insert" menu
b. Select "Symbol"
c. Select "More Symbols"
d. Select "AutoCorrect"
e. In the "Replace" box, type the letters to be replaced.
f. Choose "Plain Text"
g. In the "With" box, type the words that the letters will expand into.
h. Choose "Add"
i. Choose "Ok"

List any special autocorrect shortcuts used by you or your employer here:

_____

_____

_____

_____

_____

_____

_____

_____

_____

_____

_____

_____

Keyboard and Mouse Shortcuts

Many word processing tasks can be completed faster using keyboard shortcuts. The following shortcuts work with Microsoft Word, but most also work with WordPerfect, Google Docs, LibreOffice, OpenOffice, and other word processors. They are grouped by function and usefulness instead of being in alphabetical order.

Keys	Action	Why you want to know it.
Ctrl+a	Highlight all text.	Change all fonts, spacing, etc. or copy all text to a new document.
Ctrl+c	Copy text	Faster than choosing from the menu.
Ctrl+x	Cut text	Faster than choosing from the menu.
Ctrl+v	Paste text	Faster than choosing from the menu.
Ctrl+i	Make text italic	Use for case and code citations
Ctrl+m	Indent	Faster than choosing from the menu.
Ctrl+z	Undo	Undo a mistake.
Ctrl+y	Redo	Redo an accidental Ctrl-z.
Ctrl+End	Move to end of document	Faster than scrolling.
Ctrl+Home	Move to the start of the document	Faster than scrolling.
Shift+f5	Jump	Jumps between recently edited places. Note that this feature is buggy in some versions of Office.
Ctrl+1	Single space	Good for long quotes
Ctrl+2	Double space	Most text will be double space
Ctrl+5	1.5 line spacing	This seems to be rarely used in the trial courts
Shift+f3	Uppercase	Changes to all upper case and back
Ctrl+Enter	New page	Force the text onto the next page
Shift+Alt+D	Insert the date	Faster than typing and fewer mistakes
Ctrl+Mouse wheel	Zoom	Easy way to get the exact size you want when viewing a document.

H. PLEADINGS

Introduction

Legal pleadings include Complaints, Informations, Petitions, Waivers, Stipulations, Declarations, Motions, and other such forms. The most common pleading prepared by a Criminal Defense Paralegal is a motion.

A motion is a request that the court issue an order. Motions before trial are those motions that make requests in preparation for trial. These motions are generally not heard by the judge who will preside over trial; instead, they are heard by a motions judge.

Notice Requirements

"Notice" simply means providing a copy of a motion to other interested parties. In most cases, this means giving a copy of your motion to the district attorney, but some motions must also be served on the probation department, a law enforcement agency, the city attorney, county counsel, or someone else.

Generally, a defendant cannot serve his own pleadings, and most law firms use a messenger service to pick up and deliver pleadings. The service picks up pleadings from the law firm, serves all required parties, files the pleadings with the court, and then returns endorsed copies to the law firm.

Service of motions on counsel for codefendants is technically not required for most motions, but local rules often require service on counsel for co-defendants, so it is generally the best practice to always serve each attorney for each codefendant.

It is easier to serve a motion on extra people than it is to enforce technical rules, so non-essential parties are shown in the chart on the next page.

Service times refer to personal service, but the court may require an additional five days if service is by mail.

The number of days refers to court days – days the court is in session. The chart on the following page summarizes notice requirements and recommendations.

Motion	Who to Serve	Notice	Notes
General Rule	District Attorney	10 days	*Rule of Court 4.111*; Unless noted, motions require ten-day notice
Pitchess (Discover Personnel Files)	District Attorney, Police Agency, and Agency's Attorney	16 days	*Code of Civil Procedure §1005(b)*, Service on the District Attorney is not technically required, but clerks may insist.
Suppress Evidence	District Attorney	10 days	*Penal Code §1538.5* Time is reduced to five days if the motion is brought before preliminary hearing.
Ex Parte	None	None	Applies to few motions – mostly requests for funds.
Continuance	District Attorney	2 days	Also serve the probation department if motion is brought after conviction
Expunge Conviction	District Attorney, Probation Department	15 days	*Penal Code §1203.4*
Declare Defendant Incompetent	District Attorney	None	*Penal Code §1367 or 1368*
Withdraw Plea	District Attorney, Probation Department	10 days	*Penal Code §1018.* Some courts do not require advance notice, but best practice is to serve and file at least ten day before hearing.
Substitute Attorney	District Attorney, Prior Attorney	None	Best practice is to file at least 2 days before hearing.
Waiver of Appearance	None – Give to judge at hearing	None	*Penal Code §977* – Generally only applies to misdemeanors
Strike Prior Convictions	District Attorney, Probation	2 days	Commonly known as a *Romero, Rule 4.437(a)*
Statement in Mitigation	District Attorney, Probation	4 days	*Rule 4.437(a)*
Return Property	District Attorney, the agency holding the property	3 days	*Code of Civil Procedure §1201.5*
Substitute Attorney	District Attorney	None	Best to give two days' notice

Sample Pleadings

Many motions and pleadings before trial are fact specific to a case, so it is not possible to present "ready to file" or completely generic examples. The motions offered here are examples of some of the common types of motions that may be filed, but the list is more exhaustive that the motions filed by most criminal defense attorneys.

Even if the criminal defense attorney makes it a habit to only file a few types of motions, such as discovery and suppress, a Criminal Defense Paralegal should have a more expansive collection of standard pleading templates so case-specific motions, waivers, and other pleadings can be prepared quickly without the need for reinvention.

The motions in this section are modified versions of pleadings filed in the Superior Court related to preliminary matters, trial, sentencing, and post-conviction proceedings. Some pleadings were created from scratch, but many pleadings come from court records used as starting points for future motions. A Criminal Defense Paralegal should, when possible, build on the work of others. Fully formatted and customized electronic versions of these pleadings can be ordered at BakersfieldParalegal.com.

This book only contains a cursory overview of motions in limine, which are covered in detail in *California Criminal Defense Motions in Limine* (the print edition is available from most bookstores, and sample pleadings from the book are available at BakersfieldParalegal.com and 661Justice.com). Further, post-conviction challenges to the conviction, such as appeals and habeas corpus petitions, are beyond the scope of this book.

These sample motions are organized into several broad categories, but there is much overlap between categories.

- **Procedural Matters** – pleadings that generally do not have a direct effect on the outcome of a case but are used for scheduling, administrative, and similar purposes.

- **Discovery** – pleadings designed to obtain information to assist the defense.

- **Dismissals** – pleadings asking the court to dismiss the charges against the defendant.

- **Sanctions** – pleadings asking for sanctions against the prosecution based on misconduct by members of the prosecution team.

- **Third Party Requests** – pleadings concerning persons or entities who are neither members of the prosecution team nor the defense team.

- **Plea and Sentencing** – pleadings connected with a defendant's plea and sentence.

- **Defense Funding** – pleadings used to obtain funding for the defense team.

How can we organize this whole table of discovery in time for trial tomorrow?

This is my table. You have a table and six bank boxes over there.

1. Procedural Matters

a. Substitute Attorney (Consent)

Note: Courts usually allow a substitution of attorney by agreement when the substitution is made early in the proceedings and is not opposed by the current attorney. The following form will accomplish this type of substitution; however, if substitution is made on the eve of trial, preliminary hearing, or other contested matter, it is best to use a motion to make the substitution (see next form).

ROGER LAMPKIN
SB#113786
1234 L Street
Bakersfield, CA 93301
Tel: (661)633-1234
Fax: (661)863-6741
Attorney for Doug Donenabbed

IN THE SUPERIOR COURT OF THE STATE OF CALIFORNIA,
IN AND FOR THE COUNTY OF KERN

People of the State of California,	CASE NO. 123456
Plaintiffs,	SUBSTITUTION OF ATTORNEY
- v. -	
Doug Donenabbed,	
Defendant	

Defendant, Doug Donenabbed, hereby substitutes Roger Lampkin, 1234 L Street, Bakersfield, CA, 93301 as his attorney of record in place of his current counsel whose signature is below.

Dated: I request this substitution.

                                        _____

                                        By   Doug Donenabbed

Dated: I accept this substitution.

76

By   Roger Lampkin, Attorney for
Doug Donenabbed

Dated:

I consent to this substitution.

By   Deputy Public Defender

b. Motion to Substitute Attorney

ROGER LAMPKIN
SB#113786
1234 L Street
Bakersfield, CA 93301
Tel: (661)633-1234
Fax: (661)863-6741
Attorney for Doug Donenabbed

IN THE SUPERIOR COURT OF THE STATE OF CALIFORNIA, IN AND FOR THE COUNTY OF KERN

| People of the State of California,

Plaintiffs,

- v. –

Doug Donenabbed,

Defendant | CASE NO. 123456
MOTION TO SUBSTITUTE ATTORNEY

Date: August 12, 2021
Time: 8:30 a.m.
Dept: CC

Readiness: August 13, 2021
Trial: August 23, 2021 |

TO THE COURT, PRIOR DEFENSE COUNSEL, AND THE
DISTRICT ATTORNEY: PLEASE TAKE NOTICE that at the date and
time indicated above, the defendant will move for an order substituting
Roger Lampkin as attorney of record for Defendant.
Dated:

By   Roger Lampkin, Attorney for
Doug Donenabbed

c.Motion to Waive Conflict

ROGER LAMPKIN
SB#113786
1234 L Street
Bakersfield, CA 93301
Tel: (661)633-1234
Fax: (661)863-6741
Attorney for Doug Donenabbed, David Donenabbed

IN THE SUPERIOR COURT OF THE STATE OF CALIFORNIA,
IN AND FOR THE COUNTY OF KERN

People of the State of California,	CASE NO. 123456
Plaintiffs,	MOTION TO WAIVE CONFLICT OF INTERESTS
- v. —	Date: August 2, 2022
Doug Donenabbed, David Donenabbed	Time: 8:30 a.m. Dept: CC
Defendant	Readiness: August 12, 2022 Trial: August 22, 2022

TO THE COURT AND THE DISTRICT ATTORNEY:
PLEASE TAKE NOTICE that on the date and time indicated above, or as soon thereafter as the matter can be heard in the above-entitled court, the defendants will move the Court to accept defendants' waiver of any conflict of interest that may exist between defendants and counsel and allow counsel to continue to represent both defendants.

This motion will be made on the ground that defendants' right to counsel under the Sixth Amendment to the United States Constitution affords defendants the right to counsel of their own choice.

The motion will be based on this notice and attachments, on all papers and records on file in this action and on such oral and documentary evidence as may be presented at the time of the motion.

Dated:

By   Roger Lampkin, Attorney for
Doug Donenabbed

MEMORANDUM OF POINTS AND AUTHORITIES

"A court abridges a defendant's right to counsel when it removes retained defense counsel in the face of a defendant's willingness to make an informed and intelligent waiver of his right to be represented by conflict-free counsel. California decisions limit severely the judge's discretion to intrude on defendant's choice of counsel in order to eliminate potential conflicts, ensure adequate representation, or serve judicial convenience… Our courts recognize that the right of a defendant to decide for himself who best can conduct the case must be respected wherever feasible… After the trial court has fulfilled its obligation to inquire into the possibility of a conflict of interest and to act in response to what its inquiry discovers, the defendant may choose the course he wishes to take. If the court has found that a conflict of interest is at least possible, the defendant may, of course, decline or discharge conflicted counsel. But he may also choose not to do so: a defendant may waive his right to the assistance of an attorney unhindered by a conflict of interest." (*Alcocer v. Superior Court* (1988) 206 Cal.App.3rd 951, punctuation and citations omitted)

"In determining whether a defendant understands the nature of a possible conflict of interest with counsel, a trial court need not separately explore each foreseeable conflict and consequence. Nor does a defendant's waiver of conflict-free counsel extend only to matters discussed in detail on the record." (*People v. Jones* (1991) 53 Cal.3rd 1115, 1137.)

For a waiver to be valid, the potential dangers need only be "disclosed generally" to the defendant. (*Maxwell v. Superior Court* (1982) 30 Cal.3rd 606, 619)

In order to find such a waiver, "[n]o particular form of inquiry is required, but, at a minimum, the trial court must assure itself that (1) the defendant has discussed the potential drawbacks of joint representation with is attorney, or if he wishes, outside counsel, (2) that he has been made aware of the dangers and possible consequences of joint representation in this case, (3) that he knows of his right to conflict-free representation, and (4) that he voluntarily wishes to waive that right. [Citations.]" (*People v. Mroczko* (1983) 35 Cal. 3rd 86, 109-110)

→••Ω••←

Practical Tip:
The janitor in your building is a person who deserves your respect. Do something nice for the janitor, the secretary, the intern, and everyone else in your building. Learn their names and treat them with kindness.

d. Motion to be Relieved as Attorney of Record

ROGER LAMPKIN
SB#113786
1234 L Street
Bakersfield, CA 93301
Tel: (661)633-1234
Fax: (661)863-6741
Attorney for Doug Donenabbed

IN THE SUPERIOR COURT OF THE STATE OF CALIFORNIA, IN AND FOR THE COUNTY OF KERN

People of the State of California, Plaintiffs, - v. – Doug Donenabbed, Defendant	CASE NO. 123456 NOTICE OF MOTION AND MOTION TO BE RELIEVED AS ATTORNEY OF RECORD Date: August 2, 2022 Time: 8:30 a.m. Dept: CC Readiness: August 12, 2022 Trial: August 22, 2022

TO THE COURT, THE DEFENDANT, AND THE DISTRICT ATTORNEY: PLEASE TAKE NOTICE that on the date and time noted above, or as soon thereafter as the matter can be heard in the above-entitled court, Attorney Roger Lampkin will move for an order relieving him as attorney of record for defendant.

The motion will be made on the grounds that the there is an actual conflict of interests between defendant and his counsel and it appears that further action is required in this case before its conclusion.

The motion will be based on this Notice of Motion, on the attached memorandum of points and authorities and filed herewith and such supplemental memorandum of points and authorities that may be hereafter filed with the court or stated orally at the conclusion of the hearing, on all papers and records on file in this action and on such oral and documentary evidence as may be presented at the time of the motion.
Dated:

_____

By Roger Lampkin, Attorney for
Doug Donenabbed

DECLARATION OF COUNSEL

I, Roger Lampkin, declare:
1. I am an attorney at law and am the attorney for the defendant in this case.
2. An actual conflict of interests has arisen between me and defendant which requires my withdrawal from this case.
3. The conflict was unknown to me during trial, and the conflict was only recently revealed to me.
4. To disclose further details at this time would violate the attorney-client privilege.

I declare that the foregoing is true and correct.

Dated:

_____

By   Roger Lampkin, Attorney for
Doug Donenabbed

POINTS AND AUTHORITIES

Code of Civil Procedure §284 allows for a substitution of attorney, and this Court has the power to "Provide for the orderly conduct of proceedings before it" (*Code of Civil Procedure §128(a)(3)*).

There is a conflict in the present case. See the attached declaration of defense counsel. Because it is essential that the attorney-client privilege be protected, defense counsel's good faith assertion of a conflict of interest is sufficient basis for a motion to be relieved, without requiring details. (*Leverson v Superior Court* (1983) 34 Cal 3rd 530; *Aceves v Superior Court* (1996) 51 Cal App 4th 584; *Uhl v Municipal Court* (1974) 37 Cal App 3rd 526).

Practical Tip:
Learn how to properly use every piece of technology in your office. The day will come when something is due immediately and the only person who understands the required technology is out of the office. You can save the day by learning how to reset the computer network, how to perform simple copier maintenance, how to use the postage machine, how to run a video conference, how to use scanners, and how to use all the other technology in the office before an emergency comes up.

e. Waiver of Personal Appearance

Note: This waiver generally applies to misdemeanor cases, and the court may not allow a waiver in certain types of cases. The defendant will most likely have to personally appear in court if "charged with a misdemeanor offense involving domestic violence" or "with a misdemeanor offense involving driving under the influence." See *Penal Code §977* in the chapter entitled Select Legal Authorities.

ROGER LAMPKIN
SB#113786
1234 L Street
Bakersfield, CA 93301
Tel: (661)633-1234
Fax: (661)863-6741
Attorney for Doug Donenabbed

IN THE SUPERIOR COURT OF THE STATE OF CALIFORNIA,
IN AND FOR THE COUNTY OF KERN

People of the State of California,	CASE NO. 123456
Plaintiffs,	WAIVER OF PERSONAL APPEARANCE
- v. -	
Doug Donenabbed,	
Defendant	

The undersigned defendant, having been advised of his or her right to be present at all stages of the proceedings, including, but not limited to, presentation of and arguments on questions of fact and law, and to be confronted by and cross-examine all witnesses, hereby waives the right to be present at the hearing of any motion or other proceeding in this cause.

The undersigned defendant hereby requests the court to proceed during every absence of the defendant that the court may permit pursuant to this waiver, and hereby agrees that his or her interest is represented at all times by the presence of his or her attorney the same as if the defendant were personally present in court, and further agrees that notice to his or her attorney that his or her presence in court on a particular day at a particular time is required is notice to the defendant of the requirement of his or her appearance at that time and place.

Dated:

_____

By   Doug Donenabbed

f. Motion to Recall Warrant

An arrest warrant may be issued if a person is charged but not arrested, if a person fails to appear in court when required, or if a bondsman revokes a defendant's bond. If a defendant is out of custody but aware that an arrest warrant has been issues, a motion to recall warrant can be used to remedy the issue.

Before filing a motion to recall warrant, it is good to check to make sure the defendant has arranged for bail or is prepared to go into custody should the court not grant an own recognizance release.

If the court exonerated a bail bond, the bail company may need to issue a resumption of bail, sometimes at a substantial cost to the defendant. If the bail company does not issue a resumption or otherwise post bail, the court may take the defendant into custody because there is no valid bail bond on file.

If the warrant was issued because the defendant failed to appear for court, be the motion gives an explanation as to why the defendant failed to appear and what efforts the defendant made to remedy the failure.

There is always a danger that the court will deny the motion and take the defendant into custody, but the chances of it being granted are higher if bail issues have been resolved before hearing. Do not give an opinion as to whether or not the defendant will be taken into custody, even if the defendant or his family pressures you for such an opinion. If a defendant asks, "will the court take me into custody?" good answers are:

- I hope the court lets you out, but I don't know what they will do.
- The attorney will argue that you should not go into custody, but it is up to the judge.
- I don't know, but you may want to discuss it with the attorney if you have more concerns.

ROGER LAMPKIN
SB#113786
1234 L Street
Bakersfield, CA 93301
Tel: (661)633-1234
Fax: (661)863-6741

Attorney for Doug Defendant

IN THE SUPERIOR COURT OF THE STATE OF CALIFORNIA,

IN AND FOR THE COUNTY OF KERN

People of the State of California, Plaintiffs, - v - Doug Donenabbed, Defendant	CASE NO. 123456 MOTION TO RECALL WARRANT Date: August 2, 2022 Time: 8:30 a.m. Dept: CC Readiness: August 12, 2022 Trial: August 22, 2022

TO THE COURT AND THE DISTRICT ATTORNEY: PLEASE TAKE NOTICE that at the date and time indicated above, the defendant will move the Court for an order to recall the warrant and set dates for further proceedings.

  This motion shall be based on this Notice of Motion, all attached papers, all papers and pleadings on file with the court, and such oral and documentary evidence as may be presented at the hearing.

Dated:

_____
By   Roger Lampkin, Attorney for
     Doug Donenabbed

84

DECLARATION IN SUPPORT OF MOTION

I, Roger Lampkin, Attorney for Defendant, declare:
1. I am the attorney for Defendant in the above-entitled matter.
2. The arraignment in this matter was set for December 22, 2021.
3. Due to an illness, Defendant was unable to attend, and the court issued a warrant.
4. Defendant's wife called the same day and informed me of the illness and Defendant's inability to attend.
5. I request that the warrant be recalled and that the matter be set for further proceedings.

I declare that I am informed and believe that the foregoing is true and correct.

Dated:

_____

By   Roger Lampkin, Attorney for
Doug Donenabbed

POINTS AND AUTHORITIES

"Every court shall have the power to… provide for the orderly conduct of proceedings before it, or its officers." (*Code of Civil Procedure §128*)

→ • • Ω • • ←

A pair of eagles may help fight the case, but I said, "I need paralegals."

g. Motion to Reduce Bail

ROGER LAMPKIN
SB#113786
1234 L Street
Bakersfield, CA 93301
Tel: (661)633-1234
Fax: (661)863-6741
Attorney for Doug Donenabbed

IN THE SUPERIOR COURT OF THE STATE OF CALIFORNIA,
IN AND FOR THE COUNTY OF KERN

People of the State of California,	CASE NO. 123456
Plaintiffs,	NOTICE OF MOTION FOR OWN RECOGNIZANCE RELEASE OR, IN THE ALTERNATIVE, MOTION TO REDUCE BAIL
- v. -	
Doug Donenabbed,	
Defendant	Date: August 2, 2022 Time: 8:30 a.m. Dept: CC
	Readiness: August 12, 2022 Trial: August 22, 2022

TO THE COURT AND THE DISTRICT ATTORNEY: PLEASE TAKE NOTICE that at the date and time indicated above, or as soon thereafter as the matter can be heard in the above-entitled court, the defendant will move for an order reducing the amount of bail set in this matter.

Current Bail: $195,000

Requested Bail: $20,000 or less

Prior Bail Motions: None

Current Charges
  Penal Code §246.3(A)   Recklessly Discharge a Firearm
  Penal Code §246   Shoot at Inhabited Vehicle

Penal Code §245(A)(2)   Assault with Firearm on Person

The motion will be made on the grounds that the bail set is excessive within the meaning of the Eighth Amendment to the United States Constitution and of Article I, §12 of the California Constitution.

The motion will be based on this notice of motion, all attached documents, the records on file in this action, and on such matters as may be presented at the hearing.

Dated:

_____

By   Roger Lampkin, Attorney for
Doug Donenabbed

DECLARATION IN SUPPORT OF BAIL MOTION

I, Roger Lampkin, Attorney for Defendant, declare that I am informed and believe:
1.   Defendant has no prior criminal arrests or convictions.
2.   Defendant has extensive ties to the community including church membership, participating in local amateur sports leagues, and membership in Kiwanis.
3.   Defendant's mother, father, three grandparents, and two siblings live in town and have regular family meetings with Defendant.
4.   Defendant is gainfully employed at Taffy Truck, earning approximately $42,000 per year.
5.   Defendant has been married for three years and has two children.
6.   Defendant is, therefore, not a flight risk.

I so declare based on information and belief.

Dated:

_____

By   Roger Lampkin,
Attorney for Doug Donenabbed

POINTS, AUTHORITIES, AND ARGUMENT

The California Constitution contains two bail sections - Article I, §12 and Article I, §28.

Section 12 "was intended to abrogate the common law rule that bail was a matter of judicial discretion by conferring an absolute right to bail except in a narrow class of cases." (*In re Law* (1973) 10 Cal. 3rd 21, 25). The section "establishes a person's right to obtain release on bail from pretrial custody, identifies certain categories of crime in which such bail is unavailable, prohibits the imposition of excessive bail as to other crimes, sets forth the factors a court shall take into consideration in fixing the amount of the required bail, and recognizes that a person 'may be released on his or her own recognizance in the court's discretion." (*In re York* (1995) 9 Cal.4th 1133, 1139-1140, fn. omitted).

Even if the charged offenses involve serious violence, the Court cannot deny bail unless it "finds based upon clear and convincing evidence that there is a substantial likelihood the person's release would result in great bodily harm to others" (California Constitution, Article 1, §12(b)&(c))

When "fixing the amount of bail, the court shall take into consideration the seriousness of the offense charged, the previous criminal record of the defendant, and the probability of his or her appearing at the trial or hearing of the case." (Article 1, §12(c); see also *Penal Code §1275*).

Article 1 §28(f)(3), provides that "In setting, reducing or denying bail, the judge or magistrate shall take into consideration the protection of the public, the safety of the victim, the seriousness of the offense charged, the previous criminal record of the defendant, and the probability of his or her appearing at the trial or hearing of the case. Public safety and the safety of the victim shall be the primary considerations. A person may be released on his or her own recognizance in the court's discretion, subject to the same factors considered in setting bail…" (see also *Penal Code §§ 1268–1276.5*).

However, in *In re Humphrey* (2021) 11 Cal 5th 135, 143, the California Supreme Court found that, "The common practice of conditioning freedom solely on whether an arrestee can afford bail is unconstitutional. Other conditions of release — such as electronic monitoring, regular check-ins with a pretrial case manager, community housing or shelter, and drug and alcohol treatment — can in many cases protect public and victim safety as well as assure the arrestee's appearance at trial. What we hold is that where a financial condition is nonetheless necessary, the court must consider the arrestee's ability to pay the stated amount of bail — and may not effectively detain the arrestee 'solely because' the arrestee 'lacked the resources' to post bail."

"[T]he court may neither deny bail nor set it in a sum that is the functional equivalent of no bail" (*In re Christie* (2001) 92 Cal. App. 4th 1105, 1109). "[T]he setting of bond unreachable because of its amount would be tantamount to setting no conditions at all" (*United States v. Leathers* (D.C. Cir. 1969) 412 F.2nd 169, 171).

"Principles of equal protection and substantive due process likewise converge in the money bail context. The accused retains a fundamental constitutional right to liberty. Further, the state's interest in the bail context is not to punish — it is to ensure the defendant appears at court proceedings and to protect the victim, as well as the public, from further harm. Yet if a court does not consider an arrestee's ability to pay, it cannot know whether requiring money bail in a particular amount is likely to operate as the functional equivalent of a pretrial detention order. Detaining an arrestee in such circumstances accords insufficient respect to the arrestee's crucial state and federal equal protection rights against wealth-based detention as well as the arrestee's state and federal substantive due process rights to pretrial liberty." (*Humphrey*, supra, citations omitted).

Because bail was set per the county schedule, the amount was set without the court's attention to this individual Defendant.

In the instant case, Defendant is charged with a three felony counts related to allegations that he fired a gun at his own house. Bail has been set in an amount more than double Defendant's annual income.

The charges in this case are serious, but the other factors weigh in favor of a bail reduction. (1) Defendant did not harm anyone, (3) Defendant's previous criminal record is non-existent, and (4) Defendant's ties to the community make the probability of him appearing for future hearings very high.

Bail in this case is excessive and is the equivalent of "no bail." Defendant, therefore, should be released on his own recognizance, or bail should be reduced to a reasonable amount.

h. Motion to Release from Custody (Extradition)

ROGER LAMPKIN
SB#113786
1234 L Street
Bakersfield, CA 93301
Tel: (661)633-1234
Fax: (661)863-6741
Attorney for Doug Donenabbed

IN THE SUPERIOR COURT OF THE STATE OF CALIFORNIA, IN AND FOR THE COUNTY OF KERN

People of the State of California,	CASE NO. 123456
Plaintiffs,	DEFENDANT DOUG DONENABBED'S MOTION FOR RELEASE FROM CUSTODY
- v. -	[Extradition Proceedings]
Doug Donenabbed,	
Defendant	Date: August 2, 2022 Time: 8:30 a.m. Dept: CC

TO THE COURT AND THE DISTRICT ATTORNEY: PLEASE TAKE NOTICE that at the date and time indicated above, the Defendant will move the Court for an order releasing Defendant from custody.

The motion will be made on the grounds that the state seeking to extradite Defendant has failed to do so and more than thirty days have passed.

This motion will be based on this notice, all papers and pleadings on file with the court, and such oral and documentary evidence as may be presented at the hearing.

Dated:

_____
By   Roger Lampkin, Attorney for
Doug Donenabbed

POINTS AND AUTHORITIES

Following an identity hearing, the Court must discharge the defendant (if identity is not established), admit the defendant on bail, or "commit him to the county jail for such a time, not exceeding thirty days and specified in the warrant, as will enable the arrest of the accused to be made under a warrant of the Governor on a requisition of the executive authority of the State having jurisdiction of the offense..." (Penal Code §1552) "If the accused is not arrested under warrant of the Governor by the expiration of the time specified in the warrant, bond, or undertaking, a magistrate may discharge him or may recommit him for a further period of 60 days...." (*Penal Code §1552.2*)

The maximum time a defendant may be held awaiting a governor's warrant is, therefore, ninety days; however, at the end of the first thirty days the court must discharge the defendant or use the court's discretion to "recommit him for a further period of 60 days..."

In the instant case, the thirty days has run without action by the state seeking extradition. It would, consequently, be an abuse of discretion for the court to recommit.

It is, therefore, respectfully submitted that Defendant should be discharged from custody.

In the alternative, Defendant should be released on sufficient sureties under *Penal Code §1552.1*, which holds that, "the magistrate may admit the person arrested to bail by bond or undertaking, with sufficient sureties, and in such sum as he deems proper, conditioned upon the appearance of such person before him at a time specified in such bond or undertaking, and for his surrender upon the warrant of the Governor of this state."

i. Joinder

ROGER LAMPKIN
SB#113786
1234 L Street
Bakersfield, CA 93301
Tel: (661)633-1234
Fax: (661)863-6741

Attorney for Doug Donenabbed

IN THE SUPERIOR COURT OF THE STATE OF CALIFORNIA,

IN AND FOR THE COUNTY OF KERN

People of the State of California,	CASE NO. 123456
Plaintiffs,	DEFENDANT DOUG DONENABBED'S JOINDER IN DEFENDANT' JOHN SMITH'S MOTION TO SUPPRESS
- v. -	
Doug Donenabbed,	Date: August 2, 2022 Time: 8:30 a.m. Dept: CC
Defendant	
	Readiness: August 12, 2022 Trial: August 22, 2022

TO THE COURT, COUNSEL FOR CODEFENDANT, AND THE
DISTRICT ATTORNEY: Please take notice that Defendant Doug
Donenabbed hereby joins in codefendant John Smith's Motion to Suppress,
currently set as noted above.

Dated:

_____

By   Roger Lampkin, Attorney for
Doug Donenabbed

j. Not Competent to Stand Trial

ROGER LAMPKIN
SB#113786
1234 L Street
Bakersfield, CA 93301
Tel: (661)633-1234
Fax: (661)863-6741
Attorney for Doug Donenabbed

IN THE SUPERIOR COURT OF THE STATE OF CALIFORNIA,
IN AND FOR THE COUNTY OF KERN

People of the State of California,	CASE NO. 123456
Plaintiffs,	DEFENDANT DOUG DONENABBED'S MOTION FOR HEARING ON COMPETENCY
- v. -	(Penal Code §1368)
Doug Donenabbed,	
Defendant	Date: August 2, 2022 Time: 8:30 a.m. Dept: CC

TO THE ABOVE-ENTITLED COURT AND THE DISTRICT ATTORNEY OF KERN COUNTY: PLEASE TAKE NOTICE that at the date and time indicated above, the defendant will move for an order that a trial be set on the issue of defendant's competency to stand trial.

The motion will be based on the grounds that due to a mental disorder and/or developmental disability, the defendant is unable to understand the nature of the proceedings or to assist counsel in the conduct of the defense.

The motion will be based on this Notice of Motion, all attached papers, all papers and records on file in this action and on such oral, and documentary evidence as may be presented at the time of the motion.

Dated:

_____
By   Roger Lampkin, Attorney for
Doug Donenabbed

MEMORANDUM OF POINTS AND AUTHORITIES

If the Court receives substantial evidence that a defendant's mental ability is impaired, the court must conduct a hearing to determine whether the defendant understands the proceedings and is able to assist in the defense. In *People v. Pennington* (1967) 66 Cal. 2nd 508, 518, our Supreme Court noted "that an accused has a constitutional right to a hearing on present sanity if he comes forward with substantial evidence that he is incapable, because of mental illness, of understanding the nature of the proceedings against him or of assisting in his defense. Once such substantial evidence appears, a doubt as to the sanity of the accused exists, no matter how persuasive other evidence -- testimony of prosecution witnesses or the court's own observations of the accused -- may be to the contrary."

DECLARATION

I, Roger Lampkin, declare:

I am the attorney representing the defendant in this action.

I based on conversations with the defendant and his actions, it is my opinion that the defendant is, because of mental illness, incapable of understanding the nature of the proceedings against him or assisting in a defense at this stage of the proceedings.

I am informed and believe that the foregoing is true and correct.

Dated:

_____
By   Roger Lampkin, Attorney for
      Doug Donenabbed

Practical Tip:
Accept the fact that you will be doing jobs that are beneath you. Change copier paper, take out the trash, deliver inmate clothes, fetch coffee, pick up lunch, redact discovery, vacuum the conference room, and do the other menial tasks that are required to keep an office running smoothly. This is not to say that you should be subservient to an overbearing attorney or that you should subvert the efforts of a cleaning service or someone assigned to do such jobs, but everyone in a criminal defense office, including the attorney, should work together to ensure that the office runs smoothly.

k. Motion for Probable Cause Hearing

ROGER LAMPKIN
SB#113786
1234 L Street
Bakersfield, CA 93301
Tel: (661)633-1234
Fax: (661)863-6741
Attorney for Doug Donenabbed

IN THE SUPERIOR COURT OF THE STATE OF CALIFORNIA, IN AND FOR THE COUNTY OF KERN

People of the State of California,	CASE NO. 123456
Plaintiffs,	DEFENDANT DOUG DONENABBED'S MOTION FOR PROBABLE CAUSE HEARING
- v. -	
Doug Donenabbed,	
	Date: August 2, 2022
Defendant	Time: 8:30 a.m.
	Dept: CC

TO THE COURT AND THE DISTRICT ATTORNEY: PLEASE TAKE NOTICE that at the date and time indicated above, or as soon thereafter as the matter can be heard in the above-entitled court, the defendant will move the Court under *Penal Code §991* for a probable cause hearing on the Complaint, alleging a violation of *Penal Code §242*, battery.

The motion will be based on this notice, all attached documents, the records on file in this action, and on such matters as may be presented at the hearing.

Dated:

_____

By   Roger Lampkin, Attorney for
      Doug Donenabbed

POINTS, AUTHORITIES, AND ARGUMENT

Penal Code §991 explicitly allows for a probable cause hearing on a misdemeanor charge at the time a defendant is arraigned. By implication, *Section 991* also allows a defendant to make a later request for a probable cause hearing if the defendant remains in custody.

As noted in *In re Walters* (1975) 15 Cal. 3rd 738, "a judicial determination of probable cause to hold an arrestee for trial on a misdemeanor charge must be made if the arrestee requests that determination, unless pending trial he is released on his own recognizance."

"[T]he legislative history is replete with evidence that section 991 was intended not only to codify Walters, but also to weed out groundless charges." (*People v. McGowan* (2015) 242 Cal. App.4th 377).

"[S]ections 991 and 995 were meant to serve analogous purposes in the misdemeanor and felony contexts, [therefore] the rules of statutory construction demand that we harmonize the two provisions whenever possible." (id.) This leads to the conclusion that "section 991 permits the court to dismiss individual charges from the complaint." (id.)

Commitment without reasonable or probable cause occurs if there is insufficient proof to establish a reasonable belief that an offense has been committed and the defendant is guilty of the offense charged. (*Caughlin v Superior Court of San Diego County* (1971) 4 Cal 3rd 461; *People v Hernandez* (1978) 90 Cal App 3rd 309).

There must be some evidence to support each element of an offense, or the finding must fall. (*Panos v. Superior Court* (1984) 156 Cal. App. 3rd 626; *People v. Superior Court (Mendella)* (1983) 33 Cal. 3rd 754; *People v. Shirley* (1978) 78 Cal. App. 3rd 424).

Based on the foregoing, it is respectfully submitted that there is not probable cause to believe that Defendant violated *Penal Code §242,* and he should be discharged on that count.

1. Motion to Release Subpoenaed Documents

ROGER LAMPKIN
SB#113786
1234 L Street
Bakersfield, CA 93301
Tel: (661)633-1234
Fax: (661)863-6741
Attorney for Doug Donenabbed

IN THE SUPERIOR COURT OF THE STATE OF CALIFORNIA,
IN AND FOR THE COUNTY OF KERN

People of the State of California, Plaintiffs, - v. - Doug Donenabbed, Defendant	CASE NO. 123456 DEFENDANT DOUG DONENABBED'S MOTION TO RELEASE SUBPOENAED RECORDS Date: August 2, 2022 Time: 8:30 a.m. Dept: CC

TO THE COURT AND THE DISTRICT ATTORNEY:
PLEASE TAKE NOTICE that at the date and time indicated above, Defendant will move the Court for an order releasing documents subpoenaed by the Defense.

The motion will be made on the ground that records were subpoenaed by the Defense and delivered to the Court. An in camera hearing is, therefore, required prior to release of the records to the Defense.

The motion will be based on this Notice of Motion, on the attached memorandum of points and authorities and filed herewith and such supplemental memorandum of points and authorities that may be hereafter filed with the court or stated orally at the conclusion of the hearing, on all papers and records on file in this action and on such oral and documentary evidence as may be presented at the time of the motion.

Dated:

_____
By   Roger Lampkin, Attorney for
      Doug Donenabbed

POINTS AND AUTHORITIES

Penal Code §1326(c) provides in part:

> When a defendant has issued a subpoena to a person or entity that is not a party for the production of books, papers, documents, or records, or copies thereof, the court may order an in camera hearing to determine whether or not the defense is entitled to receive the documents. The court may not order the documents disclosed to the prosecution except as required by Section 1054.3.

→••Ω••←

Attorney Anthony: Hey, Paul, remember when I asked you about your plans for the holidays and you didn't know what you were going to do?

Paralegal Paul: Vaguely…

Attorney Anthony: Well, have I got something to make your holiday memorable…. [shouting over his shoulder] bring in the rest of the boxes.

Paralegal Paul: What?

Attorney Anthony: Oh, I forgot to mention. The firm bought you a subscription to *Jelly of the Month Club*. Happy holidays.

m. Motion to Return Property

ROGER LAMPKIN
SB#113786
1234 L Street
Bakersfield, CA 93301
Tel: (661)633-1234
Fax: (661)863-6741
Attorney for Doug Donenabbed

IN THE SUPERIOR COURT OF THE STATE OF CALIFORNIA,
IN AND FOR THE COUNTY OF KERN

People of the State of California,	CASE NO. 123456
Plaintiffs,	DEFENDANT DOUG DONENABBED'S MOTION
- v. -	FOR RETURN OF PROPERTY (Penal Code §1536) Date: August 2, 2022
Doug Donenabbed,	Time: 8:30 a.m.
Defendant	Dept: CC
	Readiness: August 12, 2022 Trial: August 22, 2022

TO THE ABOVE-ENTITLED COURT AND THE DISTRICT
ATTORNEY OF KERN COUNTY: PLEASE TAKE NOTICE that at
the date and time indicated above, the defendant will move the Court for an
order directing the Kern County Sheriff, the office of the District Attorney
of Kern County, and their agents to release to the defendant the following
property that was seized from Defendant on or about May 23, 2020:
1. $1,000,000 in United States currency
2. Ford Mustang, VIN#123456789
3. Personal papers, letters, and notes

This Motion will be made on the ground that the there are no civil
forfeiture proceedings related to the seized items, and the items are not
needed for the instant prosecution.

The motion will be based on this notice of motion, the attached
declaration, the memorandum of points and authorities served and filed
herewith, the records on file in this action and on such oral and

documentary evidence as may be presented at the hearing.

Dated:

_____

By   Roger Lampkin, Attorney for
Doug Donenabbed

POINTS, AUTHORITIES, AND ARGUMENT

A court has authority to order the return of seized property to the persons entitles to it on a showing of ownership. As *Penal Code §1536* explains, "All property or things taken on a warrant must be retained by the officer in his custody, subject to the order of the court to which he is required to return the proceedings before him, or of any other court in which the offense in respect to which the property or things taken is triable."

"Section 1536 was enacted in order to provide controls over those officials in possession of property seized pursuant to a search warrant, pending resolution of the disposition of the property, either through an order granting a motion for release of improperly seized materials or an order admitting the items seized into evidence." (*People v. Von Villas* (1992) 10 Cal. App. 4th 201).

In addition to the statutory authority, the court has an inherent power to hold hearings and issue orders for the return of seized property (see *In re Seizure of Approximately 28 Grams of Marijuana* (N.D.Cal.2003) 278 F.Supp.2nd 1097).

"Case law clearly establishes that both during and after the pendency of a criminal action, section 1536 empowers the court to entertain a summary proceeding by "nonstatutory" motion, for the release of property seized under a search warrant. An officer who takes such property does so on behalf of the court for use in a judicial proceeding, and he must respond, as does any custodian, to the orders of the court for which he acted." (*People v. Icenogle* (1985) 164 Cal. App. 3rd 620, citations and punctuation omitted).

"[D]enial of the motion [to return currency] upon the ground the seized currency should be retained in custody because there was some 'color' upon which it could be admitted in evidence, constituted an abuse of discretion as a matter of law." (*Buker v. Superior Court* (1972) 25 Cal. App. 3rd 1085)

In the instant case, the return indicates that officers seized the items, but no forfeiture proceedings are pending and there is no indication that the Prosecution intends to admit any of the seized items into evidence.

The items should, therefore, now be returned.

n. Motion to Continue Trial

ROGER LAMPKIN
SB#113786
1234 L Street
Bakersfield, CA 93301
Tel: (661)633-1234
Fax: (661)863-6741
Attorney for Doug Donenabbed

IN THE SUPERIOR COURT OF THE STATE OF CALIFORNIA, IN AND FOR THE COUNTY OF KERN

People of the State of California,	CASE NO. 123456
Plaintiffs,	DEFENDANT DOUG DONENABBED'S MOTION TO CONTINUE TRIAL
- v. -	Date: August 2, 2022
Doug Donenabbed,	Time: 8:30 a.m.
	Dept: CC
Defendant	
	Readiness: August 12, 2022
	Trial: August 22, 2022

TO THE ABOVE-ENTITLED COURT AND THE DISTRICT ATTORNEY OF KERN COUNTY: PLEASE TAKE NOTICE that at the date and time indicated above, the defendant will move that the Court continue the Readiness and Trial dates in the above-entitled matter.

The motion will be made on the grounds that a continuance is necessary to preserve the ends of justice by allowing the defense opportunity to properly prepare for trial.

The motion will be based on this notice of motion, the attached declaration, the memorandum of points and authorities served and filed herewith, the records on file in this action and on such oral and documentary evidence as may be presented at the hearing.

Dated:

_____
By   Roger Lampkin, Attorney for
      Doug Donenabbed

ATTORNEY DECLARATION

I, Roger Lampkin, declare:

I am the attorney of record for Defendant.

The court appointed investigator has requested an additional thirty days to complete his investigation.

Further, the Prosecution produced an additional 650 pages of discovery on September 15, 2022.

Based on the foregoing, I request a reasonable continuance and a new motions date.

I suggest a trial date in late October.

Dated:

_____

By   Roger Lampkin, Attorney for
Doug Donenabbed

→••Ω••←

Yes, in limine does mean
"at the threshold" but can you
stop taking it literally and just
deliver the motions to the judge?

o. Motion to Set Motions Date

ROGER LAMPKIN
SB#113786
1234 L Street
Bakersfield, CA 93301
Tel: (661)633-1234
Fax: (661)863-6741
Attorney for Doug Donenabbed

IN THE SUPERIOR COURT OF THE STATE OF CALIFORNIA, IN AND FOR THE COUNTY OF KERN

People of the State of California,	CASE NO. 123456
Plaintiffs,	DEFENDANT DOUG DONENABBED'S MOTION TO SET MOTIONS DATE
- v. -	
Doug Donenabbed,	Date: August 2, 2022 Time: 8:30 a.m.
Defendant	Dept: CC
	Readiness: August 12, 2022 Trial: August 22, 2022

TO THE COURT AND THE DISTRICT ATTORNEY: PLEASE TAKE NOTICE that at the date and time indicated above, or as soon thereafter as the matter can be heard in the above-entitled court, the defendant will move that the Court set a Motions date.

The motion will be based on this notice of motion, all attached documents, the records on file in this action, and on such matters as may be presented at the hearing.

Dated:

_____

By   Roger Lampkin, Attorney for
Doug Donenabbed

ATTORNEY DECLARATION

I, Roger Lampkin, declare:

I am an attorney at law and am the attorney for the defendant in this case.

Additional motions are needed to prepare this matter for trial. I specifically anticipate filing:

Motion to Set Aside the Information (*Penal Code §995*)
Motion to Compel Discovery

I, therefore, request a new motions date.

Dated:

_____

By   Roger Lampkin, Attorney for
Doug Donenabbed

MEMORANDUM OF POINTS AND AUTHORITIES

Code of Civil Procedure §128, holds that "Every court shall have the power... To provide for the orderly conduct of proceedings before it... [and] To amend and control its process and orders so as to make them conform to law and justice..."

Many courts do not require a specific "motions date."

Instead, courts often have standing orders with reserved dates and times for hearing of motions, such as "Motions not requiring testimony will be heard Tuesdays, Wednesdays, and Thursdays at 8:30 a.m. Motions requiring testimony will be heard on those same days at 10:00 a.m."

A given county may have dozens of such rules, and the hearing dates and times may vary between judges in the same courthouse. Therefore, the following page has space to list details of local motion date rules.

List any local motions date rules here:

_____

_____

_____

_____

_____

_____

_____

_____

_____

_____

_____

_____

_____

_____

_____

_____

_____

_____

_____

_____

p. Petition to Determine Restitution

ROGER LAMPKIN
SB#113786
1234 L Street
Bakersfield, CA 93301
Tel: (661)633-1234
Fax: (661)863-6741

Attorney for Doug Donenabbed

IN THE SUPERIOR COURT OF THE STATE OF CALIFORNIA,
IN AND FOR THE COUNTY OF KERN

People of the State of California, Plaintiffs, - v. - Doug Donenabbed, Defendant and Petitioner	CASE NO. 123456 PETITION TO DETERMINE RESTITUTION Date: June 3, 2019 Time: 8:30 a.m. Dept: 21

PLEASE TAKE NOTICE that at the date and time indicated above, or as soon thereafter as the matter can be heard in the above-entitled court, the Defendant and Petitioner, Doug Donenabbed, will move the Court to determine restitution in the above-entitled case.

The Petition will be based on this notice, all attached documents, the records on file in this action, and on such matters as may be presented at the hearing.

Date:

_____
Roger Lampkin,
Attorney for Defendant

POINTS, AUTHORITIES, AND ARGUMENT

Penal Code §1202.4(f)(1) provides in part: "The defendant has the right to a hearing before a judge to dispute the determination of the amount of restitution. The court may modify the amount, on its own motion or on the motion of the district attorney, the victim or victims, or the defendant. If a motion is made for modification of a restitution order, the victim shall be notified of that motion at least 10 days prior to the proceeding held to decide the motion…"

Penal Code §1203.1k provides in part: "The defendant shall have the right to a hearing before the judge to dispute the determinations made by the probation officer in regard to the amount or manner in which restitution is to be made to the victim or the Restitution Fund, to the extent that the victim has received payment from the Victims of Crime Program. If the court orders restitution to be made to the Restitution Fund, the court, and not the probation officer, shall determine the amount and the manner in which restitution is to be made to the Restitution Fund."

The "court must consider ability to pay in ordering restitution." (*People v. Whisenand* (1995) 37 Cal.App.4th 1383). A defendant has the right to a judicial determination of the propriety of restitution and its amount in light of his culpability and ability to pay. (*People v. Sandoval* (1989) 206 Cal. App. 3rd 1544). "In calculating ability to pay, 'the court [must] consider what resources the defendant has available and which of those resources can support the required payment,' including both the defendant's likely income and his or her assets." (*People v. Verduzco* (2012) 210 Cal.App.4th 1406, quoting *People v. Smith* (2000) 81 Cal.App.4th 630, 642).

Practical Tip:

Make a copy. Make another copy. Make a copy of the copy.

Criminal defense clients, especially those in custody, like to see progress on their cases. Inmates also share pleadings with one another, which can be free advertising for the attorneys you work with. For these reasons, it is a good idea to send copies of noticed motions to clients. Ex parte motions should not be sent.

Papers sometimes get lost in the system, so an attorney may show up to court for a hearing only to learn that the judge, prosecutor, or one of the attorneys for a codefendant does not have a copy of the motion. It is, therefore, helpful for the attorney to have an extra copy of all motions that are scheduled.

2. Discovery

a. Generic Discovery Motion

ROGER LAMPKIN
SB#113786
1234 L Street
Bakersfield, CA 93301
Tel: (661)633-1234
Fax: (661)863-6741
Attorney for Doug Donenabbed

IN THE SUPERIOR COURT OF THE STATE OF CALIFORNIA, IN AND FOR THE COUNTY OF KERN

People of the State of California,	CASE NO. 123456
Plaintiffs,	MOTION TO COMPEL DISCOVERY
- v. -	[*Brady Motion, Penal Code §1054.5*]
	DATE: October 16, 2019
	TIME: 8:30 a.m.
Doug Donenabbed,	DEPT: CC
Defendant	Trial date: October 31, 2019
	Readiness date: October 30, 2019

TO THE COURT AND THE DISTRICT ATTORNEY:

PLEASE TAKE NOTICE that at the date and time indicated above, the defendant will move the Court for an order compelling discovery.

The motion will be made on the ground that the Deputy District Attorney personally, or through other members of the Prosecution team, has in their actual or constructive possession certain items of evidence which defense counsel is legally entitled to inspect; the defense has informally requested said evidence, but the District Attorney has not provided said evidence to the defense.

The motion will be based on this notice of motion, all attached documents, the records on file in this action, and on such matters as may be presented at the hearing.

Dated: _____

                        By   Roger Lampkin, Attorney for Doug Donenabbed

POINTS, AUTHORITIES, AND ARGUMENT

DUE PROCESS REQUIRES THE PROSECUTION TO PROVIDE DISCOVERY IN ORDER TO PROTECT DEFENDANT'S RIGHT TO PRESENT A DEFENSE AND RIGHT TO A FAIR TRIAL

"(T)he interest of the prosecution is not that it shall win the case, but that it shall bring forth the true facts surrounding the commission of the crime so that justice shall be done ..." (*Berger v. United States* (1934) 295 U.S. 78, 88)

The purpose of the discovery process in criminal cases is to guarantee a defendant a fair trial by giving him equal access to information so that he may be permitted to present all relevant evidence in his behalf. This aim was emphasized in *U.S. v. Nixon* (1974) 418 U.S. 683, 709, where the United States Supreme Court stated:

> We have elected to employ an adversary system of criminal justice in which the parties contest all issues before a court of law. The need to develop all relevant facts in the adversary system is both fundamental and comprehensive. The ends of criminal justice would be defeated if judgments were to be founded on a partial or speculative presentation of the facts. The very integrity of the judicial system and public confidence in the system depend on full disclosure of all the facts, within the framework of the rules of evidence. To ensure that justice is done, it is imperative to the function of courts that compulsory process be available for the production of evidence needed by the prosecution or by the defense.

The sources in expanding criminal discovery can be found in the "Due Process Clause" of the 5th and 14th Amendments to the United States Constitution, and in the 6th Amendment to the United States Constitution.

The United States Supreme Court also stated in Nixon, supra, that to vindicate these guarantees, the courts have a "manifest duty" to ensure that all relevant and admissible evidence be produced. (id.)

Brady v. Maryland (1963) 373 U.S. 83, and its progeny, explain that the prosecution violates a defendant's Due Process rights when it fails to disclose to the defendant prior to trial, "evidence favorable to an accused. . . where the evidence is material either to guilt or to punishment, irrespective of the good faith or bad faith of the prosecution." (id. at 87). This is the "Brady Rule."

The Brady Rule is not intended "to displace the adversary system as the primary means by which truth is uncovered, but to ensure that a miscarriage of justice does not occur" (*U.S. v. Bagley* (1985) 473 U.S. 667, 675). This limited departure from the adversary system "illustrates the special role played by the American prosecutor in the search for truth in criminal trials" (*Strickler v. Greene* (1999) 527 U.S. 263). The prosecutor's unique role "transcends that of an adversary: [the prosecutor] is the representative not of an ordinary party to a controversy, but of a sovereignty . . . whose interest . . . in a criminal prosecution is not that it shall win a case, but that justice shall be done.' " *Bagley*, supra at 675, fn.6 (quoting *Berger v. United States* (1935) 295 U.S. 78, 88; see also *Kyles v. Whitley* (1995) 514 U.S. 419, 437).

Due Process requires fundamental fairness in the prosecution of a criminal case (*Lisenba v. California* (1941) 314 U.S. 219, 236). Implicit in the concept of fundamental fairness is the idea that the defendant must have the opportunity to present a complete defense (*California v. Trombetta* (1984) 467 U.S. 479, 485). The prosecution can ensure that a defendant has the opportunity to present a complete defense by providing access to favorable evidence (*Brady, supra*).

The United States Supreme Court has held that "[s]uppression by the prosecution of evidence favorable to an accused who has requested it violates Due Process where the evidence is material either to guilt or to punishment, irrespective of the good faith or bad faith of the prosecution." (*Brady, supra*). It is the character of the evidence, rather than the character of the prosecutor, that determines whether the suppression of favorable evidence results in constitutional error (*U.S. v. Agurs* (1976) 427 U.S. 97, 110).

The proper inquiry where the question is whether the prosecution violated a defendant's right to Due Process by withholding evidence is:
    (1) whether the evidence was favorable to the defendant; and,
    (2) whether the evidence was material to guilt or punishment.
        (See *United State v. Bagley* (1985) 473 U.S. 667).

For purposes of this analysis, it does not matter whether the evidence was suppressed by the prosecutor or by the other agents on the case (*Kyles v. Whitley* (1995) 514 U.S. 419). Rather, the question is whether the evidence was suppressed by the prosecution, for which both the prosecutors and the investigators serve as agents. (id.)

The ultimate responsibility for ensuring that exculpatory evidence is provided in accordance with Brady rests with the prosecutor (id. at 438). A miscommunication between the prosecutor and the investigators that results in the suppression of exculpatory evidence is no excuse for a Brady violation (id.).

As the Supreme Court explained in *Kyles v. Whitley*, since "the prosecutor has the means to discharge the government's Brady responsibility if he will, any argument excusing a prosecutor from disclosing what he does not happen to know about boils down to a plea to substitute the police for the prosecutor, and even for the courts themselves, as the final arbiters of the government's obligation to ensure fair trials." (id.)

THE PROSECUTION'S DISCOVERY DUTY OF DISCLOSURE EXTENDS TO ALL MEMBERS OF THE PROSECUTION TEAM

The Prosecution has a duty to seek out and disclose all discoverable materials held by members of the "prosecution team."

The prosecutors assigned to try a case have the duty "to learn of any favorable evidence known to others acting on the government's behalf in the case" (*Kyles v. Whitley* (1995) 514 U.S. 419, 437).

Accordingly, the Brady/Kyles rule extends to all members of the "prosecution team," which includes both investigative and prosecutorial personnel (*U.S. v. Morris* (7th Cir. 1996) 80 F. 3rd 1151, 1170 (citing with favor *Carey v. Duckworth* (7th Cir. 1984) 738 F. 2nd 875, 878, for proposition that prosecution team includes federal DEA agents and local police)).

The Prosecution is not required to review the files of agencies that have no involvement in the investigation or prosecution (*Morris, supra*), but prosecutors are required to examine the files of those entities who actively participate in the investigation or prosecution of a case (See *Kyles*, supra; *Morris*, supra at 1169).

It is well established that a prosecutor is deemed to have "control" over all members of an investigatory team and that evidence maintained by cooperating entities falls within the scope of the Prosecution's Brady obligation (*Kyles*, supra, at pp. 437-438 ("any favorable evidence known to the others acting on the government's behalf is imputed to the prosecution."; *U.S. v. Zuno-Arce* (9th Cir. 1995) 44 F. 3rd 1420 ("Exculpatory evidence cannot be kept out of the hands of the defense just because the prosecutor does not have it, where an investigating agency does.")

DEFENDANT SPECIFICALLY REQUESTS DISCLOSURE OF THE
FOLLOWING EVIDENCE:

First.   Records of convictions

   Defendant seeks discovery of the date and nature of any felony or
misdemeanor arrest or conviction of any participant in or witness to the
alleged crime.

   Penal Code §1054.1 provides for defense discovery of "felony convictions
of material witnesses whose credibility is likely to be critical to the outcome
of the trial." *Evidence Code §780* and *People v. Castro* (1985) 38 Cal 3rd 301,
211, allow impeachment of any witness by felony convictions involving
"moral turpitude." Impeachment of any witness by prior conduct not
amounting to a felony and involving "moral turpitude" is also proper.
(*People v. Wheeler* (1992) 4 Cal 4th 284) Accordingly, records of arrests and
convictions of witnesses for felonies and misdemeanors are discoverable, at
least if the conduct involves "moral turpitude." (*People v. Santos* (1994) 30
Cal App 4th 169.)

   In *Hill v. Superior Court of Los Angeles County* (1974) 10 Cal 3rd 812, 817, the
California Supreme Court held that the felony conviction records and the
records of arrests and detentions of prospective witnesses are discoverable
by the defendant, upon a showing of good cause, for the purpose of
impeachment.

Second. Identity of percipient witnesses

   Defendant seeks discovery of the names, addresses and telephone
numbers of any and all persons who were percipient witnesses to the
offense alleged, including all persons who were held in the same cell with
Defendant at the time of his arrest and all persons present when Defendant
was examined in any way.

   Persons held in the same cell with Defendant at the time of his arrest may
be able to testify as to his state of sobriety, his demeanor, any apparent
injury he suffered, any statements he made, or any statements made to him
by law enforcement. Such evidence may be used to impeach Prosecution
witnesses.

   Penal Code §1054.1(a) provides that the Prosecution must disclose the
names and addresses of persons intended to be called as witnesses. No
legitimate reason exists to withhold discovery of their telephone numbers,

and inconvenience to the witnesses will result from unannounced contacts by a defense investigator. Additionally, *Penal Code §§841.5(c)* & *1054.2* implicitly recognize the right of defense counsel to obtain the telephone numbers of victims and witnesses.

Third. Dispatch records

Defendant seeks discovery of any dispatch recordings or records relative to the incident within the subject matter of this action.

Recordings or records of radio transmissions concerning the facts underlying the charges against the defendant may be relevant to the credibility of witnesses and are therefore discoverable. (*United States v. Strifler* (9th Cir 1988) 851 F 2nd 1197; *Davis v. Alaska* (1974) 415 US 308.)

Recordings of radio and telephone calls to the police department and the times of police responses are public records within the meaning of *Government Code §6200* and may not be destroyed for at least two years (*80 Ops Atty Gen 908* (1981)).

Fourth. Recordings of communication between any officer and the communication center and between officers involved in the incident that is the subject matter of this action.

See authority under the Third request.

Fifth. Any calls to 911 or law enforcement concerning the subject matter of this action.

See authority under the Third request.

Sixth. Any documents including, but not limited to, curriculum vitaes, and written reports and/or notes for any expert witness the prosecution intends to call as a witness at trial.

Penal Code §1054.1(f), by implication, provides for defense discovery of identifying information regarding experts. In *People v. Johnson* (1974) 38 Cal App 3rd 228, the Court of Appeal stated:

> Where it is appropriate, the defendant may discover the reports of the state's experts concerning their examination of real evidence [citation omitted]; discovery of the identity of state experts is analogous.

Evidence that tends to impeach the reliability of the state's expert is "exculpatory evidence" which the state is obligated to turn over to the defendant. (*People v. Garcia* (1993) 17 Cal. App. 4th 1169).

Seventh. All real evidence seized or obtained as a part of the investigation of the offenses charged.

Penal Code §1054.1(c) provides for such discovery.

Eighth. All evidence, however stored, that any defendant, former defendant, person associated with any defendant or former defendant, or any witness in this matter was a gang member, associate of a gang, or in any way affiliated with a gang before the incident leading to the instant case.

Penal Code §1054.1(c) and (e) allow for such discovery. Defendant specifically requests:

All evidence, however stored, that Defendant, any codefendant, and any witness was a gang member, an associate of a gang, or in any way affiliated with a gang before the incident leading to the instant case.

All evidence, however stored, that any person identified in Defendant's Facebook or other social media account was a gang member, an associate of a gang, or in any way affiliated with a gang before the incident leading to the instant case.

All evidence, however stored, that Eastside Boys or that any member, associate or other person believed by law enforcement to be related to that group participates in any crime charged herein for the benefit of Eastside Boys.

Ninth. An opportunity to examine all demonstrative and real evidence, including charts, diagrams and other exhibits, whether obtained as part of the investigation of the offenses charged or not, that the Prosecution intends to offer in evidence at trial or to be viewed by the jury.

The Prosecution's duty to disclose includes trial exhibits because the defense must disclose defense trial exhibits to the prosecution (*Penal Code §1054.3(b)*; *Izazaga v. Superior Court* (1991) 54 Cal. 3rd 356, 375).

Tenth. Any original notes taken by any police officer relating to the interview of any witness intended to be called by the District Attorney to testify against any defendant.

In *People v. Angeles* (1985) 172 Cal App 3rd 1203, the Court of Appeal stated, " '… [Law enforcement officers] must take reasonable precautions to preserve for trial [their] original handwritten notes made in the course of interrogating a criminal defendant unless the interrogation is tape recorded and the tape is preserved.' …"

Due process requires disclosure of any evidence that may undermine the credibility or probative value of prosecution evidence. (*United States v. Strifler* (9th Cir 1988) 851 F 2nd 1197.)

Additionally, the original notes of police officers are reports and contain statements whose disclosure is required by *Penal Code §1054.1(f)*.

In *Funk v. Superior Court of Los Angeles County* (1959) 52 Cal 2nd 423, the court noted that the defendant "moved for an order directing that he be allowed to examine the original notes made by the officers and to inspect and copy written statements prepared from the notes… The showing made by petitioner is sufficient to entitle him to production of the documents he wishes to inspect. It is settled that, during trial, an accused can compel the People to produce written statements of prosecution witnesses relating to the matters covered in their testimony. [Citation omitted.] As recent decisions of this court illustrate, there is no sound basis for applying a different rule merely because production is requested prior to, rather than during trial."

Eleventh.   Promises, offers, or inducements

The prosecutor has a duty to disclose any explicit promise, offer, or inducement extended to prosecution witnesses. In *U.S. v. Bagley* (1985) 473 U.S. 667, the Supreme Court found a *Brady* violation for a failure to disclose written contracts with informant witnesses. In *In re Sassounian* (1995) 9 Cal. 4th 535 the California Supreme Court concluded the prosecution withheld favorable evidence when it failed to disclose evidence of benefits provided, and promises made, to a jailhouse informant.

The prosecution has a duty to disclose any "implied promise," such as when the words are not expressed but the substance implies the witness will receive a benefit. In *Giglio v. U.S.* (1972) 405 U.S. 150, the Supreme Court found a Brady violation for the failure to disclose that a prosecution witness had been told to rely on the government's good judgment whether he would be prosecuted if he agreed to testify.

The prosecutor cannot evade the duty to disclose promises by extending such offers in secret to the witness' attorney (*People v. Phillips* (1985) 41 Cal. 3rd 29, 47; full disclosure of any agreement between the prosecution and a witness or the witness's attorney is required, regardless of whether the witness has been fully informed of the agreement).

Twelfth. Promises in prior cases

When a prosecution witness, who is currently facing prosecution, has received benefits to cooperate with law enforcement in prior cases, the prosecution has a duty to disclose this fact. In *People v. Kasim* (1997) 56 Cal. App. 4th 1360, 1382, a prosecution witness, currently facing prosecution, had received benefits in the past by cooperating with law enforcement and thus had reason to believe they would in the instant case. The court concluded this evidence must be disclosed because the jury "was entitled to know about all historical events bearing on these witnesses' propensity to be truthful or untruthful."

Thirteenth.   Pending charges

In *People v. Coyer* (1983) 142 Cal. App. 3rd 839, 842, the court held that "a defendant is entitled to discovery of criminal charges currently pending against prosecution witnesses anywhere in the state" because "the pendency of criminal charges is material to a witness' motivation in testifying even when no express 'promise of leniency or immunity' have been made." This decision was reaffirmed in *People v. Hayes* (1992) 3 Cal. App. 4th 1238.

Fourteenth.   Parole or probation status

In *Davis v. Alaska* (1974) 415 U.S. 308, 319, the United States Supreme Court held that a defendant has the right to prove at trial that a prosecution witness is on probation, in order to establish that the witness' testimony is biased.

In *People v. Price* (1991) 1 Cal. 4th 324, 486, the California Supreme Court held that a defendant is entitled to prove that a prosecution witness is on parole "to show the witness' potential bias resulting from concern about possible revocation."

Fifteenth.   Drug or alcohol use

Evidence that a prosecution witness is addicted to, or affected by, alcohol or an illegal drug is admissible to impeach the credibility of that witness when there is evidence that the witness was under the influence of alcohol or another drug when the events occurred about which the witness would testify, or when the witness' mental faculties were actually impaired by the drug habit (*People v. Smith* (1970) 4 Cal. App. 3rd 403, 412; *People v. Hernandez* (1976) 63 Cal. App. 3rd 393, 405.

Sixteenth. Training and certification records regarding the use and operation of any testing equipment for the person or persons who conducted any testing concerning any evidence related to this matter.

Presumably, testing equipment will not give accurate results if it is not properly operated. The qualifications of the persons performing the tests on seized items are discoverable for impeachment purposes and as being exculpatory (*Brady, supra, Penal Code §1054.1(e)*).

Seventeenth. Any photographs taken of the Defendant at or near the time of the Defendant's arrest on these charges.

Penal Code §1054.1(c) requires the prosecution to disclose real evidence obtained as part of the investigation of the offenses charged. This, obviously, includes any photographs the Prosecution team took of the Defendant.

Eighteenth. A listing of any codes, shorthand, messages, and acronyms used in any report, computer file, or other document used or prepared in the investigation of this case.

The codes are foundational information under *People v. Adams* (1976) 59 Cal App 3rd 559. Due process forbids the Prosecution from using codes to keep information from the Defense.

Nineteenth. Any evidence to be used in rebuttal of the defense case.

The identities and statements of witnesses whom the prosecution intends to call in rebuttal of the defense are discoverable. (*Izazaga v. Superior Court* (1991) 54 Cal 3rd 356)

The Prosecution's duty to disclose evidence applies to evidence to be used as part of their case-in-chief as well as rebuttal evidence (*People v. Hammond* (1994) 21 Cal. App. 4th 1611).

b. Discovery Prior to Preliminary Hearing

Note: This motion is most often filed in in cases where the Prosecution has obviously overproduced or underproduced discovery. For example, if the Prosecution produces thousands of pages of discovery and hundreds of recordings, it is unrealistic for the Defense to review the discovery before the preliminary hearing, so this motion asks the Court to require the Prosecution to identify relevant evidence. Conversely, the motion can be used to discover obvious missing items, such as a search warrant affidavit or a video recording, if the item is mentioned in discovery but not produced in discovery.

ROGER LAMPKIN
SB#113786
1234 L Street
Bakersfield, CA 93301
Tel: (661)633-1234
Fax: (661)863-6741
Attorney for Doug Donenabbed

IN THE SUPERIOR COURT OF THE STATE OF CALIFORNIA,

IN AND FOR THE COUNTY OF KERN

People of the State of California,	CASE NO. 123456
Plaintiffs,	DEFENDANT'S MOTION FOR PRE-PRELIMINARY HEARING
- v. -	DISCOVERY
Doug Dave,	[Brady Motion, *Penal Code §1054.5*] Date: August 2, 2022
Defendant	Time: 8:30 a.m. Dept: CC

TO THE COURT AND THE DISTRICT ATTORNEY:
PLEASE TAKE NOTICE that at the date and time indicated above, or as soon thereafter as the matter can be heard in the above-entitled court, Defendant will move the Court for an order compelling pre-preliminary hearing discovery.

The motion will be made on the ground that the District Attorney has in her actual or constructive possession certain items of evidence which defense counsel is legally entitled to inspect and the defense has informally requested said evidence.

The motion will be based on this Notice of Motion, on the attached memorandum of points and authorities and filed herewith and such supplemental memorandum of points and authorities that may be hereafter filed with the court or stated orally at the conclusion of the hearing, on all papers and records on file in this action and on such oral and documentary evidence as may be presented at the time of the motion.

Dated: _____

By   Roger Lampkin,
Attorney for Doug Donenabbed

MEMORANDUM OF POINTS AND AUTHORITIES

DUE PROCESS REQUIRES THE PROSECUTION TO PROVIDE DISCOVERY IN ORDER TO PROTECT DEFENDANT'S RIGHT TO PRESENT A DEFENSE AND RIGHT TO A FAIR TRIAL

"(T)he interest of the prosecution is not that it shall win the case, but that it shall bring forth the true facts surrounding the commission of the crime so that justice shall be done ..." (*Berger v. United States* (1934) 295 U.S. 78, 88)

The purpose of the discovery process in criminal cases is to guarantee a defendant a fair trial by giving him equal access to information so that he may be permitted to present all relevant evidence in his behalf. This aim was emphasized in *U.S. v. Nixon* (1974) 418 U.S. 683, 709, where the United States Supreme Court stated:

> "We have elected to employ an adversary system of criminal justice in which the parties contest all issues before a court of law. The need to develop all relevant facts in the adversary system is both fundamental and comprehensive. The ends of criminal justice would be defeated if judgments were to be founded on a partial or speculative presentation of the facts. The very integrity of the judicial system and public confidence in the system depend on full disclosure of all the facts, within the framework of the rules of evidence. To ensure that justice is done, it is imperative to the function of courts that compulsory process be available for the production of evidence needed by the prosecution or by the defense."

The sources in expanding criminal discovery can be found in the "Due Process Clause" of the 5th and 14th Amendments to the United States Constitution, and in the 6th Amendment to the United States Constitution. The United States Supreme Court also stated in *Nixon* that to vindicate these guarantees, the courts have a "manifest duty" to ensure that *all* relevant and admissible evidence be produced. (*id.*)

Clearly established law, explained in *Brady v. Maryland* (1963) 373 U.S. 83, and its progeny, provides that the prosecution violates a defendant's Due Process rights when it fails to disclose to the defendant prior to trial, "evidence favorable to an accused. . . where the evidence is material either to guilt or to punishment, irrespective of the good faith or bad faith of the prosecution." (*id.* at 87). The *Brady* rule is not intended "to displace the adversary system as the primary means by which truth is uncovered, but to ensure that a miscarriage of justice does not occur" (*U.S. v. Bagley* (1985) 473 U.S. 667, 675). This limited departure from the adversary system "illustrates the special role played by the American prosecutor in the search for truth in criminal trials" (*Strickler v. Greene* (1999) 527 U.S. 263). The prosecutor's unique role "transcends that of an adversary: [the prosecutor] is the representative not of an ordinary party to a controversy, but of a sovereignty . . . whose interest . . . in a criminal prosecution is not that it shall win a case, but that justice shall be done.' " *Bagley*, 473 U.S. at 675 fn.6 (quoting *Berger v. United States* (1935) 295 U.S. 78, 88; see also *Kyles v. Whitley* (1995) 514 U.S. 419, 437).

Due Process requires fundamental fairness in the prosecution of a criminal case (*Lisenba v. California* (1941) 314 U.S. 219, 236). Implicit in the concept of fundamental fairness is the idea that the defendant must have the opportunity to present a complete defense (*California v. Trombetta* (1984) 467 U.S. 479, 485). The prosecution can ensure that a defendant has the opportunity to present a complete defense by providing access to favorable evidence (*Brady*, supra).

The United States Supreme Court has held that "[s]uppression by the prosecution of evidence favorable to an accused who has requested it violates Due Process where the evidence is material either to guilt or to punishment, irrespective of the good faith or bad faith of the prosecution." (*Brady, supra*). It is the character of the evidence, rather than the character of the prosecutor, that determines whether the suppression of favorable evidence results in constitutional error(*U.S. v. Agurs* (1976) 427 U.S. 97, 110).

The proper inquiry where the question is whether the prosecution

violated a defendant's right to Due Process by withholding evidence is:
  (1) whether the evidence was favorable to the defendant; and,
  (2) whether the evidence was material to guilt or punishment.
        (See *United State v. Bagley* (1985) 473 U.S. 667).

For purposes of this analysis, it does not matter whether the evidence was suppressed by the prosecutor or by the other agents on the case (*Kyles v. Whitley* (1995) 514 U.S. 419). Rather, the question is whether the evidence was suppressed by the prosecution, for which both the prosecutors and the investigators serve as agents.(*id.*)

The ultimate responsibility for ensuring that exculpatory evidence is provided in accordance with *Brady* rests with the prosecutor (*id.* at 438). A miscommunication between the prosecutor and the investigators that results in the suppression of exculpatory evidence is no excuse for a *Brady* violation (id.). As the Supreme Court explained in *Kyles v. Whitley*, since "the prosecutor has the means to discharge the government's *Brady* responsibility if he will, any argument excusing a prosecutor from disclosing what he does not happen to know about boils down to a plea to substitute the police for the prosecutor, and even for the courts themselves, as the final arbiters of the government's obligation to ensure fair trials." (id.)

THE PROSECUTION'S DISCOVERY DUTY OF DISCLOSURE INCLUDES THE DUTY TO DISCLOSE MATERIALS IN THE ACTUAL OR CONSTRUCTIVE POSSESSION OF ALL MEMBERS OF THE PROSECUTION TEAM

The Prosecution has a duty to seek out and disclose all discoverable materials held by members of the "prosecution team," including the evidence held by each investigative agency.

The prosecutors assigned to try a case have the duty "to learn of any favorable evidence known to others acting on the government's behalf in the case" (*Kyles v. Whitley* (1995) 514 U.S. 419, 437). Accordingly, the *Brady/Kyles* rule extends to all members of the "prosecution team," which includes both investigative and prosecutorial personnel (*U.S. v. Morris* (7th Cir. 1996) 80 F.3rd 1151, 1170 (citing with favor *Carey v. Duckworth* (7th Cir. 1984) 738 F.2nd 875, 878, for proposition that prosecution team includes federal DEA agents and local police)).

The Prosecution is not required to review the files of agencies that have no involvement in the investigation or prosecution (*Morris, supra*), but prosecutors are required to examine the files of those entities who actively participate in the investigation or prosecution of a case (See *Kyles, supra* 514 U.S. 419; *Morris,* supra 80 F. 3rd at 1169).

It is well established that a prosecutor is deemed to have "control" over all members of an investigatory team and that evidence maintained by cooperating entities falls within the scope of the Prosecution's *Brady* obligation (*Kyles, supra,* 514 U.S. at pp. 437-438 ("any favorable evidence known to the others acting on the government's behalf is imputed to the prosecution."; *U.S. v. Zuno-Arce* (9th Cir.1995) 44 F. 3rd 1420 ("Exculpatory evidence cannot be kept out of the hands of the defense just because the prosecutor does not have it, where an investigating agency does.")

PROPOSITION 115 DID NOT ELIMINATE A DEFENDANT'S RIGHT TO DISCOVERY BEFORE THE PRELIMINARY HEARING

Our appellate courts have never held that discovery procedures were unavailable or inappropriate in advance of the preliminary examination. Instead the courts have simply cautioned magistrates not to grant discovery motions "in the absence of a showing that such discovery is reasonably necessary to prepare for the preliminary examination" and observed that "[p]retrial discovery is aimed at facilitating the swift administration of justice, not thwarting it" (*Holman v. Superior Court* (1981) 29 Cal. 3rd 480; *Alvarado v. Superior Court* (2000) 23 Cal. 4th 1121).

Penal Code §1054(e) and *Penal Code §1054.7* do state that the prosecution must provide the required information to the defense "at least 30 days before trial." However, our appellate courts have held that *Penal Code §1054.7* "does not preclude a defendant from making an earlier discovery motion under Pen. Code, §1054.5, nor does it preclude such a motion from being granted more than 30 days in advance of trial" (*Magallan v. Superior Court* (2011) 192 Cal. App. 4th 1444 - preliminary hearing magistrate had the power to grant discovery in support of defendant's motion to suppress evidence at the preliminary hearing)).

The *Magallan* court also held that defense discovery under *Penal Code §1054.1* was not limited to a "trial setting" which did not include the preliminary hearing (*Magallan,* supra at p. 1458).

Most important, the *Magallan* court reaffirmed the continuing viability of *Holman v. Superior Court* (1981) 29 Cal. 3rd 480, 485 which was decided prior to enactment of the statutory scheme and held that a defendant is entitled to pre-preliminary hearing discovery upon "a showing that such discovery is reasonably necessary to prepare for the preliminary examination."

THE DEFENDANT HAS THE RIGHT TO DISCOVERY BEFORE THE PRELIMINARY HEARING IN ORDER TO EXERCISE SPECIFIC STATUTORY RIGHTS

The changes Proposition 115 made to the nature of preliminary examinations did not result in magistrates lacking the power to order discovery. Proposition 115 did not eliminate a criminal defendant's right to present specific statutory motions at the preliminary examination. Hence, the need for discovery in support of such motions is left unchanged by Proposition 115's other changes to the nature of preliminary examinations (*Magallan v. Superior Court*, 192 Cal. App. 4th 1444 (2011)). The appellate courts have reasoned it would defy common sense that the Legislature would provide rights under certain statutes but at the same time deny the defendant any means to pursue those rights.

Although *Magallan* and its progeny have not endorsed an expansive power to grant discovery prior to the preliminary hearing, the decisions have held that *Penal Code §1054(e)* itself specifically recognizes that certain discovery is exempted from the Prop 115 structure where it is necessitated by other express statutory provisions, such as *Penal Code §1538.5* suppression motions (*Magallan v. Superior Court* (2011) 192 Cal. App. 4th 1444, 1458, and *Evidence Code, §§1043 to 1045 Pitchess* motions (*Galindo v. Superior Court* (2010) 50 Cal. 4th 1). In addition, discovery must be permitted before a preliminary hearing to exercise rights "mandated by the Constitution of the United States," such as *Brady* obligations to disclose material evidence favorable to the accused (*Galindo v. Superior Court* (2010) 50 Cal. 4th 1, 13).

A DEFENDANT HAS THE RIGHT TO DISCOVERY BEFORE THE PRELIMINARY HEARING IN ORDER TO SUPPORT A PENAL CODE §1538.5 MOTION

Under *Penal Code §1538.5(f)(1)* a defendant is statutorily authorized to bring a motion to suppress evidence at the preliminary examination, if the prosecution seeks to introduce, at the preliminary examination, evidence that the defense claims is the product of an unreasonable search and seizure. Therefore, a defendant's right to due process under the California Constitution takes precedence over the discovery statutes and entitles the defense to the discovery necessary to support a *Penal Code §1538(f)* motion at the preliminary hearing, even if the requested material is not enumerated in *Penal Code §1054*. In *Magallan v. Superior Court*, 192 Cal. App. 4th 1444, 1460 (2011), the court held the preliminary hearing magistrate had the power to grant discovery in support of a defendant's statutory right to move to suppress evidence at the preliminary hearing.

Proposition 115 did not eliminate a criminal defendant's right to bring a suppression motion at the preliminary examination. Hence, the need for discovery in support of such a motion was left unchanged by Proposition 115's other changes to the nature of preliminary examinations.

A defendant's right to due process under the California Constitution takes precedence over *Proposition 115* and entitles the defense to the discovery necessary to support a *Penal Code §1538.5(f)* motion. The California Supreme Court has long recognized that a criminal defendant has a right to due process under the California Constitution at a suppression hearing.

> [T]he spirit and the purpose of the right to due process under the California Constitution is to assure to everyone a full and ample opportunity to be heard before he can be deprived of his liberty or his property [citation]. However, the procedures at a suppression hearing before a judge need not be the same as those available to a defendant at trial [citations]. Nonetheless, at a suppression hearing, the defendant must have a fair opportunity to litigate the claim.
>
> (*People v. Hansel*, 1 Cal. 4th 1211, 1219-1220 (1992)).

THE DUTY TO DISCLOSE FAVORABLE EVIDENCE EXISTS PRIOR TO THE PRELIMINARY HEARING

In *Stanton v. Superior Court*, 193 Cal. App. 3rd 265, 267 (1987), the court held that the prosecution's duty to disclose material evidence that is favorable to the defense under *Brady v. Maryland*, 373 U.S. 83 (1963) applies at the time of the preliminary hearing. In *Stanton*, the court struck an element of the charged offense because of "the prosecution's failure to disclose evidence material to defense cross-examination of eyewitnesses at a preliminary hearing."

The enactment of Proposition 115 (*Cal. Const. art. I, §3(b), (c)*) which authorized the use of hearsay evidence at preliminary hearings and the new criminal discovery statutes (*Penal Code §§1054 et seq.*) did not abrogate the prosecutor's *Brady* obligations at the preliminary hearing (*People v. Gutierrez* (2010) 214 Cal. App. 4th 343, 350).

A defendant has a due process right to the disclosure of evidence, prior to a preliminary hearing, that is both favorable to the defense and material to the magistrate's determination of whether probable cause exists to hold the defendant to answer (*Bridgeforth v. Superior Court* (2013) 214 Cal. App. 4th 1074, 1087).

DUE PROCESS MANDATES DISCLOSURE OF EVIDENCE THAT UNDERMINES THE CREDIBILITY OF PROSECUTION WITNESSES

In the landmark case of *Brady v. Maryland*, 373 U.S. 83, 87 (1963), the United States Supreme Court held that the suppression of material evidence favorable to the defendant violates the guarantees of due process:

> We now hold that the suppression by the prosecution of evidence favorable to an accused upon request violates due process where the evidence is material either to guilt or to punishment, irrespective of the good faith or bad faith of the prosecution.

In *Giglio v. U.S.*, 405 U.S. 150, 154 (1972) the United States Supreme Court held that evidence that affects the credibility of a witness whose testimony might impact upon the defendant's guilt or innocence falls within the *Brady* rule of compelled disclosure. The Giglio holding was reaffirmed in *U.S. v. Bagley*, 473 U.S. 667, 676 (1985): "Impeachment evidence, however, as well as exculpatory evidence, falls within the Brady rule [citation]. Such evidence is 'evidence favorable to an accused' [citation]."

The California Supreme Court adopted this reasoning in *People v. Pensinger*, 52 Cal. 3rd 1210, 1272 (1991), holding that "[t]he duty to disclose evidence favorable to the accused extends to the disclosure of evidence relating to the credibility of witnesses."

A DEFENDANT HAS THE RIGHT TO DISCOVERY BEFORE THE PRELIMINARY HEARING IN ORDER TO SUPPORT A PITCHESS MOTION

A defendant is statutorily empowered to seek disclosure of a peace officer's personnel records upon a proper showing in order to support his defense (*Evidence Code §§1043 to 1045*; *Penal Code §§832.7 to 832.8*). Because Pitchess discovery is authorized by an express statutory provision, reciprocal discovery statutes do not preclude the defendant from obtaining such discovery. Our Supreme Court has held that a defendant may file such a motion before the preliminary hearing is held (*Galindo v. Superior Court* (2010) 50 Cal. 4th 1, 11).

"The Pitchess discovery statutes (Evid. Code, §§1043 to 1045; Pen. Code,

§§832.7 to 832.8) do not restrict the use of evidence obtained through such discovery to any particular proceeding. As there is no legislative prohibition against the filing of a Pitchess discovery motion before a preliminary hearing is held, we conclude that such a filing is permissible." (id.)

PRODUCING IRRELEVANT MATERIALS OUTSIDE THE RECOGNIZED DISCOVERY SCHEME DENIES DEFENDANT A FAIR TRIAL

Penal Code §1054.1 requires the Prosecution to produce certain evidence to the Defense. In the instant case, the Prosecution appears to be attempting to fulfil their obligation under §1054.1 by producing evidence, but the Prosecution appears to have also produced voluminous evidence related to all defendants in all cases connected to the Operation known as Blind Mice. This overproduction of evidence denies Defendant due process in that it hides relevant and material evidence from the Defense.

"A keyword in Penal Code §1054.1(c) is 'relevant.' The prosecution must produce 'All relevant real evidence seized or obtained as a part of the investigation of the offenses charged.' This should not be interpreted to give them leave to hide a grain of relevant evidence in a mountain of irrelevant evidence." (*A View From the Bottom – Discovery* [1])

"When a statute is susceptible to more than one construction, a court must give it an interpretation that will avoid confusion and absurdity and must adopt an interpretation that is consistent with sound reason (*Cilibrasi v. Reiter* (1951) 103 Cal. App. 2nd 397). A statute should not be construed in such a manner as to result in a palpable absurdity (*Kauke v. Lindsay Unified School Dist.* (1941) 46 Cal. App. 2nd 176). Where the meaning of a statute is doubtful, any construction which would lead to absurd results should be rejected (*Aggeler v. Dominguez* (1933) 217 Cal. 429)." (id)

"Interpreting *Penal Code §1054.1* to allow for the production of mass quantities of irrelevant evidence along with the relevant evidence is an interpretation that leads to confusion and absurd results..." (id.)

---

[1] *A View From the Bottom – Discovery*, 661Justice.com/discovery-abuse (View) last visited 12/19/2021.

"…the idea that the discovery process should not create "undue burden and expense" is consistent with the concept that a trial is a search for the truth and should be fair (*People v. Bell* (2004) 118 Cal. App. 4th 249). The overproduction of irrelevant evidence creates an "undue burden and expense" that is borne by the county for indigent defendants, and is neither consistent with the search for the truth not fundamental fairness." (id.)

"One of the purposes of the discovery scheme is "To promote the ascertainment of truth in trials by requiring timely pretrial discovery." (*Penal Code §1054(a)*). A trial is a search for the truth, and the discovery rules are designed to ensure that the search is fair (*People v. Bell* (2004) 118 Cal. App. 4th 249; *People v. Superior Court* (2000) 78 Cal. App. 4th 403)…" (id.)

If a case involves a large number of documents, mere access to the documents is not adequate to inform a defendant what exactly he is accused of doing and what evidence will be offered to prove the allegations. Merely giving access to documents impermissibly shifts the burden to a defendant. (*U.S. v. Bortnovsky* (2nd Cir. 1987) 820 F. 2nd 572, 575; *U.S. v. Davidoff* (2nd Cir. 1988) 845 F. 2nd 1151).

The evidence the Prosecution may produce related to defendants in other cases does not appear to be relevant to the instant prosecution, does not appear to be *Brady* material, and does not appear to be evidence that the Prosecution could possibly intend to introduce during trial in this matter. Discovery should be limited to relevant evidence and evidence that would logically lead to the discovery of relevant evidence.

DEFENDANT SPECIFICALLY REQUESTS DISCLOSURE OF THE FOLLOWING EVIDENCE:

ONE - LEGIBLE COPIES OF ALL POLICE REPORTS

The Defense requests legible copies of all police reports, in a standard format, without removal of fonts and metadata.

Penal Code §1054.1 (f) requires the Prosecution to disclose "Relevant written or recorded statements of witnesses or reports of the statements of witnesses whom the prosecutor intends to call at the trial, including any reports or statements of experts made in conjunction with the case, including the results of physical or mental examinations, scientific tests, experiments, or comparisons which the prosecutor intends to offer in evidence at the trial."

The Prosecution has been known to produce electronic records that have been scanned in low resolution, which makes portions of the reports unintelligible. The originals of such documents often contained font and character information, making them searchable. Such information is automatically created when the documents are created, but this information may be stripped from copies produced to the Defense. Further, the resolution of such documents is often of such poor quality that standard Optical Character Recognition software is unable to properly recreate the missing information. The defense, therefore, requests that discovery of documents be in original format without loss of data.

TWO – WITNESS INFORMATION

The Defense requests names and contact information for each trial witness.

Penal Code §1054.1(a) requires the Prosecution to disclose "The names and addresses of persons the prosecutor intends to call as witnesses at trial." The discovery provided by the Prosecution identifies possible witnesses. It is highly unlikely that the more than a few of the persons identified are actually witnesses to anything relevant or material in this matter. The large number of people disclosed the actual witness information that the Prosecution is required to disclose. The Defense, therefore, seeks an order requiring the Prosecution to disclose which witnesses it actually intends to call without including names of persons it does not intend to call, unless such disclosure is pursuant to *Brady*.

THREE - CONSPIRATOR NAMES AND DATES

The Defense requests the name of each alleged conspirator and approximate dates each entered any conspiracy alleged against Defendant.

"[D]efendants must be provided with certain information in order to permit them to prepare adequately for trial. Specifically, they are entitled to… the names of all persons the government would claim at trial were co-conspirators (whether or not they will be called as trial witnesses), the approximate dates and locations of any meetings or conversations not already identified in the indictment in which each defendant allegedly participated, and the approximate date on which each defendant allegedly joined the conspiracy." (*U.S. v. Ramirez* (1999) 54 F.Supp.2nd 25)

FOUR – WARRANTS AND ATTACHMENTS

The Defense requests all warrants and attachments to all relevant warrants.

c.Motion to Unseal Affidavit (Hobbs Motion)

ROGER LAMPKIN
SB#113786
1234 L Street
Bakersfield, CA 93301
Tel: (661)633-1234
Fax: (661)863-6741
Attorney for Doug Donenabbed

IN THE SUPERIOR COURT OF THE STATE OF CALIFORNIA, IN AND FOR THE COUNTY OF KERN

People of the State of California, Plaintiffs, - v. - Doug Donenabbed, Defendant	CASE NO. 123456 DEFENDANT'S MOTION TO UNSEAL THE AFFIDAVIT DATE: December 16, 2021 TIME: 10:00 a.m. DEPT: CC Trial date: January 17, 2022 Readiness date: January 7, 2022

TO THE COURT AND THE DISTRICT ATTORNEY:

PLEASE TAKE NOTICE that at the date and time indicated above, or as soon thereafter as the matter can be heard in the above-entitled court, the defendant will move that the Court unseal the affidavit used to support the search warrant used in this case. An in camera hearing is requested pursuant to *People v. Hobbs* (1994) 7 Cal. 4th 948, to rule on the propriety of the concealing portions of the affidavit from the defendant.

The motion will be based on this notice of motion, all attached documents, the records on file in this action, and on such matters as may be presented at the hearing.

Dated:

                        _____

                        By   Roger Lampkin,
                        Attorney for Doug Donenabbed

DECLARATION IN SUPPORT OF MOTION TO
UNSEAL THE AFFIDAVIT

I, Roger Lampkin, Attorney for Defendant, declare:

1. According to the affidavit in support of the search warrant in this case (attached), officers received information from a witness only identified as "X" that several people were involved in trafficking methamphetamine, including Defendant.
2. The officer begins by referring to X in the singular, but then changes to the plural form, thus indicating that X actually refers to more than one person: "X told me they know a white male subject... they told me they recently have seen [Defendant] in possession of a large amount of methamphetamine."
3. The affidavit goes on to explain that it is actually Bart Baddy who "holds the methamphetamine at his residence..."
4. These informants are alleged to have had knowledge as to who was in the home, who owned the home, and who was selling narcotics.
5. Defendant contends that another person was responsible for the drug sales (possibly one of the informants or Bart) and that Defendant had no connection with the narcotics.
6. A reasonable possibility exists that one or more of the informants, whose true number is unknown, was also an eyewitness to the crimes alleged and could give evidence on the issue of guilt or innocence in this action that would result in the exoneration of the Defendant.
7. Significantly, the informants each appear to know that "Bart" possessed the methamphetamine. This gives rise to an obvious third party culpability defense, and these informants can each give exculpatory testimony.
8. At a minimum, the informants should be able to testify that Bart owned the residence and possessed the methamphetamine that was found therein.
9. Further, the affiant makes conclusory statements concerning the reliability of the informants, but it is clear that X is representative of multiple people, some of whom may not be reliable and/or may have themselves been involved in the sales of methamphetamine. The affidavit is unclear as to how many people are represented by X, why the officer believes one or more of them is reliable, and what portion of the information he received from each person represented by X.
10. The affidavit contains an attachment, B, which has been sealed and withheld from Defendant. Attachment B may contain:
    a. Information related to Bart, his ownership of the house, and/or his possession of methamphetamine. This information would

be exculpatory as to Defendant.

b. Information related to the reliability or lack thereof of informants represented by X. This too would be exculpatory to Defendant in that if the informants are reliable, their statements as to Bart owning the residence and possessing methamphetamine would tend to exonerate Defendant. If the informants are not reliable, the warrant was issued without probable cause.

c. False statements of material facts or material omissions that could negate probable cause.

d. Other information that is otherwise exculpatory and discovery is required under Brady.

Dated:

_____

By   Roger Lampkin,
      Attorney for Doug Donenabbed

POINTS, AUTHORITIES, AND ARGUMENT

WHERE AN AFFIDAVIT IN SUPPORT OF A WARRANT HAS BEEN SEALED, AN IN CAMERA HEARING MUST BE HELD BY THE COURT

In *Franks v. Delaware* (1978) 438 U.S. 154, 155-157, the United States Supreme Court held that a defendant may challenge the veracity of a facially valid warrant affidavit on a substantial preliminary showing that (1) the affiant made statements that were deliberately false or in reckless disregard of the truth; and (2) the affidavit's remaining content is insufficient to justify a finding of probable cause. The Fourth Amendment requires that a hearing be held at the defendant's request, where such a showing is made. The rule enunciated in *Franks* is, moreover, applicable to affidavits marred by omissions of fact (*U.S. v. Lefkowitz* (9th Cir 1980) 618 F. 2nd 1313, 1317).

However, our courts have recognized that when the defendant moves to traverse or quash a warrant on the grounds of material false statements or omissions in the application and the entire affidavit supporting it is sealed, the defendant may not be able to make even the minimal showing required by *People v. Luttenberger* (1990) 50 Cal. 3rd 1. Our Supreme Court has devised a procedure to address this issue. In this situation, the court is required to conduct an in camera hearing and failure to do so is reversible error (*People v. Galland* (2004) 116 Cal. App. 4th 489, 490-491).

No preliminary showing is required by the defendant to be entitled to an in camera hearing. By filing the motion, the court is required to treat the matter as if the defendant had made the requisite preliminary showing called for in *Luttenberger* (*People v. Hobbs* (1994) 7 Cal. 4th 948, 972).

THE COURT SHOULD FOLLOW A THREE-PART PROCEDURE FOR THE IN CAMERA HEARING

In *People v. Hobbs* (1994) 7 Cal. 4th 948, 974-975 the court set forth the procedure for the in camera hearing. The prosecutor is present at the hearing and the defense excluded, unless the prosecutor consents to their presence. At the hearing the court should inform the prosecution what materials and witnesses it requires. The prosecution may present testimony. After examining the warrant and any supporting material or testimony, the court must determine the following:

> First, whether the affidavit is properly sealed, that is, whether sufficient grounds exist for maintaining the confidentiality of the informant's identity and whether a portion of the sealed information may be disclosed without compromising the informant's identity.

> Second, if the court finds that the affidavit, or a major part of it, has been properly sealed, the court proceeds to the next step, which requires the court to determine whether "there is a reasonable probability the defendant would prevail" on his suppression motion. The "precise standard of review" applied by the court at this stage of the *Hobbs* procedure depends on whether the defendant has noticed a motion to quash the warrant or to traverse it.

> Third, if the affidavit is found to be properly sealed and the defendant has filed a motion to traverse, the court must determine whether the defendant's allegations of material misrepresentations or omissions are supported by the record under the standards set out in *Franks v. Delaware* (1978) 438 U.S. 154, 155-156, which is that the affidavit supporting the search warrant contained inaccurate statements or omissions from the affidavit that rendered it substantially misleading, meaning that there was a substantial possibility that the misrepresentations would have altered a reasonable magistrate's probable cause determination.

The instant motion goes to the first step, with the expectation that a motion to traverse (steps two and three) may be brought based on the contents of the sealed affidavit, if such is disclosed.

Since the defendant is completely ignorant of all critical portions of the affidavit (and, as a result, the defense is unable to specify what materials the court should reveal in camera), the court must take it upon itself both to examine the affidavit for possible inconsistencies or insufficiencies regarding the showing of probable cause and inform the prosecution of the materials or witnesses it requires. The materials will invariably include such items as relevant police reports and other information regarding the informant and the informant's reliability (*People v. Hobbs* (1994) 7 Cal. 4th 948, 973).

Furthermore, because the defendant's access to the "essence of the affidavit" has been eliminated, the court may, in its discretion, find it necessary and appropriate to call and question the affiant, the informant, or any other witness whose testimony it deems necessary to rule upon the issues. Where feasible, the court may also, in its discretion, order the tape recording or videotaping of all or any portion of the in camera proceeding (*People v. Hobbs* (1994) 7 Cal. 4th 948).

→••Ω••←

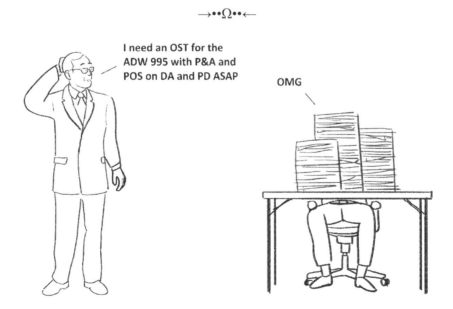

I need an OST for the ADW 995 with P&A and POS on DA and PD ASAP

OMG

d. Motion for Bill of Particulars

ROGER LAMPKIN
SB#113786
1234 L Street
Bakersfield, CA 93301
Tel: (661)633-1234
Fax: (661)863-6741
Attorney for Doug Donenabbed

IN THE SUPERIOR COURT OF THE STATE OF CALIFORNIA,
IN AND FOR THE COUNTY OF KERN

People of the State of California,	CASE NO. 123456
Plaintiffs,	DEFENDANT DOUG DONENABBED'S MOTION FOR BILL OF PARTICULARS
- v. -	
Doug Donenabbed,	Date: August 2, 2022 Time: 8:30 a.m.
Defendant	Dept: CC
	Readiness: August 12, 2022 Trial: August 22, 2022

TO THE COURT AND THE DISTRICT ATTORNEY:
PLEASE TAKE NOTICE that at the date and time indicated above, the defendant will move for an order requiring the Prosecution to prepare a Bill of Particulars describing the allegations against Defendant in a sufficient manner to satisfy the requirements of the Sixth Amendment to the United States Constitution.

The motion will be made on the grounds that the charging document does not give Defendant adequate notice of the accusations against him.

The motion will be based on this notice of motion, all attached documents, the records on file in this action, and on such matters as may be presented at the hearing.

Dated: _____

                By   Roger Lampkin,
                      Attorney for Doug Donenabbed

POINTS, AUTHORITIES, AND ARGUMENT

"In all criminal prosecutions, the accused shall enjoy the right ... to be informed of the nature and cause of the accusation." (U.S. Const. amend. VI.)

"Due process of law requires that an accused be advised of the charges against him in order that he may have a reasonable opportunity to prepare and present his defense and not be taken by surprise by evidence offered at his trial." (*People v. West* (1970) 3 Cal 3rd 595, quoting *In re Hess* (1955) 45 Cal. 2nd 171)

Penal Code §952 generally abolishes the formalistic pleading requirements of the common law, but to satisfy the Sixth Amendment right to adequate notice, "the charging document need not contain a citation to the specific statute at issue; the substance of the information, however, must in some appreciable way apprise the defendant of the charges against him so that he may prepare a defense accordingly." (*Gautt v. Lewis* (9th Cir. 2007) 489 F.3rd 993, 1004).

Ross v. Municipal Court (1975) 49 Cal. App. 3rd 575 is instructive. In *Ross*, the prosecution charged the defendant with being under the influence (*Health & Safety Code §11550*) without identifying the controlled substance involved. The reviewing court explained, "Nevertheless we are definitely of the view that, upon appropriate pre-trial motion therefor, petitioner should be granted promptly discovery of all information bearing upon the possible identity of the controlled substance involved that the People possess. He is entitled to this information so that he may the more readily prepare his defense... This information would serve the function of a bill of particulars. The denial of such a bill in a criminal case has been upheld in this state on the ground of lack of statutory authority therefor. [citations] But since such a bill represents a form of discovery as well as being a pleading, production of this information would no longer appear subject to such a limitation in California. [citations] In at least one other state a bill of particulars in the situation before us had long been required. [citation]..." (*Ross v. Municipal Court* (1975) 49 Cal. App. 3rd 575, footnote included).

In *People v. Lewelling* (2017) 16 Cal. App. 5th 276, the court noted in passing that, "Prior to trial, defendant moved for a bill of particulars, claiming it was impossible from the information to understand the theory of the... charge. A hearing was held, at which the court confirmed defendant's position that 'the defense is unclear of what specific acts constitute each count.' The court then asked the prosecutor for her response…"

In *Sheppard v. Rees* (9th Cir. 1989) 909 F. 2nd 1234, the defendant argued that "he did not receive adequate notice to enable him to prepare a proper defense to the theory of felony-murder" during his California state court trial. "The State of California originally took the position in this court that [defendant's] Sixth Amendment right to be informed of the nature and cause of the accusation against him had not been violated. The State argued that the general allegation of murder in the primary charging document was constitutionally sufficient in itself to put the defendant on notice that he may have to defend against a charge of felony-murder."

The court reversed the defendant's conviction and noted, "An accused could be adequately notified of the nature and cause of the accusation by other means—for example, a complaint, an arrest warrant, or a bill of particulars…. Similarly, it is possible that an accused could become apprised of the particular charges during the course of a preliminary hearing. Any or all of these sources—or perhaps others—might provide notice sufficient to meet the requirements of due process, although precise formal notice is certainly the most reliable way to comply with the Sixth Amendment. The Constitution itself speaks not of form, but of substance." (id. at footnote 2).

The Complaint in this case does not give Defendant adequate notice of what he is alleged to have done.

This case involves allegations that a medical doctor ordered unnecessary laboratory tests and overbilled insurance carriers; however, Defendant does not have the ability to order laboratory tests or bill insurance carriers. He is not a doctor or laboratory worker. Defendant is alleged to be a sales representative for a laboratory. He has no knowledge of what tests are medically necessary, and he has no ability to order or bill for any type of medical or laboratory tests. In this context, the counts alleged against Defendant are constitutionally deficient.

As an example, Count 1 alleges a conspiracy between Defendant and the doctor. Overt acts alleged against Defendant are that he:

1. Established a fraudulent business relationship by completing unnecessary medical treatment…

The defense is unable to understand what a "fraudulent business relationship" is. Is the Prosecution alleging that Defendant and the doctor had a false (i.e. non-existent) business relationship, that the doctor defrauded Defendant into believing there was a business relationship, or something else?

Nevertheless, it is not alleged that Defendant is a medical doctor or otherwise has any ability to complete "unnecessary medical treatment" of any kind. Without proper licensing, Defendant cannot order or perform medical treatment, unnecessary or otherwise, and without medical training, Defendant cannot be expected to know what treatment is proper, recommended, or necessary.

Further, it is unclear what is meant by unnecessary. Withholding of a certain treatment may have adverse effects, but no medical treatment can be deemed necessary without clarification. Is the treatment "necessary" to preserve life, "necessary" to dissuade patient fears, "necessary" to diagnose a disease, or "necessary" for some other purpose? It simply cannot be determined what improper conduct is being attributed to Defendant.

2. Billed for unnecessary medical treatment…

Again, use of the word "unnecessary" is unnecessarily confusing in the context of this case. It is also unclear who Defendant allegedly billed. Defendant is not a doctor and is not able to bill, prescribe, order, authorize, or perform for any medical treatment.

Count 1 further claims that the "violation was not discovered until September 16, 2020," but it is unclear who "discovered" the alleged violation. This information is essential to the defense because it can be used to establish that the statute of limitations has run.

As shown by these examples, the Complaint in this case does not give Defendant adequate notice of what he is alleged to have done. The Complaint does appear to allege that Codefendant Doc Ock submitted insurance claims that the Prosecution disagrees with, but it is unclear what Defendant is alleged to have done.

Based on the foregoing, Defendant respectfully requests a bill of particulars that clearly states Defendant's alleged involvement in any crime.

e. Motion to Disclose Evidence Needed for Demurrer

ROGER LAMPKIN
SB#113786
1234 L Street
Bakersfield, CA 93301
Tel: (661)633-1234
Fax: (661)863-6741
Attorney for Doug Donenabbed

IN THE SUPERIOR COURT OF THE STATE OF CALIFORNIA,

IN AND FOR THE COUNTY OF KERN

People of the State of California,	CASE NO. 123456
Plaintiffs,	REQUEST FOR EVIDENTIARY HEARING IN ANTICIPATION OF DEMURRER [Zamora Motion]
- v. -	
Doug Donenabbed,	Date: August 2, 2022
Defendant	Time: 8:30 a.m. Dept: CC
	Readiness: August 12, 2022 Trial: August 22, 2022

TO THE ABOVE-ENTITLED COURT AND THE DISTRICT ATTORNEY OF KERN COUNTY: PLEASE TAKE NOTICE that at the date and time indicated above, or as soon thereafter as the matter can be heard in the above-entitled court, the defendant will request an evidentiary hearing in anticipation of a Demurrer to the Complaint.

The motion will be made on the grounds that the charging document does not sufficiently allege that the charges come within the applicable statute of limitations, and it would be in the interest of judicial economy to determine the jurisdiction of the court at the earliest opportunity.

The motion will be based on this notice of motion, all attached documents, the records on file in this action, and on such matters as may be presented at the hearing.

Dated: _____

By   Roger Lampkin,
      Attorney for Doug Donenabbed

STATEMENT OF THE CASE

Defendant is charged with various financial crimes allegedly committed on or about and between May 1, 2004 and August 1, 2018. A portion of this time frame appears to be beyond the applicable statute of limitations.

POINTS, AUTHORITY, AND ARGUMENT

Penal Code §1004(5) provides in part: "The defendant may demur to the accusatory pleading at any time prior to the entry of a plea, when it appears upon the face thereof …. that the court has no jurisdiction of the offense charged therein…That it contains a matter which, if true, would constitute a… legal bar to the prosecution." Running of the statute of limitations deprives the court of jurisdiction (*In re Demillo* (1975) 14 Cal. 3rd 598.

A complaint must allege facts on its face showing that the prosecution is not barred by the applicable statute of limitations. (*People v Crosby* (1962) 58 Cal. 2nd 713, 724).

The Prosecution has alleged that the applicable statute of limitations was tolled until discovery of the offenses pursuant to *Penal Code §803(c)(6)*. *Penal Code §803(c)* does not define the "discovery of an offense" or specify who qualifies as a discoverer.

In *People v. Zamora* (1976) 18 Cal. 3rd 538, 564, the California Supreme Court, held that the "following facts [must] be alleged in an accusatory pleading which seeks to avoid the bar of the statute of limitations by pleading the "discovery" provision of section 800: (1) the date on which the offense was "discovered"; (2) how and by whom the offense was "discovered"; (3) lack of knowledge, both actual or constructive, prior to the date of "discovery"; (4) the reason why the offense was not "discovered" earlier."

The *Zamora* court noted that "the limitation question is a basic jurisdictional issue and the bar thereof is aimed as much at the prevention of untimely prosecutions as it is at the prevention of untimely convictions. If it appears possible that the evidence will establish as a matter of law that the period of limitation has run, then judicial economy may be far better served if the issue is resolved at the earliest possible stage of the proceedings… We conclude therefore that a trial court has within its discretion the power to hold an evidentiary hearing for purposes of determining whether as a matter of law the statute of limitations bars the prosecution."

For reasons of judicial economy, it is within the discretion of the court to hold an evidentiary hearing to determine whether as a matter of law the statute of limitations bars the prosecution. (*People v. Zamora* (1976) 18 Cal. 3rd 538, 564).

Based on the foregoing, Defendant respectfully requests an evidentiary hearing.

→•••Ω•••←

"Sorry, as a paralegal, I am not allowed to give an opinion as to whether the jury will believe your statement."

f. Motion to Discover Evidence of Selective Prosecution

ROGER LAMPKIN
SB#113786
1234 L Street
Bakersfield, CA 93301
Tel: (661)633-1234
Fax: (661)863-6741
Attorney for Doug Donenabbed

IN THE SUPERIOR COURT OF THE STATE OF CALIFORNIA,

IN AND FOR THE COUNTY OF KERN

People of the State of California,	CASE NO. 123456
Plaintiffs,	MOTION TO DISCOVER EVIDENCE OF SELECTIVE PROSECUTION [*Murgia*]
- v. -	
Doug Donenabbed,	Date: August 2, 2022
Defendant	Time: 8:30 a.m. Dept: CC
	Readiness: August 12, 2022 Trial: August 22, 2022

TO THE ABOVE-ENTITLED COURT AND THE DISTRICT ATTORNEY OF KERN COUNTY: PLEASE TAKE NOTICE that at the date and time indicated above, or as soon thereafter as the matter can be heard in the above-entitled court, the defendant will move for an order requiring the Prosecution to provide evidence of selective prosecution, including but not limited to:

1. All departmental standards and guidelines for selection of cases for prosecution.
2. Statistical data for all arrests, prosecutions, and dismissals for the same offense for the past five years, including the sex and race of the accused.
3. Any records produced in response to a *Murgia* motion brought in any case in the past five years.

The motion will be based on the grounds that Defendant has cause to believe that he has been deliberately singled out for prosecution on the basis of some invidious criterion.

The motion will be based on this Notice of Motion, on all attached papers filed herewith or later filed, on all papers and records on file in this action and on such oral and documentary evidence as may be presented at the time of the motion.

Dated: _____

By   Roger Lampkin,
     Attorney for Doug Donenabbed

DECLARATION OF COUNSEL

I, Roger Lampkin, declare:
1. I am an attorney at law and am the attorney for the defendant in this case.
2. I am informed and believe that the following facts establish a plausible showing that Defendant has been deliberately singled out for prosecution on the basis of some invidious criterion.
    a. Defendant is of African descent.
    b. Officers stopped Defendant's 2020 Mercedes based on an anonymous tip that a "Black man is driving a stolen luxury car through the neighborhood."
    c. No additional information was given about the vehicle, its occupant, or how the anonymous person came to believe the vehicle was stolen.
    d. The vehicle was registered to Defendant, but officers nonetheless demanded that he exit the vehicle and consent to a search.
    e. Defendant withheld consent and was arrested for obstruction.

I declare that I am informed and believe the foregoing is true and correct.

Dated: _____

By   Roger Lampkin,
     Attorney for Doug Donenabbed

MEMORANDUM OF POINTS AND AUTHORITIES

In its landmark decision in *Yick Wo v. Hopkins* (1886) 118 U.S. 356, the Supreme Court declared that the Constitution's promise of equal protection under the laws compels the law not only to "be fair on its face and impartial in appearance," but to be "applied and administered by public authority with an [honorable] eye and an [equal] hand." (id. at 373–374.) In *Two Guys from Harrison–Allentown, Inc. v. McGinley* (1961) 366 U.S. 582 and *Oyler v. Boles* (1962) 368 U.S. 448, 456, the court condemned selective prosecution, holding that deliberate invidious discrimination in the prosecution of a criminal charge is a ground for dismissal of the charge.

In order to establish a claim of discriminatory prosecution, " 'the defendant must prove: (1) "that he has been deliberately singled out for prosecution on the basis of some invidious criterion"; and (2) that "the prosecution would not have been pursued except for the discriminatory design of the prosecuting authorities." ' " (*Baluyut v. Superior Court* (1996) 12 Cal.4th 826, 832).

" '[A]n invidious purpose for prosecution is one that is arbitrary and thus unjustified because it bears no rational relationship to legitimate law enforcement interests ....' [Citation.]" (*Manduley v. Superior Court* (2002) 27 Cal.4th 537, 568–569.)

In *Murgia v. Municipal Court* (1975) 15 Cal. 3rd 286, the California Supreme Court held that, upon a sufficient showing, a defendant is entitled to obtain discovery in support of a claim of discriminatory prosecution. The showing required to invoke the discovery rights that *Murgia* provides is discussed in *United States v. Armstrong* (1996) 517 U.S. 456 and requires that defendants must produce some evidence of differential treatment of similarly situated members of other races or protected classes.

A *Murgia* motion must "describe the requested information with at least some degree of specificity and must be sustained by plausible justification" (*Griffin v. Municipal Court* (1977) 20 Cal. 3rd 300, 306).

Our Supreme Court has held a showing of "plausible justification" requires a defendant to "show by direct or circumstantial evidence that prosecutorial discretion was exercised with intentional and invidious discrimination in his case" (*People v. Montes* (2014) 58 Cal. 4th 809).

g. Motion to Discover Prosecution Agreements

ROGER LAMPKIN
SB#113786
1234 L Street
Bakersfield, CA 93301
Tel: (661)633-1234
Fax: (661)863-6741
Attorney for Doug Donenabbed

IN THE SUPERIOR COURT OF THE STATE OF CALIFORNIA,
IN AND FOR THE COUNTY OF KERN

| People of the State of California,

Plaintiffs,

- v. -

Doug Donenabbed,

Defendant | CASE NO. 123456

DEFENDANT DOUG DONENABBED'S MOTION TO DISCOVER PROSECUTION AGREEMENTS

Date: August 2, 2022
Time: 8:30 a.m.
Dept: CC

Readiness: August 12, 2022
Trial: August 22, 2022 |

TO THE COURT AND THE DISTRICT ATTORNEY:
PLEASE TAKE NOTICE that at the date and time indicated above, Defendant will move the Court for an order requiring the Prosecution to disclose all agreements, warnings in lieu of prosecution, witness fees, reduced charges, dismissed charges, and other forms of compensation, however slight, given to any witness concerning the subject matter of this action.

The motion will be based on this notice and attached papers, on all papers and records on file in this action, and on such oral and documentary evidence as may be presented at the time of the motion.

Dated: _____

By   Roger Lampkin,
Attorney for Doug Donenabbed

MEMORANDUM OF POINTS AND AUTHORITIES

The prosecutor has a duty to disclose any inducement offered to any witness (*U.S. v. Bagley* (1985) 473 U.S. 667; *In re Sassounian* (1995) 9 Cal. 4th 535).

The prosecution has a duty to disclose any implied promises or benefits. For example, in *Giglio v. U.S.* (1972) 405 U.S. 150, the prosecutor told a witness that he would "definitely be prosecuted if he did not testify and that if he did testify he would be obliged to rely on the 'good judgment and conscience of the Government' as to whether he would be prosecuted." The Supreme Court ruled that failure to disclose this information to the defense was reversible error.

Penal Code §1127a requires the prosecution to provide the defendant with a "written statement setting out any and all consideration promised to, or received by" an in-custody informant, and the statute defines consideration as "any plea bargain, bail consideration, reduction or modification of sentence, or any other leniency, benefit, immunity, financial assistance, reward, or amelioration of current or future conditions of incarceration in return for, or in connection with, the informant's testimony in the criminal proceeding in which the prosecutor intends to call him or her as a witness" (id.) However, this statutory duty does not fully encompass the scope of required disclosure. "A prosecutor's duty to disclose evidence favorable to the accused extends to evidence reflecting on the credibility of a material witness. This includes any inducements made to prosecution witnesses for favorable testimony" (*People v. Kasim* (1997) 56 Cal. App. 4th 1360 [internal citations omitted]).

The prosecution must even disclose inducements received in prior cases because the jury is "entitled to know about all historical events bearing on these witnesses' propensity to be truthful or untruthful" (*People v. Kasim* (1997) 56 Cal. App. 4th 1360, 1382).

Practical Tip:

Don't leave it on a desk.

The attorneys you work with may already have a system for the exchange of papers – most often a simple "in box" – but often papers are simply left on an attorney's desk until she returns. This is a bad practice for multiple reasons. First, papers that require immediate action may not receive the needed attention. If something needs immediate attention, it should be handed to the attorney with an explanation of the urgency. Second, papers on a desk tend to become piles on a desk. Clutter begets clutter. Mail also stacks up, but most mail directed to an attorney should be opened and processed by someone else. Ask the attorney his preference. The attorney's desk should be clear so she can meet with clients at any time without the appearance of clutter. Third, papers tend to be stacked. If the attorney sits down to meet with a client, papers on the desk will often be stacked and shoved to the side – out of sight and out of mind. Fourth, paper piles may violate confidentiality. If a client can view papers on the attorney's desk during a consultation, the client may see a bit too much.

h. Motion to Discover Witness Criminal Records

ROGER LAMPKIN
SB#113786
1234 L Street
Bakersfield, CA 93301
Tel: (661)633-1234
Fax: (661)863-6741
Attorney for Doug Donenabbed

IN THE SUPERIOR COURT OF THE STATE OF CALIFORNIA,

IN AND FOR THE COUNTY OF KERN

People of the State of California,	CASE NO. 123456
Plaintiffs,	DEFENDANT DOUG DONENABBED'S MOTION TO DISCOVERY RECORDS RELATED TO WITNESS'S CRIMINAL HISTORY [Brady Motion, Penal Code §1054.5]
- v. -	
Doug Donenabbed,	
Defendant	Date: August 2, 2022
Time: 8:30 a.m.
Dept: CC
	Readiness: August 12, 2022
Trial: August 22, 2022

TO THE COURT AND THE DISTRICT ATTORNEY: PLEASE TAKE NOTICE that at the date and time indicated above, or as soon thereafter as the matter can be heard in the above-entitled court, Defendant will move the Court for an order compelling discovery of police and investigative reports related to alleged criminal conduct by Vicky Vick, a witness in this action.

The motion will be made on the ground that the District Attorney has in his actual or constructive possession certain items of evidence which defense counsel is legally entitled to inspect and the defense has informally requested said evidence.

The motion will be based on this Notice of Motion, on the attached memorandum of points and authorities and filed herewith and such supplemental memorandum of points and authorities that may be hereafter filed with the court or stated orally at the conclusion of the hearing, on all papers and records on file in this action and on such oral and documentary evidence as may be presented at the time of the motion.

Dated: _____

        By   Roger Lampkin,
           Attorney for Doug Donenabbed

MEMORANDUM OF POINTS AND AUTHORITIES

DUE PROCESS REQUIRES THE PROSECUTION TO PROVIDE DISCOVERY IN ORDER TO PROTECT DEFENDANT'S RIGHT TO PRESENT A DEFENSE AND RIGHT TO A FAIR TRIAL

"(T)he interest of the prosecution is not that it shall win the case, but that it shall bring forth the true facts surrounding the commission of the crime so that justice shall be done ..." (*Berger v. United States* (1934) 295 U.S. 78, 88)

The purpose of the discovery process in criminal cases is to guarantee a defendant a fair trial by giving him equal access to information so that he may be permitted to present all relevant evidence on his behalf. This aim was emphasized in *U.S. v. Nixon* (1974) 418 U.S. 683, 709, where the United States Supreme Court stated:

> "We have elected to employ an adversary system of criminal justice in which the parties contest all issues before a court of law. The need to develop all relevant facts in the adversary system is

both fundamental and comprehensive. The ends of criminal justice would be defeated if judgments were to be founded on a partial or speculative presentation of the facts. The very integrity of the judicial system and public confidence in the system depend on full disclosure of all the facts, within the framework of the rules of evidence. To ensure that justice is done, it is imperative to the function of courts that compulsory process be available for the production of evidence needed by the prosecution or by the defense."

Clearly established law, explained in *Brady v. Maryland* (1963) 373 U.S. 83, and its progeny, provides that the prosecution violates a defendant's Due Process rights when it fails to disclose to the defendant prior to trial, "evidence favorable to an accused. . . where the evidence is material either to guilt or to punishment, irrespective of the good faith or bad faith of the prosecution." (*id.* at 87). The *Brady* rule is not intended "to displace the adversary system as the primary means by which truth is uncovered, but to ensure that a miscarriage of justice does not occur" (*U.S. v. Bagley* (1985) 473 U.S. 667, 675). This limited departure from the adversary system "illustrates the special role played by the American prosecutor in the search for truth in criminal trials" (*Strickler v. Greene* (1999) 527 U.S. 263). The prosecutor's unique role "transcends that of an adversary: [the prosecutor] is the representative not of an ordinary party to a controversy, but of a sovereignty . . . whose interest . . . in a criminal prosecution is not that it shall win a case, but that justice shall be done.' " *Bagley*, 473 U.S. at 675 fn.6 (quoting *Berger v. United States* (1935) 295 U.S. 78, 88; see also *Kyles v. Whitley* (1995) 514 U.S. 419, 437).

Due Process requires fundamental fairness in the prosecution of a criminal case (*Lisenba v. California* (1941) 314 U.S. 219, 236). Implicit in the concept of fundamental fairness is the idea that the defendant must have the opportunity to present a complete defense (*California v. Trombetta* (1984) 467 U.S. 479, 485). The prosecution can ensure that a defendant has the opportunity to present a complete defense by providing access to favorable evidence (Brady, supra).

The United States Supreme Court has held that "[s]uppression by the prosecution of evidence favorable to an accused who has requested it violates Due Process where the evidence is material either to guilt or to punishment, irrespective of the good faith or bad faith of the prosecution." (*Brady, supra*). It is the character of the evidence, rather than the character of the prosecutor, that determines whether the suppression of favorable evidence results in constitutional error (*U.S. v. Agurs* (1976) 427 U.S. 97,

110).

THE PROSECUTION'S DISCOVERY DUTY OF DISCLOSURE INCLUDES THE DUTY TO DISCLOSE MATERIALS IN THE ACTUAL OR CONSTRUCTIVE POSSESSION OF ALL MEMBERS OF THE PROSECUTION TEAM

The Prosecution has a duty to seek out and disclose all discoverable materials held by members of the "prosecution team," including the evidence held by law enforcement agencies.

The prosecutors assigned to try a case have the duty "to learn of any favorable evidence known to others acting on the government's behalf in the case" (*Kyles v. Whitley* (1995) 514 U.S. 419, 437).

"Prosecutors are deemed constructively aware of Brady material known to anyone on the prosecution team and must share that information with the defense." (*Association for Los Angeles Deputy Sheriffs v. Superior Court* (2019) 8 Cal. 5th 28)

THE DEFENSE IS ENTITLED TO ACCESS TO RECORDS RELATED TO ALLEGED CRIMINAL ACTIVITY BY WITNESSES

Penal Code §1054.1 provides for defense discovery of "felony convictions of material witnesses whose credibility is likely to be critical to the outcome of the trial." Impeachment of any witness by prior conduct not amounting to a felony and involving "moral turpitude" is also proper. (*People v Wheeler* (1992) 4 Cal 4th 284). Accordingly, records of arrests and convictions of witnesses for felonies and misdemeanors are discoverable, at least if the conduct involves "moral turpitude." (*People v Santos* (1994) 30 Cal App 4th 169).

In *Hill v Superior Court of Los Angeles County* (1974) 10 Cal 3rd 812, 817, the California Supreme Court held that the felony conviction records and the records of arrests and detentions of prospective witnesses are discoverable by the defendant, upon a showing of good cause, for the purpose of impeachment.

"[S]pecific acts of aggression by the alleged victim may be admissible to show that the victim was the aggressor; such evidence would be material when the defense is self-defense, or where the defendant seeks to show mitigating circumstances to reduce the charge." (*Engstrom v. Superior Court*

(1971) 20 Cal.App.3rd 240, citing *In re Ferguson* (1971) 5 Cal.3rd 525, 534 and *People v. Smith* (1967) 249 Cal.App.2nd 395, 404-405).

In the instant case, the Prosecution has disclosed that witness Vicky Vick has a criminal history of violence. Disclosure of police reports and records related to past offenses will assist the Defense in locating witnesses to Vicky Vick's history of violence as well as assist the Defense to impeach her.

i. Motion to Discover Child Exploitation Records

ROGER LAMPKIN
SB#113786
1234 L Street
Bakersfield, CA 93301
Tel: (661)633-1234
Fax: (661)863-6741
Attorney for Doug Donenabbed

IN THE SUPERIOR COURT OF THE STATE OF CALIFORNIA,
IN AND FOR THE COUNTY OF KERN

People of the State of California, Plaintiffs, - v. - Doug Donenabbed, Defendant	CASE NO. 123456 DEFENDANT DOUG DONENABBED'S DISCOVERY MOTION [Brady Motion, *Penal Code §1054.5*] Date: August 2, 2022 Time: 8:30 a.m. Dept: CC Readiness: August 12, 2022 Trial: August 22, 2022

TO THE COURT AND THE DISTRICT ATTORNEY:
PLEASE TAKE NOTICE that at the date and time indicated above, Defendant will move the Court for an order compelling discovery.
The motion will be made on the ground that the District Attorney has in his actual or constructive possession certain items of evidence which defense counsel is legally entitled to inspect and the defense has informally requested said evidence.
The motion will be based on this Notice of Motion, on the attached

memorandum of points and authorities and filed herewith and such supplemental memorandum of points and authorities that may be hereafter filed with the court or stated orally at the conclusion of the hearing, on all papers and records on file in this action and on such oral and documentary evidence as may be presented at the time of the motion.

Dated: _____

By   Roger Lampkin,
       Attorney for Doug Donenabbed

MEMORANDUM OF POINTS AND AUTHORITIES

The purpose of the discovery process in criminal cases is to guarantee a defendant a fair trial by giving him equal access to information so that he may be permitted to present all relevant evidence in his behalf. This aim was emphasized in *U.S. v. Nixon* (1974) 418 U.S. 683, 709, where the United States Supreme Court stated:

> "We have elected to employ an adversary system of criminal justice in which the parties contest all issues before a court of law. The need to develop all relevant facts in the adversary system is both fundamental and comprehensive. The ends of criminal justice would be defeated if judgments were to be founded on a partial or speculative presentation of the facts. The very integrity of the judicial system and public confidence in the system depend on full disclosure of all the facts, within the framework of the rules of evidence. To ensure that justice is done, it is imperative to the function of courts that compulsory process be available for the production of evidence needed by the prosecution or by the defense."

Defendant specifically requests access to:
1. Audio recordings of any suspect, defendant, or former defendant in this matter.
2. Video recordings of any alleged crime in this matter.
3. Any alleged contraband.
4. All seized electronic evidence, including computers, hard drives, thumb drives, cell phones, and other electronic media.

Penal Code §1054.1(c) provides for such discovery. Pursuant to the *Adam Walsh Child Protection and Safety Act* of 2006, law enforcement and prosecutors are prohibited from providing visual depictions of suspected child exploitation exhibits to defense attorneys and defense attorney experts. The defense may not be entitled to possess the image or video physically; however, the Prosecution is required to provide the file name and file attributes related to the file to the defense.

Generally, most forensic software, such as Physical Analyzer by Cellebrite, which is used by local law enforcement, can create reports that are intended to report all relevant "evidence" or information as set forth during the report generation. This would include thumbnail images and links that would display the entire image or video. Physical Analyzer has built-in functions to assist examiners in generating reports that omit these thumbnail images, links, and files but includes associated meta data.

The Defense is entitled to these reports, and the Defense is entitled to view the actual images as they remain in Prosecution custody. Without such reports and a physical viewing, the Defense will be ambushed at trial when the Prosecution presents the images to the jury.

j. Motion for Independent Testing

ROGER LAMPKIN
SB#113786
1234 L Street
Bakersfield, CA 93301
Tel: (661)633-1234
Fax: (661)863-6741
Attorney for Doug Donenabbed

IN THE SUPERIOR COURT OF THE STATE OF CALIFORNIA,
IN AND FOR THE COUNTY OF KERN

People of the State of California,	CASE NO. 123456
Plaintiffs,	MOTION FOR RELEASE OF EVIDENCE FOR EXAMINATION AND TESTING
- v. -	
Doug Donenabbed,	Date: August 2, 2022 Time: 8:30 a.m.
Defendant	Dept: CC
	Readiness: August 12, 2022 Trial: August 22, 2022

TO THE COURT AND THE DISTRICT ATTORNEY OF KERN COUNTY: PLEASE TAKE NOTICE that at the date and time indicated above, or as soon thereafter as the matter can be heard in the above-entitled court, the defendant move the Court for an order requiring the Prosecution team to make available to the Defense team for examination and testing the following evidence:

1. A portion of the blood seized from Defendant in this case.
2. The bullet fragments seized in this case.
3. A swatch of blood-stained portion of the jacket seized in this case

The motion will be made on the grounds that independent testing of the seized items is necessary for the defense of this action.

The motion will be based on this notice and the attached papers, on all papers and records on file in this action and on such oral and documentary evidence as may be presented at the time of the request.

Dated: _____

By   Roger Lampkin,
Attorney for Doug Donenabbed

MEMORANDUM OF POINTS AND AUTHORITIES

The right to counsel includes the right to the use of experts to assist counsel in preparing a defense (*Torres v. Municipal Court* (1975) 50 Cal. App. 3rd 778, 783).

The Defense is entitled to have its own experts inspect physical evidence seized by the Prosecution team (*Prince v. Superior Court* (1992) 8 Cal. App. 4th 1176, 1180). The court in Prince explained, "[w]hile it is true the goal of the judicial process is to find the truth, allowing the defense to conduct an independent test of the [evidence] will not unfairly prejudice the People or result in injustice."

DECLARATION OF COUNSEL

I, Roger Lampkin, declare:

1. I am an attorney at law and am the attorney for the defendant in this case.
2. The Prosecution seized blood from Defendant, bullet fragments, and a blood-stained jacket seized.
3. Prosecution experts, who are expected to testify at trial, have performed various tests and examinations on these items.
4. The defense has secured the services of its own experts.
5. I am informed and believe that there is a sufficient quantity of blood for a split, and there is sufficient blood on the jacket for

swatches to be taken without depriving the Prosecution of evidence for use in its case.

6. I am informed and believe that the defense experts' examination of the bullet fragments will be non-destructive and the fragments can be returned to the Prosecution following examination.

I declare that the foregoing is true and correct.
Dated: _____

By   Roger Lampkin,
     Attorney for Doug Donenabbed

k. Motion to Disclose Informant

ROGER LAMPKIN
SB#113786
1234 L Street
Bakersfield, CA 93301
Tel: (661)633-1234
Fax: (661)863-6741
Attorney for Doug Donenabbed

IN THE SUPERIOR COURT OF THE STATE OF CALIFORNIA,

IN AND FOR THE COUNTY OF KERN

People of the State of California,	CASE NO. 123456
Plaintiffs,	DEFENDANT DOUG DONENABBED'S MOTION TO DISCOVER IDENTITY OF INFORMANT
- v. -	
Doug Donenabbed,	Date: August 2, 2022 Time: 8:30 a.m. Dept: CC
Defendant	
	Readiness: August 12, 2022 Trial: August 22, 2022

TO THE ABOVE-ENTITLED COURT AND THE DISTRICT ATTORNEY OF KERN COUNTY: PLEASE TAKE NOTICE that on the date and time noted above or as soon thereafter as counsel may be heard in the courtroom of the above-entitled court, the defendant will move for an order requiring the prosecution to either disclose to counsel for defendant the identity of the informant specified in the attached search warrant, or dismiss the charges against the defendant.

The motion will be made on the grounds that this informant is a material witness on the issue of guilt or innocence in this action and is a necessary witness regarding issues related to the validity of the search and as such, the disclosure of the informant's identity is essential to a full and fair determination of the case.

The motion will be based on this notice of motion, on the attached declaration, on the memorandum of points and authorities served and filed herewith, on all the papers and records on file in this action, and on such oral and documentary evidence as may be presented at the hearing of the motion.

Dated: _____

By   Roger Lampkin,
Attorney for Doug Donenabbed

ATTORNEY DECLARATION

I, Roger Lampkin, declare:

1.   I am the attorney representing the defendant in this action.
2.   I am informed and believe that the informant is a necessary witness for a suppression hearing to prove that some of the allegations supporting probable cause were false or misleading.
3.   The informant is needed, inter alia, to establish which defendant (or what other person) was responsible for the alleged drug sales at Defendant's home.
4.   There is no showing or allegation that the informant is reliable, and it is quite possible that the informant is someone with a grudge against defendants, received compensation for information provided, or had other reason to make false statements to law enforcement, plant evidence on defendants, or otherwise frame defendants.

Dated: _____

By   Roger Lampkin,
Attorney for Doug Donenabbed

MEMORANDUM OF POINTS AND AUTHORITIES

The identity of an informant who was an eyewitness to the crime charged against the defendant must be disclosed to the defense. In *People v. Goliday* (1973) 8 Cal. 3rd 771, 782, the Supreme Court explained:

> We emphasize that the eyewitness informers involved here acted as police agents at the time of the alleged sale. The police bear no duty to obtain information about a person who is not a material witness, who 'simply points the finger of suspicion toward a person who has violated the law.' [Citation omitted.] If, however, a material witness serves as an agent of the police and becomes a material witness on the issue of guilt, his desire for anonymity must yield to the interest of the accused in a fair trial. The police, accordingly, must undertake reasonable efforts to obtain information by which the defense may locate such an informer.

A defendant may offer evidence at a suppression hearing to prove that some of the allegations in an affidavit supporting a facially sufficient search warrant were false. Our Supreme Court has held that "a defendant possesses a limited but viable constitutional right to attempt to controvert the veracity of statements made in the affidavit. To exercise that right, the defendant requires information indicating the material falsity of the affidavit." (*People v. Luttenberger* (1990) 50 Cal. 3rd 1, 19)

Recognizing that it may be difficult for a defendant to prove police misrepresentations without discovery when probable cause is based on statements of an unidentified informant, the courts have adopt a preliminary-showing requirement that is somewhat less demanding than the "substantial showing of material falsity" required by *Franks v. Delaware*, 438 U.S. 154 (1978). A defendant who wants to obtain discovery to controvert probable cause need only "offer evidence casting some reasonable doubt on the veracity of material statements made by the affiant." (*People v. Luttenberger* (1990) 50 Cal. 3rd 1, 21)

→••Ω••←

Practical Tip:
Be aware (or beware) of your presence on social media. Are you an avid gardener? Posting garden pictures probably won't hurt your career. Are you heavily involved in politics, pro-life, or pro-choice? Posting your opinions on such topics may offend some of your clients. Are you planning a trip to Tahiti? Posting about it on social media could inform clients about your expected absence. Bought a new house in a gated community? Post about it on social media, and your clients may learn where you live.

1. Motion to Disclose Informant Reliability Records

ROGER LAMPKIN
SB#113786
1234 L Street
Bakersfield, CA 93301
Tel: (661)633-1234
Fax: (661)863-6741
Attorney for Doug Donenabbed

IN THE SUPERIOR COURT OF THE STATE OF CALIFORNIA,

IN AND FOR THE COUNTY OF KERN

People of the State of California,	CASE NO. 123456
Plaintiffs,	DEFENDANT DOUG DONENABBED'S MOTION TO DISCLOSE INFORMANT RELIABILITY RECORDS
- v. -	
Doug Donenabbed,	[Luttenberger]
Defendant	Date: August 2, 2022 Time: 8:30 a.m. Dept: CC
	Readiness: August 12, 2022 Trial: August 22, 2022

TO THE ABOVE-ENTITLED COURT AND THE DISTRICT ATTORNEY OF KERN COUNTY: PLEASE TAKE NOTICE that at the date and time indicated above, or as soon thereafter as the matter can be heard in the above-entitled court, the defendant will move for an order requiring the Prosecution to disclose informant reliability records.

The motion will be based on the grounds that a search was conducted based on an allegedly reliable informant and the requested records are needed to challenge the search.

The motion will be based on this Notice of Motion, on the attached memorandum of points and authorities and filed herewith and such supplemental memorandum of points and authorities that may be hereafter filed with the court or stated orally at the conclusion of the hearing, on all papers and records on file in this action and on such oral and documentary evidence as may be presented at the time of the motion.

Dated:

_____

By   Roger Lampkin,
        Attorney for Doug Donenabbed

MEMORANDUM OF POINTS AND AUTHORITIES

"[A] defendant possesses a limited but viable constitutional right to attempt to controvert the veracity of statements made in the affidavit. To exercise that right, the defendant requires information indicating the material falsity of the affidavit." (*People v. Luttenberger* (1990) 50 Cal. 3rd 1, 19).

"To justify in camera review and discovery, preliminary to a subfacial challenge to a search warrant, a defendant must offer evidence casting some reasonable doubt on the veracity of material statements made by the affiant... Thus, before an in camera review may be ordered, the defendant must raise some reasonable doubt regarding either the existence of the informant or the truthfulness of the affiant's report concerning the informant's prior reliability or the information he furnished." (id)

DECLARATION IN SUPPORT OF MOTION

I, Roger Lampkin, declare:
1. I am attorney for the Defendant.
2. The affiant to the search warrant in this case alleges an informant told an officer that he had purchased marijuana at the property officers sought to search. Presumably, multiple officers participated in the surveillance of the location over the course of multiple days, but only one officer "found" an informant.
3. The informant was allegedly found in possession of marijuana, but was not searched prior to being near the location, and no information is provided to indicate that the informant did or did not have a medical marijuana recommendation.
4. The time and date the informant allegedly provided information to law enforcement is not given nor is information about pending charges against the informant, other than the fact that he had committed an offense and was being detained. The immediate threat of prosecution and inferred promise of leniency give the informant

158

motive to provide false information.

5. The affiant does not claim to know the informant or have had any other contact with the informant, and the informant is neither named nor described.

6. Based on the foregoing, I am informed and believe that the informant in the instant case either does not exist or is not reliable.

I declare under penalty of perjury that I am informed and believe that the foregoing is true and correct.

Dated: _____

By   Roger Lampkin,
Attorney for Doug Donenabbed

→ • • Ω • • ←

3. Dismissals

a. Demurrer – Jurisdiction

Note: A demurrer is a challenge to the charging document that does not deny the truth of the allegations; rather, it argues that even if everything in the charging document were true, the defendant still could not be charged. A demurrer is generally limited to the charging document itself and matters that the court can take judicial notice of (see Judicial Notice under Important Terms above).

An exception to this general rule is when the charging document is ambiguous regarding the jurisdiction of the court. The following motion is a request that the court either establish jurisdiction or dismiss the charges.

ROGER LAMPKIN
SB#113786
1234 L Street
Bakersfield, CA 93301
Tel: (661)633-1234
Fax: (661)863-6741
Attorney for Doug Donenabbed

IN THE SUPERIOR COURT OF THE STATE OF CALIFORNIA,

IN AND FOR THE COUNTY OF KERN

People of the State of California,	CASE NO. 123456
Plaintiffs,	DEFENDANT DOUG DONENABBED'S MOTION
- v. -	FOR HEARING ON JURISDICTION AND
Doug Donenabbed,	DEMURRER
Defendant	Date: August 2, 2022 Time: 8:30 a.m. Dept: CC

TO THE COURT AND THE DISTRICT ATTORNEY OF KERN COUNTY: PLEASE TAKE NOTICE that Defendant moves the Court an order for a hearing to establish jurisdiction of the Court in the instant case and thereafter sustain Defendant's demurrer and dismiss the Complaint against Defendant.

This motion is made on the ground that Defendant contends that the prosecution is barred by the statute of limitations or other defects that deprive the Court of jurisdiction in this matter, and Defendant is, therefore, entitled to dismissal or an evidentiary hearing to establish jurisdiction.

The motion will be based on this notice and all attached papers, on all papers and records on file in this action, and on such oral and documentary evidence as may be presented at the time of the motion.

Dated: _____

By   Roger Lampkin,
Attorney for Doug Donenabbed

POINTS, AUTHORITIES, AND ARGUMENT

Penal Code §1004 allows a defendant to "demur to the accusatory pleading at any time prior to the entry of a plea, when it appears upon the face thereof... that the court has no jurisdiction of the offense charged therein."

"[T]he limitation question is a basic jurisdictional issue and the bar thereof is aimed as much at the prevention of untimely prosecutions as it is at the prevention of untimely convictions. If it appears possible that the evidence will establish as a matter of law that the period of limitation has run, then judicial economy may be far better served if the issue is resolved at the earliest possible stage of the proceedings rather than waiting until an entire trial on multiple issues is completed. Moreover, the determination of the trial court after such a hearing will be similar to that on a motion for a directed verdict (§§ 1118, 1118.1) without the necessity of first litigating the merits of the case. We conclude therefore that a trial court has within its discretion the power to hold an evidentiary hearing for purposes of determining whether as a matter of law the statute of limitations bars the prosecution." (*People v. Zamora* (1976) 18 Cal.3rd 538)

"The words "jurisdictional territory" when used with reference to a court, mean the city and county, county, city, township, or other limited territory over which the criminal jurisdiction of the court extends, as provided by law, and in case of a superior court mean the county in which the court sits." *(Penal Code §691(b))*.

The Prosecution has burden of proof to establish jurisdiction by a preponderance of the evidence *(Zamora,* supra, at 564; see also *People v. Castillo* (2008) 168 Cal. App. 4th 364, 369).

In the instant case, the Complaint alleges that on or about January 1, 2010, Defendant made terrorist threats to the alleged victim, but no allegations are made that the conduct occurred within the territorial jurisdiction of this Court or within the statute of limitations. Defendant, therefore, requests a hearing to establish jurisdiction.

b. Demurrer – Misjoinder

Note: A demurrer requests that the charging document be dismissed, but the district attorney may still be allowed to proceed with the prosecution by filing an amended Complaint. The following demurrer, if granted, would most likely result in the Complaint being dismissed but amended Complaints being filed to separate the charges.

ROGER LAMPKIN
SB#113786
1234 L Street
Bakersfield, CA 93301
Tel: (661)633-1234
Fax: (661)863-6741
Attorney for Doug Donenabbed

IN THE SUPERIOR COURT OF THE STATE OF CALIFORNIA,

IN AND FOR THE COUNTY OF KERN

People of the State of California,	CASE NO. 123456
Plaintiffs,	DEFENDANT DOUG DONENABBED'S DEMURRER
- v. -	[Misjoinder]
Doug Donenabbed,	Date: August 2, 2022 Time: 8:30 a.m.
Defendant	Dept: CC

TO THE COURT AND THE DISTRICT ATTORNEY: PLEASE TAKE NOTICE that at the date and time indicated above, or as soon thereafter as the matter can be heard in the above-entitled court, the defendant will Demurrer to the Information.

The demurrer will be made on the ground that the Information does not substantially conform to the provisions of *Penal Code §950*.

The demurrer will be based on this notice of demurrer, all attached documents, the records on file in this action, and on such matters as may be presented at the hearing.

Dated: _____

By   Roger Lampkin,
Attorney for Doug Donenabbed

POINTS, AUTHORITIES, AND ARGUMENT

Penal Code "Section 954 provides that an accusatory pleading may 'charge two or more different offenses connected together in their commission ... or two or more different offenses of the same class of crimes or offenses....' " (*People v. Mendoza* (2000) 24 Cal.4th 130, 160).

Offenses are " ' "connected together in their commission" when they are [ ] linked by a " 'common element of substantial importance.' " ' " (Id. at 160; see *People v. Kemp* (1961) 55 Cal. 2nd 458, 476; Alcala v. Superior Court (2008) 43 Cal. 4th 1205, 1217).

Offenses are of the same class when they possess common characteristics or attributes. (*People v. Kraft* (2000) 23 Cal.4th 978, 1030).

A demurrer is the proper way to challenge the improper joinder of counts. "[M]isjoinder is not one of the grounds upon which the information may be attacked under section 995 of the Penal Code. That objection to the information may be only raised by demurrer." (*People v. Cummings* (1959) 173 Cal. App. 2nd 721).

THE CHARGES AGAINST THE DEFENDANT ARE UNCONNECTED IN THEIR COMMISSION AND ARE NOT THE SAME CLASS OF CRIMES

Defendant is charged by Information with eight felony counts stemming from the alleged theft of a piece of construction equipment, a separate incident where he allegedly threatened someone, and a third incident where he allegedly possessed a firearm. Counts are as follows:

1. Take Vehicle without Owner's Consent (*Penal Code §10851(a)*)
2. Vandalism (*Penal Code §594(B)(1)*)
3. Grand Theft Embezzlement (*Penal Code §487(B)(3)*)
4. Grand Theft Automobile (*Penal Code §487(D)(1)*)
5. Embezzlement (*Penal Code §503*)
6. Possession of Stolen Vehicle (*Penal Code §496D(A)*)
7. Terrorist Threats (*Penal Code §422*)
8. Possession of Firearm by Felon (*Penal Code §12021(A)(1)*)

Counts 1 through 6 are properly joined because each count concerns the alleged theft of a piece of construction equipment. Count 7 is not connected in time or classification. Count 8 is not connected in time or classification. Evidence tending to prove guilt on Counts 1 through 6 would not be admissible to prove Counts 7 or 8.

c. Demurrer – Ambiguous

ROGER LAMPKIN
SB#113786
1234 L Street
Bakersfield, CA 93301
Tel: (661)633-1234
Fax: (661)863-6741
Attorney for Doug Donenabbed

IN THE SUPERIOR COURT OF THE STATE OF CALIFORNIA,

IN AND FOR THE COUNTY OF KERN

People of the State of California,	CASE NO. 123456
Plaintiffs,	DEFENDANT DOUG DONENABBED'S DEMURRER [Ambiguous]
- v. -	
Doug Donenabbed,	Date: August 2, 2022 Time: 8:30 a.m.
Defendant	Dept: CC

TO THE COURT AND THE DISTRICT ATTORNEY: PLEASE TAKE NOTICE that at the date and time indicated above, or as soon thereafter as the matter can be heard in the above-entitled court, the defendant will Demurrer to the Complaint.

The demurrer will be made on the ground that the Complaint does not adequately notify Defendant of the charges against him.

The demurrer will be based on this notice of demurrer, all attached documents, the records on file in this action, and on such matters as may be presented at the hearing.

Dated: _____

                        By   Roger Lampkin,
                        Attorney for Doug Donenabbed

POINTS, AUTHORITIES, AND ARGUMENT

THE CHARGING DOCUMENT IS AMBIGUOUS

In Counts One and Two, Defendant is charged with violating Bakersfield Municipal Codes; however, there is no allegation that either offense was committed within the city limits of Bakersfield. There is no indication where the offenses are alleged to have been committed other than somewhere within the county.

DEFENDANT MAY DEMURRER TO AN AMBIGUOUS CHARGING DOCUMENT

Penal Code §1004 allows a defendant to "demur to the accusatory pleading at any time prior to the entry of a plea, when it appears upon the face thereof... That it does not substantially conform to the provisions of Sections 950 and 952 , and also Section 951 in case of an indictment or information."

"When any of the objections mentioned in Section 1004 appears on the face of the accusatory pleading, it can be taken only by demurrer..." (*Penal Code §1012*)

Penal Code §950 requires that "The accusatory pleading must contain:... A statement of the public offense or offenses charged therein."

"The substantial facts necessary to constitute the crime charged, must appear in the indictment with sufficient certainty to enable the Court to pronounce a proper judgment, and the party to defend against the charge; but they need not be stated with the particularity required at common law." (*People v. Dolan* (1858) 9 Cal. 576).

A "defendant's remedy for obtaining more specific notice… is provided by the special demurrer procedure authorized by section 1012" (*People v. Equarte* (1986) 42 Cal. 3rd 456)

A defendant is entitled to be advised with some particularity which factual theories the Prosecution will rely on (*Lamadrid v. Municipal Court* (1981) 118 Cal. App. 3rd 786, 791). A pleading couched in the statutory language does not always give adequate notice for purposes of trial (id.)

DEFENDANT SHOULD BE ALLOWED TO WITHDRAW HIS PLEA FOR PURPOSE OF ENTERING A DEMURRER

Errors in the accusatory pleading are not waived by Defendant's failure to file timely demurrer. (*People v. Churchill* (1967) 255 Cal.App. 2nd 448; see also *People v. Paul* (1978) 78 Cal.App. 3rd 32).

Defendant's failure to timely demurrer in the instant case should be excused in that he was arraigned prior to counsel being given adequate time to read and consider the charging document and related discovery. Counsel was, therefore, unaware of the basis of this demurrer and was, therefore, unable to file said demurrer prior to arraignment.

CONCLUSION

Defendant should be allowed to withdraw his not guilty plea and enter a demur to the Complaint because the Complaint does not properly and sufficiently give notice of a public offense.

A demurrer based on ambiguity is very case-specific and may be defeated by the Prosecution by simply clarifying any areas of ambiguity prior to hearing of the demurrer.

d. Demurrer – Facial Defect

ROGER LAMPKIN
SB#113786
1234 L Street
Bakersfield, CA 93301
Tel: (661)633-1234
Fax: (661)863-6741
Attorney for Doug Donenabbed

IN THE SUPERIOR COURT OF THE STATE OF CALIFORNIA,

IN AND FOR THE COUNTY OF KERN

People of the State of California, Plaintiffs, - v. - Doug Donenabbed, Defendant	CASE NO. 123456 DEFENDANT DOUG DONENABBED'S DEMURRER Date: August 2, 2022 Time: 8:30 a.m. Dept: CC

TO THE COURT AND THE DISTRICT ATTORNEY: PLEASE TAKE NOTICE that at the date and time indicated above, or as soon thereafter as the matter can be heard in the above-entitled court, the defendant will Demurrer to the Complaint.

The demurrer will be made on the ground that the Complaint contains on its face a legal bar to prosecution.

The demurrer will be based on this notice of demurrer, all attached documents, the records on file in this action, and on such matters as may be presented at the hearing.

Dated: _____

_____
By   Roger Lampkin,
Attorney for Doug Donenabbed

MEMORANDUM OF POINTS AND AUTHORITIES

In Count Two of the sworn Complaint in this action, Defendants are charged with violating *Kern County Ordinance 19.08.055(b)*, which holds:

> Businesses conducting commercial recreational cannabis activity <u>licensed under the Medicinal and Adult-Use Cannabis Regulation and Safety Act</u> are prohibited in all zone districts. No local authorization for any of the activities covered by the license classifications identified in Business and Professions Code 26050 shall be granted for any zone district in the unincorporated area of the County of Kern.
>
> (*Ordinance 19.08.055(b)*, emphasis added)

Count Two contains the Prosecution's admission that Defendants' alleged conduct was "licensed under the Medicinal and Adult-Use Cannabis Regulation and Safety Act."

Count One, however, alleges that Defendants possessed cannabis for sale in violation of *Health & Safety Code §11359(b)*, which holds:

> Every person who possesses for sale any cannabis, <u>except as otherwise provided by law</u>, shall be punished as follows:... (b) Every person 18 years of age or over who possesses cannabis for sale shall be punished by imprisonment in a county jail for a period of not more than six months or by a fine of not more than five hundred dollars ($500), or by both such fine and imprisonment.
>
> (*§11359*, emphasis added)

Because the activity alleged in Count Two is "licensed under the Medicinal and Adult-Use Cannabis Regulation and Safety Act," the sales as alleged in Count One are authorized as being "otherwise provided by law."

The Prosecution's admission in Count Two establishes that the conduct alleged in Count One does not constitute a crime (See Compassionate Use Act, *Health & Safety Code §§11362.5*, et seq., and the Medical Marijuana Program Act, *Health & Safety Code §§11362.7*, et seq., two of the programs coming under the "otherwise provided by law" provision of *Health & Safety Code §11359*.

As the California Supreme Court has explained, "[a]mong other things, these statutes exempt the 'collective[ ] or cooperative[ ] cultiva[tion]' of medical marijuana by qualified patients and their designated caregivers from prosecution or abatement under specified state criminal and nuisance laws that would otherwise prohibit those activities." (*City of Riverside v. Inland Empire Patients Health & Wellness Ctr., Inc.* (2013) 56 Cal. 4th 729, 737; see also *People v. London* (2014) 228 Cal.App.4th 544; *People v. Ahmed* (2018) 25 Cal.App.5th 136).

Prosecution on Count One is, therefore, barred by the admission in Count Two that the activity was "licensed under the Medicinal and Adult-Use Cannabis Regulation and Safety Act."

Penal Code § 1004(5) provides in part: "The defendant may demur to the accusatory pleading at any time prior to the entry of a plea, when it appears upon the face thereof …. That it contains matter which, if true, would constitute a… legal bar to the prosecution."

Errors in the accusatory pleading are not waived by Defendant's failure to file timely demurrer. (*People v. Churchill* (1967) 255 Cal.App. 2nd 448; see also *People v. Paul* (1978) 78 Cal.App.3rd 32). Defendant should, therefore, be allowed to withdraw his not guilty plea to Count One and demurrer to the same.

→••Ω••←

A defect in the charging document that amounts to a bar to prosecution can result in a dismissal without leave to file an amended charging document. However, a demurrer to such a defect is generally highly case-specific and requires extensive legal research.

→••Ω••←

Practical Tip:

Don't wait for work to be assigned. Catch up on filing or scanning. Call clients to remind them of court dates. Call investigators and expert witnesses to get status updates and see if they need additional funding, reports, or anything else. There is always something that needs to be done, and there is always something to learn. If you have nothing to do, ask. If there is no one around to ask and you can't find any work that needs to be done, find something to study. Learn the details of all the office technology. Review a book of common pleadings. Study a case file and write a summary of any important findings. Be proactive and show initiative.

e. Motion to Dismiss for Pre-Accusation Delay

ROGER LAMPKIN
SB#113786
1234 L Street
Bakersfield, CA 93301
Tel: (661)633-1234
Fax: (661)863-6741
Attorney for Doug Donenabbed

IN THE SUPERIOR COURT OF THE STATE OF CALIFORNIA,

IN AND FOR THE COUNTY OF KERN

People of the State of California,	CASE NO. 123456
Plaintiffs,	DEFENDANT DOUG DONENABBED'S MOTION TO DISMISS FOR PRE-ACCUSATION DELAY
- v. -	
Doug Donenabbed,	
Defendant	Date: August 2, 2022 Time: 8:30 a.m. Dept: CC

TO THE ABOVE-ENTITLED COURT AND THE DISTRICT ATTORNEY OF KERN COUNTY: PLEASE TAKE NOTICE that at the date and time indicated above, the defendant will move for an order dismissing the instant action for delay in prosecution.

This motion is made on the ground that the Prosecution team intentionally and/or unreasonably delayed proceedings and Defendant was prejudiced by the delay.

The motion will be based on this Notice of Motion, all attached papers, all papers and records on file in this action, and on such oral and documentary evidence as may be presented at the time of the motion.

Dated: _____   _____

By   Roger Lampkin,
Attorney for Doug Donenabbed

MEMORANDUM OF POINTS AND AUTHORITIES

A delay between the commission of an offense and the filing of a criminal charge does not implicate the constitutional right to speedy trial, it but may implicate a defendant's right to a fair trial and due process of law. (*Scherling v. Superior Court* (1978) 22 Cal. 3rd 493, 505; *People v. Allen* (1979) 96 Cal.App.3rd 268; *People v. Nelson* (2008) 43 Cal.4th 1242, 1250.) Although the statute of limitations is the general guarantee against the bringing of criminal charges in an untimely fashion, a defendant's due process rights under the state and federal constitutions may be violated by an unreasonable delay in bringing criminal charges. (*Nelson*, supra, at 1250.)

In determining whether a criminal defendant's due process right has been violated, courts employ a three-step test. (*People v. Catlin* (2001) 26 Cal.4th 81, 107). The defendant has the initial burden of showing prejudice as a result of the delay; the prosecution then must show justification for the delay; thereafter, the court balances the harm against the justification. (*People v. Reeder* (1984) 152 Cal.App.3rd 900, 909–910; *Ibarra v. Municipal Court* (1984) 162 Cal.App.3rd 853, 858.)

If the defendant does not meet his burden of showing prejudice, there is no need to determine whether the delay was justified. (*Serna v. Superior Court* (1985) 40 Cal. 3rd 239, 249.)

"[U]nder California law, negligent, as well as purposeful, delay in bringing charges may, when accompanied by a showing of prejudice, violate due process. This does not mean, however, that whether the delay was purposeful or negligent is irrelevant… whether the delay was negligent or purposeful is relevant to the balancing process. Purposeful delay to gain an advantage is totally unjustified, and a relatively weak showing of prejudice would suffice to tip the scales towards finding a due process violation. If the delay was merely negligent, a greater showing of prejudice would be required to establish a due process violation." (*Nelson*, supra, at 1255–1256).

Prejudice may be shown by the loss of a material witness or other missing evidence or fading memory caused by lapse of time. (*Nelson*, supra, at 1251.)

The amount of time between the commission of the crime and the filing of charges is not the critical issue. (*Fowler v. Superior Court* (1984) 162 Cal.App.3rd 215, 221.) Prejudice sufficient to sustain dismissal has resulted after a delay of five months (*People v. Cave* (1978) 81 Cal.App.3rd 957), while charges filed after a delay of ten years have been upheld (*Scherling v. Superior Court*, supra, at 507).

In the instant case, Defendant allegedly assaulted his wife two years ago. He was arrested at the time, but no charges were filed. A year ago, the only independent witness to the alleged assault, Wally Wit, died. Two months ago, Defendant filed for divorce, which resulted in his arrest three days later.

f. Motion to Dismiss for Delay in Prosecution

ROGER LAMPKIN
SB#113786
1234 L Street
Bakersfield, CA 93301
Tel: (661)633-1234
Fax: (661)863-6741
Attorney for Doug Donenabbed

IN THE SUPERIOR COURT OF THE STATE OF CALIFORNIA,

IN AND FOR THE COUNTY OF KERN

People of the State of California, Plaintiffs, - v. - Doug Donenabbed, Defendant	CASE NO. 123456 DEFENDANT DOUG DONENABBED'S MOTION TO DISMISS FOR DELAY IN PROSECUTION Date: August 2, 2022 Time: 8:30 a.m. Dept: CC Readiness: August 12, 2022 Trial: August 22, 2022

TO THE ABOVE-ENTITLED COURT AND THE DISTRICT ATTORNEY OF KERN COUNTY: PLEASE TAKE NOTICE that at the date and time indicated above, or as soon thereafter as the matter can be heard in the above-entitled court, the defendant will move for an order to Dismiss for Delay in Prosecution.

This motion is made on the ground that the Prosecution team intentionally and/or unreasonably delayed proceedings and Defendant was prejudiced by the delay.

The motion will be based on this Notice of Motion, on the attached memorandum of points and authorities and filed herewith and such supplemental memorandum of points and authorities that may be hereafter filed with the court or stated orally at the conclusion of the hearing, on all papers and records on file in this action and on such oral and documentary evidence as may be presented at the time of the motion.

Dated: _____

By   Roger Lampkin,
Attorney for Doug Donenabbed

MEMORANDUM OF POINTS AND AUTHORITIES

"In a criminal action the defendant is entitled: 1. To a speedy and public trial." (*Penal Code §686*; see also U.S. Constitution, Amendment VI and Article I, section 13, of the California Constitution).

A defendant's right to a speedy trial under the California Constitution attaches when a criminal complaint is filed. (*Scherling v. Superior Court* (1978) 22 Cal. 3rd 493, 504.). To prevail on an argument their right to a speedy trial was violated, a defendant "must affirmatively demonstrate prejudice" caused by the delay. (*People v. Martinez* (2000) 22 Cal.4th 750, 767.) If prejudice is based on lost witnesses, the defense must "specifically identif[y] what witnesses might have eluded the defense or what testimony might have been lost or distorted as a result of the delay in this case." (*People v. Williams* (2013) 58 Cal.4th 197, 236.)

If the defendant can show he suffered prejudice by the delay, "the prosecution must show justification for the delay. If the prosecution does that, the trial court must balance the prejudice to the defendant resulting from the delay against the prosecution's justification for the delay. [Citation.]" (*People v. Lowe* (2007) 40 Cal.4th 937, 942.) "Whether preaccusation delay is unreasonable and prejudicial to a defendant is a question of fact. [Citation.]" (*People v. Mirenda* (2009) 174 Cal.App.4th 1313, 1330.)

Evidence of deprivation of due process sufficient to warrant dismissal does not require a showing of purposeful delay by the prosecution. Prejudicial delay caused by negligence of law enforcement agencies or by the prosecution is sufficient to deny a defendant the right to due process. (*Scherling v. Superior Court* (1978) 22 Cal. 3rd 493; *Penney v. Superior Court* (1972) 28 Cal.App. 3rd 941, 953).

Even if the delay is merely the result of administrative malfeasance or simple negligence on the part of the state or its officers, it is clear that there must, nonetheless, be a dismissal. (*Barker v. Wingo* (1972) 407 U.S. 514)

Even if the prejudice to the Defendant appears to be minimal, the court must conduct a hearing to balance the prejudice against the justification for the delay. (*Garcia v. Superior Court* (1984)163 Cal. App. 3rd 148; *Ibarra v. Municipal Court* (1984) 162 Cal. App. 3rd 853).

The delay in the instant case is excessive. Charges were filed against Defendant on or about January 1, 2019. A warrant was issued for Defendant's arrest on January 3, 2019. Defendant was finally arrested on July 4, 2020.

During this time period, Defendant lived an open and notorious life and could have easily been located by law enforcement had they merely looked to Department of Motor Vehicle records, voter registration records, utility records, phone records, or even had they merely performed a search on the Internet, but the Prosecution decided not to pursue the matter.

Had Defendant's prosecution proceeded with haste he could have possibly presented evidence to prove an alibi at the time of the alleged crime, presented evidence that he was not the suspect in question, presented evidence that his arrest or detention was unreasonable under the Fourth Amendment, or presented other such exculpatory evidence. However, such evidence has been lost, or at least deteriorated, by the passage of time.

In *People v. Hill* (1984) 37 Cal. 3rd 491, the Supreme Court stated that fading memories of prosecution witnesses that prevent adequate cross-examination on a material issue may constitute sufficient prejudice to warrant a finding of denial of due process. Likewise, in *Ibarra v. Municipal Court* (1984) 162 Cal. App. 3rd 853, the Court of Appeal stated that the fading memory of the defendant must be considered by the court in determining prejudice.

In the instant case, there appears to be no reason for the extended delay. The Prosecution simply did not take actions to arrest Defendant.

g. Motion to Dismiss for Speedy Trial Violation

ROGER LAMPKIN
SB#113786
1234 L Street
Bakersfield, CA 93301
Tel: (661)633-1234
Fax: (661)863-6741
Attorney for Doug Donenabbed

IN THE SUPERIOR COURT OF THE STATE OF CALIFORNIA,

IN AND FOR THE COUNTY OF KERN

People of the State of California,	CASE NO. 123456
Plaintiffs,	DEFENDANT'S MOTION TO DISMISS FOR SPEEDY TRIAL VIOLATION
- v. -	*(Penal Code §1382)*
Doug Donenabbed,	Date: August 2, 2022
Defendant	Time: 8:30 a.m.
	Dept: CC
	Readiness: August 12, 2022
	Trial: August 22, 2022

TO THE ABOVE-ENTITLED COURT AND THE DISTRICT ATTORNEY OF KERN COUNTY: PLEASE TAKE NOTICE that on the date and time noted above or as soon thereafter as counsel may be heard in the courtroom of the above-entitled court, the defendant will move the Court for an order dismissing the instant case because Defendant's right to a speedy trial has been violated.

The motion will be based on this notice of motion, all attached documents, the records on file in this action, and on such matters as may be presented at the hearing.

Dated: _____

_____
By   Roger Lampkin,
Attorney for Doug Donenabbed

SUMMARY OF TIMELINE

Defendant's arraignment on the Information was conducted on January 29, 2019.

Proceedings were suspended on March 19, 2020 pursuant to *Penal Code §1368* and reinstated on April 4, 2020; thus, arguably eliminating that time period from Speedy Trial calculations.

The days charged against Defendant's right to a speedy trial are, therefore, as follows:

January 30 & 31	2 days
February	28 days
March 1 – 18	17 days
April 5 – 30	25 days
May 1 – 20	20 days
Total	92 days

POINTS, AUTHORITIES, AND ARGUMENT

Penal Code § 1382 holds in part: "(a) The court, unless good cause to the contrary is shown, shall order the action to be dismissed in the following cases:… (2) In a felony case, when a defendant is not brought to trial within 60 days of the defendant's arraignment on an indictment or information…"

The Prosecution may argue that good cause exists because Defendant has changed counsel; however, such changes are standard practice at the public defender's office and for alternate defense programs. However, the inability of defense attorneys to be prepared for trial due to changes in counsel do not constitute good cause for a Speedy Trial violation.

In *People v. Johnson* (1980) 26 Cal. 3rd 557, 571–73, our Supreme Court held that a criminal case may be dismissed if there are too few appointed attorneys to give a defendant a speedy trial.

In *Johnson*, the defendant, charged with robbery, was not brought to trial within sixty days of arraignment. Over the defendant's objection, the court repeatedly continued the case at the request and to accommodate scheduling conflicts of defense counsel (Id. at 563–66). Our Supreme Court held that an appointed attorney cannot waive a defendant's speedy trial right, over the defendant's objection, to accommodate the attorney's scheduling conflict caused by another client:

> "[W]hen a client expressly objects to waiver of his right to a speedy trial under section 1382, counsel may not waive that right to resolve a calendar conflict when counsel acts not for the benefit of the client before the court but to accommodate counsel's other clients." (Id. at 561–62).

Our Supreme Court also held that when a defendant is incarcerated, the fact that his appointed attorney is unavailable due to scheduling conflicts with other clients is insufficient to constitute good cause:

> "[A]t least in the case of an incarcerated defendant, the asserted inability of the public defender to try such a defendant's case within the statutory period because of conflicting obligations to other clients does not constitute good cause to avoid dismissal of the charges." (Id. at 562).

Such scheduling conflicts are the fault of the state:

> The [speedy trial] right may also be denied by failure to provide enough public defenders or appointed counsel, so that an indigent must choose between the right to a speedy trial and the right to representation by competent counsel. "(U)nreasonable delay in run-of-the-mill criminal cases cannot be justified by simply asserting that the public resources provided by the State's criminal-justice system are limited and that each case must await its turn." (Id. at 571, quoting *Barker v. Wingo* (1972) 407 U.S. 514, 538 (White. J., conc.)).

Changes in counsel caused by administrative procedures and delays related to those changes, such as delay in transferring the file to new counsel, delay in transfer of the preliminary hearing transcript, and other such delays caused by the logistics of transferring cases are also not good cause to violate a defendant's right to a speedy trial. (see *People v. Hajjaj* (2010) 50 Cal.4th 1184, 1190, where the California Supreme Court held that a criminal case may be dismissed if the courtroom is too far away for a defendant to have a speedy trial.).

In the instant case, Defendant's rights have been repeatedly violated. He did not have a speedy arraignment, a speedy preliminary hearing, or a speedy trial. Based on the foregoing, Defendant respectfully requests that his motion be granted, and the Information be dismissed.

h. Motion to Dismiss - Speedy Preliminary Examination

ROGER LAMPKIN
SB#113786
1234 L Street
Bakersfield, CA 93301
Tel: (661)633-1234
Fax: (661)863-6741
Attorney for Doug Donenabbed

IN THE SUPERIOR COURT OF THE STATE OF CALIFORNIA, IN AND FOR THE COUNTY OF KERN

People of the State of California,	CASE NO. 123456
Plaintiffs,	DEFENDANT'S MOTION TO DISMISS DENIAL OF SPEEDY PRELIMINARY EXAMINATION
- v. -	
Doug Donenabbed,	Date: August 2, 2022 Time: 8:30 a.m.
Defendant	Dept: CC
	Readiness: August 12, 2022 Trial: August 22, 2022

TO THE ABOVE-ENTITLED COURT AND THE DISTRICT ATTORNEY OF KERN COUNTY: PLEASE TAKE NOTICE that at the date and time indicated above, or as soon thereafter as the matter can be heard in the above-entitled court, the defendant will move for an order dismissing the instant action.

The motion will be based on the grounds that Defendant was denied a speedy preliminary examination.

The motion will be based on this notice and all attachments and on all papers and records on file in this action and on such oral and documentary evidence as may be presented at the time of the motion.

Dated: _____

By   Roger Lampkin,
Attorney for Doug Donenabbed

MEMORANDUM OF POINTS AND AUTHORITIES

Penal Code §859b provides in part: "Whenever the defendant is in custody, the magistrate shall dismiss the complaint if the preliminary examination is set or continued beyond 10 court days from the time of the arraignment, plea, or reinstatement of criminal proceedings… and the defendant has remained in custody for 10 or more court days solely on that complaint, unless either of the following occur: (a) The defendant personally waives his or her right to preliminary examination within the 10 court days. (b) The prosecution establishes good cause for a continuance beyond the 10-court-day period."

"The right is absolute and in the absence of a waiver cannot be impinged by the magistrate, even on a showing of good cause. A defendant need neither demand that the preliminary be conducted within the 10 day period nor show prejudice, since an affirmative showing of prejudice is not required where the right is absolute or mandatory in nature." (*Johnson v. Superior Court* (1979) 97 Cal. App. 3rd 682).

In the instant case, Defendant was arraigned on April 1, 2020 but the preliminary hearing was not set until May 23, 2020. The Court should, therefore, dismiss this matter.

→ • • Ω • • ←

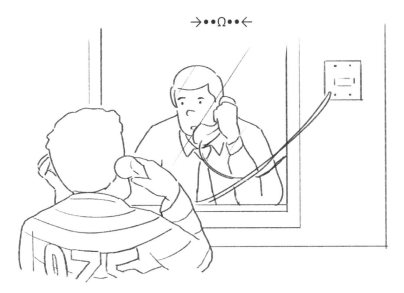

Please, Mr. Johnson, stop "taking the Fifth." Your trial starts tomorrow, and I just need to know what size suit you wear so you don't have to wear jail clothes to court.

i. Motion to Dismiss for Interrupted Preliminary Examination

ROGER LAMPKIN
SB#113786
1234 L Street
Bakersfield, CA 93301
Tel: (661)633-1234
Fax: (661)863-6741
Attorney for Doug Donenabbed

IN THE SUPERIOR COURT OF THE STATE OF CALIFORNIA,

IN AND FOR THE COUNTY OF KERN

People of the State of California,	CASE NO. 123456
Plaintiffs,	MOTION TO DISMISS FOR INTERRUPTED PRELIMINARY EXAMINATION
- v. -	
Doug Donenabbed,	Date: August 2, 2022
	Time: 8:30 a.m.
Defendant	Dept: CC
	Readiness: August 12, 2022
	Trial: August 22, 2022

TO THE ABOVE-ENTITLED COURT AND THE DISTRICT ATTORNEY OF KERN COUNTY: PLEASE TAKE NOTICE that at the date and time indicated above, the defendant will move for an order dismissing the instant action.

The motion will be based on the grounds that Defendant was denied his right to a one session preliminary examination.

The motion will be based on this Notice of Motion, all attached papers, all papers and records on file in this action, and on such oral and documentary evidence as may be presented at the time of the motion.

Dated: _____   _____

By   Roger Lampkin,
Attorney for Doug Donenabbed

MEMORANDUM OF POINTS AND AUTHORITIES

Penal Code §861 holds in part "The preliminary examination shall be completed at one session or the complaint shall be dismissed, unless the magistrate, for good cause shown by affidavit, postpones it."

The settled meaning of a single "session," for purposes of section 861, derives from *In re Karpf* (1970) 10 Cal.App.3rd 355. In *Karpf,* the court rejected the argument that the examination must be completed in a single "day." (id., at 365) Instead, the court in *Karpf* held, a "session" is " 'an actual sitting continued by adjournments in ordinary course from day to day, or over Sundays and holidays, but not interrupted by adjournment to a distant day.' " (id, quoting *United States v. Dietrich* (C.C.D.Neb.1904) 126 F. 659, 660.) Such a "postponement," the *Karpf* court noted, "is different from a temporary cessation or interruption in proceedings compelled by the needs of the human body ... or to observe a legal holiday." (id. at 366).

In *Serrato v. Superior Court* (1978) 76 Cal.App.3rd 459, 467, the court stated that although section 861 allowed normal recesses, breaks, and adjournments for nights, weekends, and holidays, the statute nonetheless "contemplate[d] a continuance of an already commenced preliminary examination from day to day, uninterrupted by any intervening judicial business."

The legislature later added subsection "b" to *Penal Code §861* to allow the court to conduct other brief business, "Nothing in this section shall preclude the magistrate from interrupting the preliminary examination to conduct brief court matters so long as a substantial majority of the court's time is devoted to the preliminary examination."

"[T]he purpose of section 861 is to ensure that, once commenced, the preliminary examination will proceed continuously onward, and be expeditiously completed, without significant interruptions to which the parties have not consented, and which are not justified by good cause." (*Stroud v. Superior Court* (2000) 23 Cal.4th 952, 967).

Good cause must be shown by affidavit (*Penal Code §861*) and is not without limits.

The court in *Kruse v. Superior Court* (2008) 162 Cal.App.4th 1364, found that neither the failure to transport the defendant nor the prosecutor's illness constituted good cause for an interrupted examination.

Similarly, the court in *Stroud*, supra, found that "A judicial officer's outside administrative duties, such as attendance to Judicial Council business, are not in and of themselves sufficient cause to delay a preliminary examination, where proper planning would have avoided the conflict." (*Stroud*, supra, at 957).

In the instant case the preliminary examination began, but an hour into it the Prosecution informed the Court that it was unprepared to proceed because a witness was unavailable. The Court continued the preliminary hearing for two days, during which time the Court heard multiple other matters.

Under these circumstances, dismissal is required.

j. Motion to Dismiss for Selective Prosecution

ROGER LAMPKIN
SB#113786
1234 L Street
Bakersfield, CA 93301
Tel: (661)633-1234
Fax: (661)863-6741
Attorney for Doug Donenabbed

IN THE SUPERIOR COURT OF THE STATE OF CALIFORNIA,

IN AND FOR THE COUNTY OF KERN

People of the State of California,	CASE NO. 123456
Plaintiffs,	MOTION TO DISMISS FOR SELECTIVE PROSECUTION [*Murgia*]
- v. -	
Doug Donenabbed,	Date: August 2, 2022 Time: 8:30 a.m.
Defendant	Dept: CC
	Readiness: August 12, 2022 Trial: August 22, 2022

TO THE ABOVE-ENTITLED COURT AND THE DISTRICT ATTORNEY OF KERN COUNTY: PLEASE TAKE NOTICE that at the date and time indicated above, or as soon thereafter as the matter can be heard in the above-entitled court, the defendant will move for an order dismissing the instant action.

The motion will be based on the grounds that Defendant has been deliberately singled out for prosecution on the basis of some invidious criterion.

The motion will be based on this Notice of Motion, on all attached papers filed herewith or later filed, on all papers and records on file in this action and on such oral and documentary evidence as may be presented at the time of the motion.

Dated: _____

By   Roger Lampkin,
Attorney for Doug Donenabbed

DECLARATION OF COUNSEL

I, Roger Lampkin, declare:
1.   I am an attorney at law and am the attorney for the defendant in this case.
2.   I am informed and believe that the following facts establish that Defendant has been deliberately singled out for prosecution on the basis of some invidious criterion.
   a. Defendant is a Black, transgender, Muslim known for his criticism of local law enforcement, courts, and politicians.
   b. On or about June 1, 2020, Defendant participated in a peaceful assembly in front of the courthouse along with more than 200 other persons.
   c. Defendant alone was arrested and charged with loitering.

I declare that the foregoing is true and correct.

Dated: _____

By   Roger Lampkin,
Attorney for Doug Donenabbed

MEMORANDUM OF POINTS AND AUTHORITIES

In its landmark decision in *Yick Wo v. Hopkins* (1886) 118 U.S. 356, the Supreme Court declared that the Constitution's promise of equal protection under the laws compels the law not only to "be fair on its face and impartial in appearance," but to be "applied and administered by public authority with an [honorable] eye and an [equal] hand." (id. at 373–374.) In *Two Guys from Harrison–Allentown, Inc. v. McGinley* (1961) 366 U.S. 582 and *Oyler v. Boles* (1962) 368 U.S. 448, 456, the court condemned selective prosecution, holding that deliberate invidious discrimination in the prosecution of a criminal charge is a ground for dismissal of the charge.

In order to establish a claim of discriminatory prosecution, " 'the defendant must prove: (1) "that he has been deliberately singled out for prosecution on the basis of some invidious criterion"; and (2) that "the prosecution would not have been pursued except for the discriminatory design of the prosecuting authorities." ' " (*Baluyut v. Superior Court* (1996) 12 Cal.4th 826, 832). " '[A]n invidious purpose for prosecution is one that is arbitrary and thus unjustified because it bears no rational relationship to legitimate law enforcement interests ....' [Citation.]" (*Manduley v. Superior Court* (2002) 27 Cal.4th 537, 568–569.) A defendant is entitled to a dismissal if a victim of discriminatory prosecution.

"Murgia v. Municipal Court, clearly stands for the proposition that a trial court has jurisdiction to determine whether the charges filed against a defendant in an action pending before it were filed as the result of unlawful discriminatory enforcement." (*People v. Shokur* (2012) 205 Cal App 4th 1398).

→ • • Ω • • ←

k. Motion to Dismiss - Charged Under General Statute

ROGER LAMPKIN
SB#113786
1234 L Street
Bakersfield, CA 93301
Tel: (661)633-1234
Fax: (661)863-6741
Attorney for Doug Donenabbed

IN THE SUPERIOR COURT OF THE STATE OF CALIFORNIA,

IN AND FOR THE COUNTY OF KERN

People of the State of California,	CASE NO. 123456
Plaintiffs,	DEFENDANT DOUG DONENABBED'S MOTION TO DISMISS FOR BEING CHARGED UNDER THE GENERAL INSTEAD OF SPECIFIC STATUTE
- v. -	
Doug Donenabbed,	
Defendant	Date: August 2, 2022 Time: 8:30 a.m. Dept: CC

TO THE COURT AND THE DISTRICT ATTORNEY OF KERN COUNTY: PLEASE TAKE NOTICE that at the date and time indicated above, the defendant will move the Court to dismiss the charges because Defendant is charged under the general instead of the specific statute.

The motion will be based on this Notice of Motion, on the attached memorandum of points and authorities and filed herewith and such supplemental memorandum of points and authorities that may be hereafter filed with the court or stated orally at the conclusion of the hearing, on all papers and records on file in this action and on such oral and documentary evidence as may be presented at the time of the motion.

Dated: _____

        By Roger Lampkin,
        Attorney for Doug Donenabbed

MEMORANDUM OF POINTS AND AUTHORITIES

"Under the Williamson rule [In re Williamson (1954) 43 Cal.2d 651, 654], if a general statute includes the same conduct as a special statute, the court infers that the Legislature intended that conduct to be prosecuted exclusively under the special statute. In effect, the special statute is interpreted as creating an exception to the general statute for conduct that otherwise could be prosecuted under either statute." (*People v. Murphy* (2011) 52 Cal.4th 81)

"The doctrine that a specific statute precludes any prosecution under a general statute is a rule designed to ascertain and carry out legislative intent. The fact that the Legislature has enacted a specific statute covering much the same ground as a more general law is a powerful indication that the Legislature intended the specific provision alone to apply." (id., citing *People v. Gilbert* (1969) 1 Cal. 3rd 475, 481; *People v. Jenkins* (1980) 28 Cal. 3rd 494, 505–506, fn. omitted.).

"Absent some indication of legislative intent to the contrary, the Williamson rule applies when (1) each element of the general statute corresponds to an element on the face of the special statute or (2) when it appears from the statutory context that a violation of the special statute will necessarily or commonly result in a violation of the general statute." (id. citing *People v. Watson* (1981) 30 Cal. 3rd 290, 295–296, punctuation omitted)

"In its clearest application, the rule is triggered when a violation of a provision of the special statute would inevitably constitute a violation of the general statute. In Williamson, for example, the defendant was convicted under the general conspiracy statute, Penal Code section 182, of conspiring to commit the crime of contracting without a license in violation of section 7028 of the Business and Professions Code. A violation of Penal Code section 182 was punishable as either a misdemeanor or a felony. The defendant argued that his conduct was punishable only under a special statute, Business and Professions Code former section 7030… which made it a misdemeanor to "conspire with another person to violate any of the provisions of this chapter." This court agreed. We explained, "To conclude that the punishment for the violation of section 7030 of the Business and Professions Code is stated in section 182 of the Penal Code, which deals with conspiracies in general, would be inconsistent with the designation of the particular conspiracy as a misdemeanor." (id. citing *Williamson*, supra, punctuation omitted).

Similarly in *Gilbert, supra,* the court held that prosecution for theft was barred by a special statute prohibiting use of false statements to obtain welfare, because "any conduct which violated [the welfare fraud statute] would also constitute a violation of the theft provision of the Penal Code".

In the instant case, the arresting officer testified at the preliminary hearing that he pulled over a Dodge Dakota pickup for no license plate (CT 11), but the vehicle did have a license plate (id. ln. 19), but the license was for a different model vehicle (RT 13).

Defendant is charged in Count Two of violating *Vehicle Code §4463(a)(1),* which holds:

> (a) A person who, with intent to prejudice, damage, or defraud, commits any of the following acts is guilty of a felony and upon conviction thereof shall be punished by imprisonment pursuant to subdivision (h) of Section 1170 of the Penal Code for 16 months, or two or three years, or by imprisonment in a county jail for not more than one year:
>
> > (1) Alters, forges, counterfeits, or falsifies a certificate of ownership, registration card, certificate, license, license plate, temporary license plate, device issued pursuant to Section 4853, special plate, or permit provided for by this code or a comparable certificate of ownership, registration card, certificate, license, license plate, temporary license plate, device comparable to that issued pursuant to Section 4853, special plate, or permit provided for by a foreign jurisdiction, or alters, forges, counterfeits, or falsifies the document, device, or plate with intent to represent it as issued by the department, or alters, forges, counterfeits, or falsifies with fraudulent intent an endorsement of transfer on a certificate of ownership or other document evidencing ownership, or with fraudulent intent displays or causes or permits to be displayed or have in his or her possession a blank, incomplete, canceled, suspended, revoked, altered, forged, counterfeit, or false certificate of ownership, registration card, certificate, license, license plate, temporary license plate, device issued pursuant to Section 4853, special plate, or permit.

Defendant is not accused of "Altering, forging, counterfeiting, or falsifying." He is accused of placing a valid license plate on the wrong vehicle. This conduct is covered by a specific statute, of which Defendant is charged in Count Three, *Vehicle Code §4462(b)*:

> (b) A person shall not display upon a vehicle, nor present to any peace officer, any registration card, identification card, temporary receipt, license plate, temporary license plate, device issued pursuant to Section 4853, or permit not issued for that vehicle or not otherwise lawfully used thereon under this code.

The Court should, therefore, dismiss the general statute of Count Two and allow the prosecution to proceed on the specific statute of Count Three.

→ • • Ω • • ←

Practical Tip:
Instead of having your full name on your business cards, consider using:
- Only your first name.
- Your middle name and last name.
- Your first name and maiden name.
- Your initials and last name.
- Something else to keep clients from finding your home address, personal phone number, and social media accounts.

l. Motion to Dismiss - Forum Shopping

ROGER LAMPKIN
SB#113786
1234 L Street
Bakersfield, CA 93301
Tel: (661)633-1234
Fax: (661)863-6741
Attorney for Doug Donenabbed

IN THE SUPERIOR COURT OF THE STATE OF CALIFORNIA,

IN AND FOR THE COUNTY OF KERN

People of the State of California,	CASE NO. 123456
Plaintiffs,	DEFENDANT DOUG DONENABBED'S MOTION TO DISMISS FOR FORUM SHOPPING
- v. -	
Doug Donenabbed,	Date: August 2, 2022
Defendant	Time: 8:30 a.m.
	Dept: CC
	Readiness: August 12, 2022
	Trial: August 22, 2022

TO THE COURT AND THE DISTRICT ATTORNEY OF KERN COUNTY: PLEASE TAKE NOTICE that at the date and time indicated above, or as soon thereafter as the matter can be heard in the above-entitled court, the defendant will move the Court to dismiss the accusatory pleading.

The motion will be based on this notice and the attached papers, on all papers and records on file in this action and on such oral and documentary evidence as may be presented at the time of the motion.

Dated: _____

By   Roger Lampkin,
Attorney for Doug Donenabbed

POINTS, AUTHORITIES, AND ARGUMENT

STATEMENT OF THE CASE

Defendant is accused of causing harm to his wife. The Prosecution filed this case in an outlying court under case number RF123456A, that the case was assigned to the Honorable John Judge for trial. The Prosecution dismissed in the interest of justice. The Prosecution then refiled in the county seat. This constitutes improper forum shopping.

FORUM SHOPPING IS NOT PROPER

The court in *Jacobs v. Superior Court* (1959) 53 Cal.2nd 187 explained the danger of courts allowing forum shopping, "Such procedure would make it possible for litigants to gamble on obtaining a favorable decision from one judge, and then, if confronted with an adverse judgment, allow them to disqualify him without presenting facts showing prejudice, in the hope of securing a different ruling from another judge in supplementary proceedings involving substantially the same issues."

The statute granting litigant right to peremptory challenge of sitting judge was enacted to prevent forum shopping and prosecutorial harassment of defendants with successive prosecutions. (*Ziesmer v. Superior Court* (2003) 107 Cal.App.4th 360). The prosecution did not elect to use a peremptory challenge in the instant case, but instead sought to bypass the peremptory challenge statute by dismissing and refiling the charges in a different court in hopes of obtaining a more favorable judge. Such back-door challenges are not available to Defendant and should not be allowed for the Prosecution.

"A primary purpose of section 1387(a) [the two dismissal rule] is to protect a defendant against harassment, and the denial of speedy-trial rights, that result from the repeated dismissal and refiling of identical charges. In particular, the statute guards against prosecutorial 'forum shopping'—the persistent refiling of charges the evidence does not support in hopes of finding a sympathetic magistrate who will hold the defendant to answer." (*People v. Traylor* (2009) 46 Cal.4th 1205, 1209).

"Section 1387 ... curtails prosecutorial harassment by placing limits on the number of times charges may be refiled ... [and] also reduces the possibility that prosecutors might use the power to dismiss and refile to forum shop," (*Burris v. Superior Court* (2005) 34 Cal. 4th 1012, 1018, citations omitted)

The Prosecution's conduct does not come under the statutory two dismissal rule of *Penal Code §1387,* but it does meet the purpose of *Penal Code §1387:* prevent forum shopping. The Prosecution dismissed and refiled in hopes of obtaining a better forum. Such conduct should not be allowed, and the instant case should be dismissed.

m. Motion to Dismiss - Suppression Forum Shopping

ROGER LAMPKIN
SB#113786
1234 L Street
Bakersfield, CA 93301
Tel: (661)633-1234
Fax: (661)863-6741
Attorney for Doug Donenabbed

IN THE SUPERIOR COURT OF THE STATE OF CALIFORNIA,

IN AND FOR THE COUNTY OF KERN

People of the State of California,	DEFENDANT DOUG DONENABBED'S MOTION TO DISMISS FOR IMPROPER SUPPRESSION FORUM SHOPPING
Plaintiffs,	
- v. -	
Doug Donenabbed,	Date: August 2, 2022 Time: 8:30 a.m. Dept: CC
Defendant	Readiness: August 12, 2022 Trial: August 22, 2022

TO THE COURT AND THE DISTRICT ATTORNEY OF KERN COUNTY: PLEASE TAKE NOTICE that at the date and time indicated above, or as soon thereafter as the matter can be heard in the above-entitled court, the defendant will move the Court to dismiss the accusatory pleading.

   The motion will be based on this notice and the attached papers, on all papers and records on file in this action and on such oral and documentary evidence as may be presented at the time of the motion.

Dated: _____

                             By   Roger Lampkin,
                             Attorney for Doug Donenabbed

POINTS, AUTHORITIES, AND ARGUMENT

STATEMENT OF THE CASE

Defendant brought a suppression motion pursuant to *Penal Code §1538.5*, which was granted by the Honorable John Judge. The Prosecution dismissed pursuant to *Penal Code §1385*. The Prosecution then refiled and attempted to relitigate the suppression issues before a different magistrate.

FORUM SHOPPING IS NOT PROPER

The court in *Jacobs v. Superior Court* (1959) 53 Cal.2nd 187 explained the danger of courts allowing forum shopping, "Such procedure would make it possible for litigants to gamble on obtaining a favorable decision from one judge, and then, if confronted with an adverse judgment, allow them to disqualify him without presenting facts showing prejudice, in the hope of securing a different ruling from another judge in supplementary proceedings involving substantially the same issues."

PENAL CODE §1538.5 PROHIBITS SUPPRESSION FORUM SHOPPING

Penal Code §1538.5(j), provides, "If the case has been dismissed pursuant to Section 1385, either on the court's own motion or the motion of the people after the special hearing, the people may file a new complaint or seek an indictment after the special hearing, and the ruling at the special hearing shall not be binding in any subsequent proceeding, except as limited by subdivision (p)."

Subdivision (p), provides, "If a defendant's motion to return property or suppress evidence in a felony matter has been granted twice, the people may not file a new complaint or seek an indictment in order to relitigate the motion or relitigate the matter de novo at a special hearing as otherwise provided by subdivision (j), unless the people discover additional evidence relating to the motion that was not reasonably discoverable at the time of the second suppression hearing. <u>Relitigation of the motion shall be heard by the same judge who granted the motion at the first hearing if the judge is available.</u>" (*Penal Code §1538.5(p)* emphasis added.)

In other words, when a defendant has successfully moved to suppress evidence, any subsequent motion made after a dismissal must be heard by the same judge who originally granted the motion. *Penal Code §1538.5*'s legislative history " 'makes it clear the Legislature intended ... to prohibit prosecutors from forum shopping.' [Citation.] To allow the prosecutor to make a judge unavailable to rehear the suppression motion simply by filing a peremptory challenge under Code of Civil Procedure section 170.6 would permit this prohibited forum shopping and 'essentially eviscerate[ ] the provisions of subdivision (p).' " (*People v. Superior Court (Jimenez)* (2002) 28 Cal.4th 798, 807).

The Prosecution failed to follow the mandate of *Penal Code §1538.5(p)*; therefore, dismissal is the appropriate remedy.

n. Motion to Dismiss for Lack of Funds

ROGER LAMPKIN
SB#113786
1234 L Street
Bakersfield, CA 93301
Tel: (661)633-1234
Fax: (661)863-6741

Attorney for Doug Donenabbed

IN THE SUPERIOR COURT OF THE STATE OF CALIFORNIA,

IN AND FOR THE COUNTY OF KERN

People of the State of California,	CASE NO. 123456
Plaintiffs,	DEFENDANT DOUG DONENABBED'S MOTION TO DISMISS OR, IN THE ALTERNATIVE, TO RECUSE THE DISTRICT ATTORNEY [Lack of defense funds and denial of right to participate in the defense]
- v. -	
Doug Donenabbed,	
Defendant	
	Date: August 2, 2022 Time: 8:30 a.m. Dept: CC
	Readiness: August 12, 2022 Trial: August 22, 2022

TO THE COURT AND THE DISTRICT ATTORNEY OF KERN COUNTY: PLEASE TAKE NOTICE that at the date and time indicated above, or as soon thereafter as the matter can be heard in the above-entitled court, the defendant will move the Court to dismiss the action because Defendant has been deprived of adequate resources to properly prepare for trial, thus violating Due Process, Equal Protection, and his right to a fair trial.

The motion will be based on this notice and the attached papers, on all papers and records on file in this action and on such oral and documentary evidence as may be presented at the time of the motion.

Dated: _____

By   Roger Lampkin,
Attorney for Doug Donenabbed

ATTORNEY DECLARATION

I, Roger Lampkin, declare:
1. Paralegals, legal secretaries, messengers, and other such support staff are available to the prosecution.
2. However, my request for minimal funds (up to $500) has been denied.
3. A court order authorizing computer use at the jail is required to take a computer into the jail to show Defendant important discovery in this case, but the court denied my request for order even though it was at no cost.
4. I do not have adequate funds or resources to properly prepare a defense in this matter, and the defendant is unable to meaningfully participate in his defense.

I declare that I am informed and believe the foregoing is true and correct.

Dated: _____

By   Roger Lampkin,
Attorney for Doug Donenabbed

MEMORANDUM OF POINTS AND AUTHORITIES

A DEFENDANT HAS THE RIGHT TO PARTICIPATE IN HIS DEFENSE

Defense counsel has a "duty to consult with the defendant on important decisions and to keep the defendant informed of important developments in the course of the prosecution" (*Strickland v. Washington* (1984) 466 U.S. 668, 688). A defendant must be given the " 'ability to communicate' with his lawyer" and the "ability to participate in his own defense" (*Deck v. Missouri* (2005) 544 U.S. 622). A defendant has the "right to be present at trial and to participate in his own defense. Once a violation of this right has been established, the defendant's conviction is unconstitutionally tainted, and reversal is required unless the State proves the error was harmless beyond a reasonable doubt." (*U.S. v. Durham* (11th Cir. 2002) 287 F.3rd 1297, citation and punctuation omitted). A defendant's " 'active assistance at trial may be key to an attorney's effective representation of his interests.' " (id., quoting *United States v. Novaton* (11th Cir.2001) 271 F.3rd 968, 1000).

The Sixth Amendment right to counsel in a criminal case includes the defendant's right to communicate and consult with his attorney during trial. (*Perry v. Leeke* (1989) 488 U.S. 272, 284; *Geders v. United States* (1976) 425 U.S. 80, 88). A defendant must have " 'sufficient present ability to consult with his lawyer with a reasonable degree of rational understanding' " (*People v. Welch* (1999) 20 Cal.4th 701, quoting *Dusky v. United States* (1960) 362 U.S. 402)

"[C]ourts have reversed convictions in cases in which the defendant was denied entirely the opportunity to consult with counsel during some stage of the court proceedings." (*U.S. v. Vasquez* (11th Cir. 1984) 732 F.2nd 846, 848, citing *Geders*, supra.)

THE STATE MUST PAY THE COST OF DEFENSE FOR AN INDIGENT DEFENDANT

"[O]ne charged with crime, who is unable to obtain counsel, must be furnished counsel by the state" (*Gideon v. Wainwright* (1963) 372 U.S. 335) "The Sixth Amendment right to counsel is a meaningless gesture if counsel for an indigent is denied the use of working tools essential to the establishment of what would appear to be a tenable or possible defense." (*People v. Gunnerson,* 74 Cal App 3rd 370, 379).

"[T]he right to effective counsel also includes the right to ancillary services necessary in the preparation of a defense." (*Keenan v Superior Court* (1982) 31 Cal 3rd 424, 428; see also *Corenevsky v. Superior Court* (1984) 36 Cal. 3rd 307, 319, *In re Ketchel* (1968) 68 Cal. 2nd 397, 399).

"As a rough benchmark, jurisdictions should provide funding for defender services that maintains parity between the defense and the prosecution with respect to workload, salaries, and resources necessary to provide quality representation (including benefits, technology, facilities, legal research, support staff, paralegals, investigators, mitigation specialists, and access to forensic services and experts). In doing so, jurisdictions must be mindful that the prosecution has access at no cost to many services for which the defense must pay." (ABA Guidelines, Guideline 9.1, Commentary, underline added for emphasis).

Due process demands "access to the raw materials integral to the building of an effective defense" (*Ake v. Oklahoma* (1985) 470 U.S. 68, 76-77).

"[S]ecretarial and paralegal services" are "necessary support services for attorneys" (*Salton Bay Marina, Inc. v. Imperial Irrigation Dist.* (1985) 172 Cal. App. 3rd 914; see also *Missouri v. Jenkins* 491 U.S. 274; *L.P. v. County of San Diego* (2014) 230 Cal. App. 4th 60.

CONCLUSION

The defense has requested funding for necessary services for preparation of a defense, but the requests have been denied. Dismissal is, therefore, the appropriate remedy.

→••Ω••←

Practical Tip:

Try to get along with everyone.

Some clients have bad tempers, have mental issues, or have other problems that make them extremely difficult to work with. If they did not have such problems, they might not be facing criminal charges. Do your best to get along with them even when they are being difficult. Empathize even if you don't sympathize. Attorneys may also be demanding, rude, and otherwise difficult to get along with, and court clerks may be overly picky and reject papers for no good reason. You should still try to get along with them. Everyone is fighting their own fight and has their own issues to deal with.

o. Motion to Dismiss for Invasion of Defense Camp

ROGER LAMPKIN
SB#113786
1234 L Street
Bakersfield, CA 93301
Tel: (661)633-1234
Fax: (661)863-6741
Attorney for Doug Donenabbed

IN THE SUPERIOR COURT OF THE STATE OF CALIFORNIA,

IN AND FOR THE COUNTY OF KERN

People of the State of California,
 	
    Plaintiffs,
 	
    - v. -
 	
Doug Donenabbed,
 	
    Defendant
	CASE NO. 123456
	
	DEFENDANT DOUG DONENABBED'S MOTION TO DISMISS OR, IN THE ALTERNATIVE, TO RECUSE THE DISTRICT ATTORNEY
	
	Date: August 2, 2022
	Time: 8:30 a.m.
	Dept: CC
	
	Readiness: August 12, 2022
	Trial: August 22, 2022

TO THE COURT AND THE DISTRICT ATTORNEY OF KERN COUNTY: PLEASE TAKE NOTICE that at the date and time indicated above, the defendant will move the Court to dismiss the instant action.

The motion will be made on the grounds that the Prosecution has intercepted attorney/client communications, has improperly obtained confidential information, has improperly made public confidential information, and/or has otherwise improperly invaded the defense camp.

The motion will be based on this notice and the attached papers, on all papers and records on file in this action and on such oral and documentary evidence as may be presented at the time of the motion.

Dated: _____   _____

By   Roger Lampkin,
Attorney for Doug Donenabbed

ATTORNEY DECLARATION

I, Roger Lampkin, declare:

I am informed and believe that the prosecution team has repeatedly interfered with the defense and invaded the defense camp as follows.

1. The defense team has repeatedly exchanged communications with the defendant including notes, police reports containing defense impressions and ideas, draft pleadings, and other documents. Members of the prosecution have repeatedly taken these papers from the defendant.

2. Members of the defense team have conducted many visits with the defendant at the Lerdo jail facility. The prosecution has tracked said visits to determine which members of the team (including confidentially appointed members) visited the defendant, when, and for how long.

3. I previously submitted to the Court confidential ex parte requests. The prosecuting attorney has been granted access to those ex parte requests through the court's CJIS system.

4. The defendant has been transferred to a jail facility wherein members of the defense team are denied confidential visits. The new facility only has a tiny paper slot for the exchange of papers. The defense is unable to pass long reports or other legal materials to the defendant without breaking the documents, books, and other materials apart, and the defense team is unable to point to places on the documents or otherwise view documents simultaneously with the defendant. The defense is also unable to hand the defendant a pen or pencil for use during interviews and the layout of the interview room makes it nearly impossible to adequately display electronic evidence for the defendant. Further, the new facility has inadequate sound dampening, so conversations can be heard by guards and other inmates.

5. The prosecution team has monitored calls from the defendant to counsel and other members of the defense team. This has caused a partial breakdown in communications and has caused the defendant a great deal of mental distress because members of the defense team have been instructed to terminate all telephone calls when they learn that the calls are being monitored.

I declare that I am informed and believe the foregoing is true and correct.
Dated: _____

By   Roger Lampkin,
Attorney for Doug Donenabbed

p. Motion to Set Aside the Information (995)

A Motion to Set Aside the Information is based only on the Information and the Preliminary Hearing transcript. The motion argues that the evidence presented at the preliminary hearing was not sufficient to support the Information. The motion cannot argue matters beyond the preliminary hearing. Even if the defendant has a perfect alibi, it cannot be argued in a Motion to Set Aside unless the evidence concerning the alibi was presented at the preliminary hearing. If the police reports show that the defendant is completely innocent of the charged offense, the issue still cannot be raised in a Motion to Set Aside. A Motion to Set Aside is limited to matters found in the preliminary hearing.

A motion brought pursuant to *Penal Code §995* is based solely on the charging document (known as the Information or Indictment) and the transcript of the preliminary hearing. The motion cannot argue any facts or evidence outside that presented at the preliminary hearing or before a grand jury.

Often, a defendant will know that the witnesses lied during the preliminary hearing, and he will have proof that they lied. A defendant may also have evidence establishing a strong alibi, or evidence proving that it was someone else who committed the crime, but none of these things can be brought up in a *Section 995* motion. Neither can a defendant show that the police reports, 911 calls, or witness statements contradict the preliminary hearing testimony. The defendant is restricted to the transcript of the proceedings and is barred from pointing out evidence that would contradict it, no matter how obvious the evidence proving the defendant's innocence.

There will be a time to raise an alibi defense. There will be a time to show that the witnesses lied. There will be a time to implicate another person for the crime. That time is most often during trial, but the time is not during the hearing of a *Section 995* motion, unless the issues were raised during the preliminary hearing or before the grand jury and are shown in the transcripts of those proceedings.

The authority for the motion is found in *Penal Code §995*, which is reprinted in the section entitled *Select Legal Authorities*.

ROGER LAMPKIN
SB#113786
1234 L Street
Bakersfield, CA 93301
Tel: (661)633-1234
Fax: (661)863-6741
Attorney for Doug Donenabbed

IN THE SUPERIOR COURT OF THE STATE OF CALIFORNIA,
IN AND FOR THE COUNTY OF KERN

People of the State of California,	CASE NO. 123456
Plaintiffs,	MOTION TO SET ASIDE THE INFORMATION
- v. -	*[Penal Code §995]* DATE: October 16, 2019
Doug Donenabbed,	TIME: 8:30 a.m. DEPT: CC
Defendant	Trial date: October 31, 2019 Readiness date: October 30, 2019

TO THE COURT AND THE DISTRICT ATTORNEY:

PLEASE TAKE NOTICE that at the date and time indicated above, or as soon thereafter as the matter can be heard in the above-entitled court, the defendant will move the Court under *Penal Code §995* to set aside the Information, alleging violations of:

1. *Penal Code § 664/212.5(c)* – Attempted Robbery
2. *Penal Code § 182(A)(1)* – Conspiracy
3. *Penal Code §487(a)* – Grand Theft

The motion will be based on this notice of motion, all attached documents, the records on file in this action, and on such matters as may be presented at the hearing.

Dated:

_____
By   Roger Lampkin,
     Attorney for Doug Donenabbed

SUMMARY OF PRELIMINARY HEARING

Officer Marks (RT 6/4) responded to Dave's Market (RT 7/5) where clerk Ravinder Singh "stated he was behind the counter of the market counting money when two individuals walked into the market… he heard his brother say he's going to shoot me and then he looked up and saw his brother in a struggle with one of the two individuals" (RT 7).

The brother of Mr. Singh told the officer that one of the suspects "reached over and grabbed a case of cigarettes that was on a stack on the floor. As he was doing that, Ravinder said he tried to stop that individual from taking the cigarettes and then the other individual grabbed the cash register at that point. He stated that he thought he had seen a bulge on one of their waistbands and the way that one of the individuals moved their hands made him believe they had a gun." (RT 8).

The officer identified defendants from a video recording of the incident (RT 10). The suspects did not take the cash register or the cigarettes (RT 11).

Officer Lorna Lang interviewed Victor Vega (RT 16) who reported that he observed two suspects exit a "red four-door Nissan Sentra," enter Dave's Market, and run out shortly thereafter. She did not identify the suspects.

Detective Mike Michaels interviewed Defendant, who admitted to being at the market, but stated that he only pushed the stack of boxes over (RT 20). Defendant denied arriving in a red Nissan (RT 21). Detective Michaels also interviewed Harry Hatt (RT 21), who claimed possession of the Nissan Sentra during the alleged altercation at the store (RT 22/6).

Officer Newt Mellon reviewed video recordings from the incident and identified Defendant (RT25). He also "also respond to a Mort's Market at 1313 Mockingbird Lane" (RT 25/21) where he interviewed Mort O'Hare who advised him "that he had walked to the rear of the store to stock items in the beer cooler and as he was doing this, he heard a commotion and looked to the front of the store and observed a subject grab cartons of cigarettes from behind his counter and run out of the store with them." (RT 26/9) The officer reviewed a video of the recording and identified Defendant Doug Donenabbed (RT 27).

POINTS, AUTHORITIES, AND ARGUMENT

Legal Standard

An Information, Indictment, or individual counts must be set aside if the defendant has been "committed without reasonable or probable cause." (*Penal Code §995(a)(2)(B)*). For a defendant to be put on trial for a particular offense, the grand jury or preliminary hearing must present "such a state of facts as would lead a man of ordinary caution or prudence to believe and conscientiously entertain a strong suspicion" that the defendant committed the crimes alleged (*People v. San Nicolas* (2004) 34 Cal. 4th 614, 654 [citation and punctuation]).

A defendant is committed "without reasonable or probable cause" unless there is sufficient proof to establish a reasonable belief that an offense has been committed and the defendant is guilty of the offense charged. (*Caughlin v. Superior Court of San Diego County* (1971) 4 Cal 3rd 461; *People v. Hernandez* (1978) 90 Cal App 3rd 309).

There must be some evidence to support every element of an offense (*Panos v. Superior Court* (1984) 156 Cal. App. 3rd 626; *People v. Superior Court (Mendella)* (1983) 33 Cal. 3rd 754; *People v. Shirley* (1978) 78 Cal. App. 3rd 424).

The identification of Doug Donenabbed fails

Officers identified Defendant from a video recording.

Officers viewed video recordings of events related to the instant case. These recordings are a "writing" as per *Evidence Code §250*. Under *Evidence Code §1520* "the content of a writing may be proved by an otherwise admissible original."

The officers described matters depicted in the recordings without offering the original or a duplicate of the recording. *Evidence Code §1521*, entitled Secondary Evidence Rule, requires that "The court shall exclude secondary evidence of the content of writing if the court determines either of the following: (1) A genuine dispute exists concerning material terms of the writing and justice requires the exclusion. (2) Admission of the secondary evidence would be unfair." The video recordings come under both prongs of the test. There is a genuine dispute as to what the recordings depict, and admission would be unfair.

Evidence Code §1521(b) holds that, "Nothing in this section makes admissible oral testimony to prove the content of a writing if the testimony is inadmissible under Section 1523 (oral testimony of the content of a writing)." As stated in the law revision commission comments, (b) explicitly establishes that *§1523*, not *§1521*, governs the admissibility of "oral testimony" to prove the content of a writing. Subdivision (c) makes clear that secondary evidence is admissible only if it is properly authenticated, i.e. the proponent must authenticate the original writing as well as establish that the proffered evidence is secondary evidence of the original.

Evidence Code §1523(a) entitled "Oral Testimony of the Content of a Writing; Admissibility" states "Except as otherwise provided by statute, oral testimony is not admissible to prove the content of a writing." (As noted in the law revision commission comments, "oral testimony of the content of a writing is less reliable than other proof of the content of a writing."

In *People v. Myers* (2014) 227 Cal. App. 4th 1219, the prosecution "sought to introduce oral testimony of the contents of a surveillance video without an audio component" the court affirmed that "Oral testimony is inadmissible as secondary evidence to prove the content of a writing or video unless 'the proponent does not have possession or control of a copy of the writing and the original is lost or has been destroyed without fraudulent intent on the part of the proponent of the evidence.'" (id. fn. 1)

Proffering testimony about what the officers claim they saw instead of introducing the recordings is improper. In *U.S. v. Bennett* (2004) 363 F. 3rd 947, the court noted the impropriety of "proffering testimony describing security camera footage of an event to prove the facts of the event instead of introducing the footage itself." The court noted that "[t]his is precisely the kind of situation in which the best evidence rule applies." The Bennett court also noted the fact that the government did not offer any "evidence that it would have been impossible or even difficult to download or print out the data…"

Defendant should, therefore, not be bound over on any charges.

There is insufficient evidence to believe Mr. Donenabbed attempted a robbery

If Mr. Donenabbed were properly identified, there is still insufficient evidence to indicate that he attempted a robbery. There was no force, and any fear by the clerk was unreasonable. The suspects were not armed, and no harm was caused to anyone.

There is insufficient evidence to believe Mr. Donenabbed was involved in a conspiracy

There was no evidence presented to indicate that the events leading to charges against Mr. Donenabbed were planned or that any agreement was made prior to the incident. The acts leading to his arrest appear to have been done on impulse without any sophistication, planning, or preparation. There was, therefore, no conspiracy.

There is insufficient evidence to believe Mr. Donenabbed committed Grand Theft

The value of the property allegedly taken was never estimated or stated in any way. There appears to be no legitimate basis to assume that the value exceeds $950 as required for Grand Theft. Nevertheless, as discussed above, the dubious identification of suspects using the video recordings negates probable cause to bind Mr. Donenabbed over on this count.

Based on the foregoing, Doug Donenabbed respectfully requests that his motion be granted and the Information be set aside.

Practical Tip:

Learn Boolean operators for legal search engines. Boolean terms and connectors are used in legal research sites, such as Westlaw and Lexis. Terms vary slightly from site to site but having a basic understanding of Boolean operators and concepts is valuable. Some common operators used with Westlaw include:

&	This **&** That	The answer has both This and That
or	This **or** That	The answer has This or That
%	This **%** That	The answer has This but not That
/s	This **/s** That	The answer has This and That in a sentence
/p	This **/p** That	The answer has This and That in a paragraph
/2	This **/2** That	This answer has This and That within two words of each other. Use this when searching names. Works with any number 1 to 255.
!	Omni!	The answer has words starting with Omni, such as Omnitel, Omnitrition, and Omnibus.

4. Sanctions

a. Motion to Suppress – No Warrant

ROGER LAMPKIN
SB#113786
1234 L Street
Bakersfield, CA 93301
Tel: (661)633-1234
Fax: (661)863-6741
Attorney for Doug Donenabbed

IN THE SUPERIOR COURT OF THE STATE OF CALIFORNIA, IN AND FOR THE COUNTY OF KERN

People of the State of California, Plaintiffs, - v. - Doug Donenabbed, Defendant	CASE NO. 123456 DEFENDANT DOUG DONENABBED'S MOTION TO SUPPRESS [*Penal Code §1538.5*] Date: August 2, 2022 Time: 8:30 a.m. Dept: CC Readiness: August 12, 2022 Trial: August 22, 2022

TO THE COURT AND THE DISTRICT ATTORNEY: PLEASE TAKE NOTICE that at the date and time indicated above, the defendant will move that the Court suppress all evidence seized in the above-entitled case including, but not limited to all officer observations, witness identifications, and all physical and intangible evidence seized or obtained as a result of search and seizure violations that occurred during all searches in this case, including the search of Defendant's home and person.

The motion will be based on this notice of motion, the attached declaration, the memorandum of points and authorities served and filed herewith, the records on file in this action and on such oral and documentary evidence as may be presented at the hearing.

Dated: _____   _____

By   Roger Lampkin,
Attorney for Doug Donenabbed

DECLARATION OF COUNSEL

I, Roger Lampkin, declare:

I am informed and believe that the search complained of was without a warrant, or that any warrant was invalid, or that the fruits of any warrant were previously suppressed, or that there are other defects in the search necessitating suppression in this matter.

Specifically, the defendant was in his house asleep when officers came to his door to inquire as to the whereabouts of his ex-wife. The defendant told officers that she did not live in the residence; she had never lived in the residence, and she was not present in the residence.

The defendant presented officers with a copy of judgement in couple's dissolution case.

Officers then removed the defendant from the home and conducted a search for the defendant's ex-wife. During the search, officers allegedly found a loaded handgun in a dresser drawer.

The defense intends to argue, inter alia, that the entry into the defendant's home was illegal, and even if it were legal, the search of the defendant's dresser was illegal because the defendant's ex-wife could not have been concealed inside the dresser.

Dated: _____

       By   Roger Lampkin,
            Attorney for Doug Donenabbed

POINTS, AUTHORITIES AND ARGUMENT

The fruits of an unlawful search must be suppressed (see *Fourth Amendment, United States Constitution*).

Penal Code § 1538.5 provides in part that "A defendant may move for the return of property or to suppress as evidence any tangible or intangible thing obtained as a result of a search or seizure on either of the following grounds:... The search or seizure without a warrant was unreasonable... If a search or seizure motion is granted pursuant to the proceedings authorized by this section, the property or evidence shall not be admissible against the movant at any trial or other hearing..."

"When a defendant moves to suppress evidence pursuant to section 1538.5, the People have "the burden of proving that the warrantless search or seizure was reasonable under the circumstances. [Citations.]" (*People v. Vannesse* (2018) 23 Cal. App. 5th 440, quoting *People v. Williams* (1999) 20 Cal. 4th 119, 130)

"A three-step allocation of the burden of producing evidence governs, with the ultimate burden of persuasion always remaining on the People. When defendants move to suppress evidence, they must set forth the factual and legal bases for the motion, but they satisfy that obligation, at least in the first instance, by making a prima facie showing that the police acted without a warrant. The prosecution then has the burden of proving some justification for the warrantless search or seizure, after which, defendants can respond by pointing out any inadequacies in that justification. The prosecution retains the ultimate burden of proving that the warrantless search or seizure was reasonable under the circumstances." (*People v. Romeo* (2015) 240 Cal.App.4th 931, 940, citations and punctuation omitted).

The court in *Wilder v. Superior Court* set forth the proper procedure for a suppression motion when the seizure complained of was made without a warrant:

The procedural problem arises from the fact that [the defendant], as the moving party, must necessarily file the first pleading-his motion to suppress evidence. Once [the defendant] has produced evidence to show that the seizure was without a warrant, [the prosecution] bears the burden of proving the only substantive issue at the hearing upon that motion-justification for the warrantless seizure. [citations]

The obvious solution to this problem is a suppression motion pleading procedure whereby [the prosecution] speaks first to the issue upon which it bears the burden of proof and [the defendant] thereafter responds...

...if [the prosecution] fails to justify the seizure, [the defendant] wins his suppression motion whether or not [the defendant] asserts subsequent specific contentions.

Wilder v. Superior Court (1979) 92 Cal.App.3rd 90

b. Motion to Suppress – Defective Warrant

ROGER LAMPKIN
SB#113786
1234 L Street
Bakersfield, CA 93301
Tel: (661)633-1234
Fax: (661)863-6741
Attorney for Doug Donenabbed

IN THE SUPERIOR COURT OF THE STATE OF CALIFORNIA,

IN AND FOR THE COUNTY OF KERN

People of the State of California, Plaintiffs, - v. - Doug Donenabbed, Defendant	DOUG DONENABBED MOTION TO SUPPRESS EVIDENCE [*Penal Code §1538.5*] Date: August 2, 2022 Time: 8:30 a.m. Dept: CC Readiness: August 12, 2022 Trial: August 22, 2022

TO THE COURT AND THE DISTRICT ATTORNEY: PLEASE TAKE NOTICE that at the date and time indicated above, or as soon thereafter as the matter can be heard in the above-entitled court, the defendant will move the Court for an order permitting cross-examination of Officer John Smith, the affiant in the affidavit filed in support of the search warrant issued and executed in this case, and for a further order permitting defendant to present evidence that a material fact was omitted from the affidavit.

Thereafter, defendant will move for an order suppressing all evidence seized pursuant to the warrant number 345678 specified in this Motion.

This Motion will be made on the ground that the evidence seized pursuant to the warrant was the product of an unreasonable search and seizure in violation of the Fourth and Fourteenth Amendments to the United States Constitution in that the affidavit in support of the above-mentioned warrant was defective by the intentional or reckless omission of material facts as described herein.

The motion will be based on this notice and the attached papers, the records on file in this action, and on such oral and documentary evidence as may be presented at the hearing.

Dated: _____

By   Roger Lampkin,
      Attorney for Doug Donenabbed

DECLARATION OF COUNSEL

I, Roger Lampkin, declare:

I am the attorney of record for Defendants.

I am informed and believe that the affidavit in support of the search warrant in the instant case omitted material facts and was crafted to mislead the issuing magistrate.

The warrant was also issued based on stale information, was not properly served, and has other defects as discussed herein.

At a minimum, the following additional facts should have been included in the affidavit in support of the warrant and presented to the magistrate:

1. The location of the proposed search, MJ Madness, is a medical marijuana dispensary.
2. The County of Kern brought a nuisance abatement action against MJ Madness (Case BCV-20-123456), which was decided against the county.
3. Angered by the adverse ruling, the City Attorney requested the search complained of in the instant case so as to render the civil action moot by seizing and destroying MJ Madness's inventory.
4. It is the intention of the City Attorney to accompany officers in the search and to bring members of the media with him.
5. This warrant is sought for a zoning violation, which are most often classified as infractions and not as criminal matters; rather, alleged zoning violations are selectively prosecuted for political reasons.
6. There are thousands of zoning violations throughout the city as described on the attached Notice of Variance List maintained by the city.
7. The request for warrant is based on unnamed informants who operate a competing marijuana cooperative who have no personal

knowledge of any alleged criminal activity.

8. MJ Madness is licensed under the Medicinal and Adult-Use Cannabis Regulation and Safety Act.
9. MJ Madness is operating under various other licenses and permits including a business license issued by the city for business as a Medical Marijuana Dispensary.

The warrant was based on unreliable, unnamed informants, used on January 1, 2020, but the warrant was not sought until January 12, 2020 and not executed until the City Attorney was available to participate in the search, January 22, 2020, a full twenty-one days after the alleged informant provided information.

The warrant was improperly executed in that non-essential, non-law enforcement personnel were allowed to participate in the execution. Specifically, the City Attorney and members of the media.

Dated: _____

By   Roger Lampkin,
      Attorney for Doug Donenabbed

→ ••Ω•• ←

No, no, no.
I said I was getting Lexis
for you.
The Lexus is for me.

No problem.
I'm on my way to give the judge
your briefs like you asked.

c. Motion to Suppress – Forced Blood Draw

ROGER LAMPKIN
SB#113786
1234 L Street
Bakersfield, CA 93301
Tel: (661)633-1234
Fax: (661)863-6741
Attorney for Doug Donenabbed

IN THE SUPERIOR COURT OF THE STATE OF CALIFORNIA,

IN AND FOR THE COUNTY OF KERN

People of the State of California,	CASE NO. 123456
Plaintiffs,	DOUG DONENABBED MOTION TO SUPPRESS EVIDENCE *[Penal Code §1538.5]*
- v. -	
Doug Donenabbed,	Date: August 2, 2022
Defendant	Time: 8:30 a.m. Dept: CC

TO THE COURT AND THE DISTRICT ATTORNEY: PLEASE TAKE NOTICE that at the date and time indicated above, the defendant will move that the Court suppress all evidence seized in the above-entitled case including, but not limited to the blood taken from defendant and all testing and testimony concerning the blood that was seized or obtained as a result of search and seizure violations that occurred during the taking of said blood.

The motion will be based on this notice of motion, the attached declaration, the memorandum of points and authorities served and filed herewith, the records on file in this action and on such oral and documentary evidence as may be presented at the hearing.

Dated: _____

By   Roger Lampkin,
Attorney for Doug Donenabbed

DECLARATION OF COUNSEL

I, Roger Lampkin, declare:

I am informed and believe that members of the Prosecution team seized blood from Defendant without a warrant and using improper procedures necessitating suppression in this matter.

Dated: _____

By   Roger Lampkin,
       Attorney for Doug Donenabbed

POINTS, AUTHORITIES AND ARGUMENT

The fruits of an unlawful search must be suppressed (see *Fourth Amendment, United States Constitution*).

Penal Code § 1538.5 provides in part that "A defendant may move for the return of property or to suppress as evidence any tangible or intangible thing obtained as a result of a search or seizure on either of the following grounds:… The search or seizure without a warrant was unreasonable… If a search or seizure motion is granted pursuant to the proceedings authorized by this section, the property or evidence shall not be admissible against the movant at any trial or other hearing…"

"When a defendant moves to suppress evidence pursuant to section 1538.5, the People have "the burden of proving that the warrantless search or seizure was reasonable under the circumstances. [Citations.]" (*People v. Vannesse* (2018) 23 Cal. App. 5th 440, quoting *People v. Williams* (1999) 20 Cal. 4th 119, 130)

Defendant did not consent to a blood test, but rather the test was taken in violation of Defendant's rights pursuant to *Vehicle Code §23612(a)(2)(A)*, which guarantees that the person "has the choice of whether the test shall be of his blood or breath and the officer shall advise the person that he or she has that choice." To save himself a short drive to the location of the breath test machine, the arresting officer ordered a non-consensual blood draw on Defendant.

This blood draw constituted a warrantless, non-consensual search of the defendant's person. Because the compelled blood test was obtained without a warrant and was without consent, it was unreasonable and violated the *Fourth and Fourteenth Amendments* to the U.S. Constitution and *Article I, §13* of the California Constitution).

"California's implied consent statute, which includes a provision allowing the arrestee a choice of tests, implies consent to the selected test, not whichever test law enforcement officials may choose to employ in violation of the statute" (*Nelson v. City of Irvine* (9th Cir. 1998) 143 F. 3rd 1196). Defendant consented to a breath test that was not given, but not to the forced blood draw.

The Prosecution may argue that exigent circumstances justified the forced blood draw, but the Supreme Court has held that "the natural dissipation of alcohol in the bloodstream does not constitute an exigency in every case sufficient to justify conducting a blood test without a warrant." (*Missouri v. McNeely* (2013) 569 U.S. 141).

Neither can the Prosecution successfully argue consent based on Defendant's failure to vigorously protest the forced blood draw because the Supreme Court has weighed in on this argument also and held that "When a prosecutor seeks to rely upon consent to justify the lawfulness of a search, he has the burden of proving that the consent was, in fact, freely and voluntarily given. This burden cannot be discharged by showing no more than acquiescence to a claim of lawful authority." (*Bumper v. North Carolina* (1968) 391 U.S. 543, 548).

The high court strongly admonished that, "Where there is coercion there cannot be consent." (id. at 550).

In the instant case, there was neither consent nor a warrant. The blood draw and all fruits springing from it must be suppressed.

→••Ω••←

Practical Tip:

Use a blue pen.

You may be asked to sign proofs of service or other documents that are filed with the court. Most court filings must be original documents. A blue pen is an easy and immediate way to tell if a document is an original or a copy. If asking anyone else to sign a document, have them use a blue pen also.

d. Motion to Dismiss for Lost Evidence - Trombetta

ROGER LAMPKIN
SB#113786
1234 L Street
Bakersfield, CA 93301
Tel: (661)633-1234
Fax: (661)863-6741
Attorney for Doug Donenabbed

IN THE SUPERIOR COURT OF THE STATE OF CALIFORNIA,

IN AND FOR THE COUNTY OF KERN

People of the State of California,	CASE NO. 123456
Plaintiffs,	DEFENDANT DOUG DONENABBED'S MOTION FOR SANCTIONS [Trombetta]
- v. -	
Doug Donenabbed,	
Defendant	

TO THE COURT AND THE DISTRICT ATTORNEY: PLEASE TAKE NOTICE that the defendant hereby moves the Court for an order dismissing the instant action based on the loss of significant exculpatory evidence.

This motion is made on the ground that the prosecution failed to provide Defendant with exculpatory evidence in the constructive hands of the prosecuting attorney and the prosecution team altered or destroyed evidence.

The motion is based on this Notice of Motion, all attached papers, all papers and records on file in this action, and on such oral and documentary evidence as may be presented at the time of the motion.

Dated: _____

        By   Roger Lampkin,
              Attorney for Doug Donenabbed

POINTS, AUTHORITIES, AND ARGUMENT

Summary of the Case

Law enforcement seized multiple pieces of exculpatory evidence in this case, including a video recording of the incident leading to Defendant's arrest and recordings of witness statements. Instead of preserving the evidence for trial, the Prosecution team disposed of it.

Authority

The law does not impose a duty on the prosecution to collect evidence that might be beneficial to the defense; however, once collected, the prosecution does have a duty to preserve material evidence. (*In re Michael L.* (1985) 39 Cal 3rd 81; *People v Hogan* (1982) 31 Cal 3rd 815, 851, disapproved on other grounds in *People v Cooper* (1991) 53 Cal 3rd 771, 836)

If the prosecution preserved and then destroyed or permanently lost evidence, the defense may make a motion for sanctions. The destroyed evidence must have been material to the defense case (*California v Trombetta* (1984) 467 US 479, 488).

The materiality of evidence in California is determined under the *Trombetta/Youngblood* federal standard (*People v Zapien* (1993) 4 Cal 4th 929, 964; *People v Cooper* (1991) 53 Cal 3rd 771, 810; *People v Johnson* (1989) 47 Cal 3rd 1194, 1233).

Material evidence is evidence that might be expected to play a significant role in the suspect's defense. It must possess an exculpatory value that was apparent before the evidence was lost or destroyed, and be of such a nature that the defendant would be unable to obtain comparable evidence by other reasonably available means (*California v Trombetta*, supra.)

To support sanctions for loss or destruction of evidence under *Trombetta* and *Youngblood*, the prosecution must have acted in bad faith in destroying the evidence (*Arizona v Youngblood* (1988) 488 US 51, 58).

In the instant case, bad faith is shown by the destruction of evidence after a Defense request for preservation.

Based on the foregoing, instant action should be dismissed. In the alternative, the Prosecution should be prohibited from making any use of the following described evidence:
1. Any description of the destroyed video recording
2. Any description of the destroyed audio recordings
3. Any statement or testimony from any witness whose interview recording was destroyed

e. Motion to Dismiss for Improper Destruction of Drugs

ROGER LAMPKIN
SB#113786
1234 L Street
Bakersfield, CA 93301
Tel: (661)633-1234
Fax: (661)863-6741
Attorney for Doug Donenabbed

IN THE SUPERIOR COURT OF THE STATE OF CALIFORNIA,

IN AND FOR THE COUNTY OF KERN

People of the State of California, Plaintiffs, - v. - Doug Donenabbed, Defendant	DEFENDANT DOUG DONENABBED'S MOTION TO DISMISS [Health & Safety Code §11479]

TO THE COURT AND THE DISTRICT ATTORNEY OF KERN COUNTY: PLEASE TAKE NOTICE that Defendant moves the Court an order dismissing the instant action because of the loss of significant exculpatory evidence.

This motion is made on the ground that the prosecution failed to provide Defendant with exculpatory evidence in the constructive hands of the prosecuting attorney and the prosecution team destroyed evidence.

The motion is based on this Notice of Motion, on the attached papers, on all papers and records on file in this action, and on such oral and documentary evidence as may be presented at the time of the motion.

Dated: _____

                        By   Roger Lampkin,
                        Attorney for Doug Donenabbed

MEMORANDUM OF POINTS AND AUTHORITIES

Summary of the Case

Law enforcement officers conducted a search at MJ Madness on or about January 22, 2020. The prosecution team seized and destroyed suspected contraband without giving Defendant an opportunity to test and otherwise demonstrate that the seized items were not contraband.

This destruction of evidence has deprived defendants of the ability to properly prepare for trial by presenting evidence to the jury that the items seized are not prohibited by law.

It is anticipated that the Prosecution will attempt to argue that destruction was authorized pursuant to *Health & Safety Code §11479*, but as discussed herein, the destruction was not authorized by *Health & Safety Code §11479* and officers failed to follow the provisions of *Health & Safety Code §11479*.

The Prosecution was Required to Preserve Seized Evidence

The law does not impose a duty on the prosecution to collect evidence that might be beneficial to the defense; however, once collected, the prosecution does have a duty to preserve material evidence. (*In re Michael L.* (1985) 39 Cal 3rd 81; *People v Hogan* (1982) 31 Cal 3rd 815, 851, disapproved on other grounds in *People v Cooper* (1991) 53 Cal 3rd 771, 836)

If the prosecution preserved and then destroyed or permanently lost evidence, the defense may make a motion for sanctions. The destroyed evidence must have been material to the defense case (*California v Trombetta* (1984) 467 US 479, 488).

The materiality of evidence in California is determined under the *Trombetta/Youngblood* federal standard (*People v Zapien* (1993) 4 Cal 4th 929, 964; *People v Cooper* (1991) 53 Cal 3rd 771, 810; *People v Johnson* (1989) 47 Cal 3rd 1194, 1233).

Material evidence is evidence that might be expected to play a significant role in the suspect's defense. It must possess an exculpatory value that was apparent before the evidence was lost or destroyed, and be of such a nature that the defendant would be unable to obtain comparable evidence by other reasonably available means (*California v Trombetta*, supra.)

To support sanctions for loss or destruction of evidence under *Trombetta* and *Youngblood*, the prosecution must have acted in bad faith in destroying the evidence (*Arizona v Youngblood* (1988) 488 US 51, 58).

In the instant the Prosecution seized multiple pieces of contraband as detailed on the attached inventory (Exhibit A). However, the Prosecution failed to properly preserve, test, or document the seized property.

The Destruction of Evidence Was Not Authorized by the Warrant

The warrant in the instant case and the return thereto (both attached as Exhibit B) specifically state that the seized property shall be maintained. The affiant did not ask permission to destroy evidence, and the Court did not grant permission to destroy evidence.

The Destruction of Evidence Was Not Authorized by Statute

Health & Safety Code §11473 allows for destruction of certain seized property "upon conviction of the owner or defendant" but only when "ordered destroyed by the court in which conviction was had." Similarly, *Health & Safety Code §11473.5* holds that "controlled substances, instruments, or paraphernalia used for unlawfully using or administering a controlled substance" may "be destroyed by order of the court, unless the court finds that the controlled substances, instruments, or paraphernalia were lawfully possessed by the defendant." In other words, destruction under either section requires order of the court.

Health & Safety Code §11479.2 allows for destruction of some controlled substances without court order, but the statute specifically holds that it is applicable to substances "except cannabis," and *Health & Safety Code §11479.1* allows for destruction of phencyclidine without court order.

Health & Safety Code §11479, however, is the destruction statute applicable to the instant case:

> Notwithstanding Sections 11473 and 11473.5, at any time after seizure by a law enforcement agency of a suspected controlled substance, except in the case of growing or harvested cannabis, that amount in excess of 10 pounds in gross weight may be destroyed without a court order by the chief of the law enforcement agency or a designated subordinate. In the case of growing or harvested cannabis, that amount in excess of two pounds, or the amount of cannabis a medicinal cannabis patient or designated caregiver is authorized to possess by ordinance in the city or county where the cannabis was seized, whichever is greater, may be destroyed without a court order by the chief of the law enforcement agency or a designated subordinate. Destruction shall not take place pursuant to this section until all of the following requirements are satisfied:
>
> (a) At least five random and representative samples have been taken, for evidentiary purposes, from the total amount of suspected controlled substances to be destroyed. These samples shall be in addition to the 10 pounds required above. When the suspected controlled substance consists of growing or harvested cannabis plants,

at least one 2-pound sample or a sample in the amount of medicinal cannabis a medicinal cannabis patient or designated caregiver is authorized to possess by ordinance in the city or county where the cannabis was seized, whichever is greater, shall be retained. This sample may include stalks, branches, or leaves. In addition, five representative samples of leaves or buds shall be retained for evidentiary purposes from the total amount of suspected controlled substances to be destroyed.

(b) Photographs and videos have been taken that reasonably and accurately demonstrate the total amount of the suspected controlled substance to be destroyed.

(c) The gross weight of the suspected controlled substance has been determined, either by actually weighing the suspected controlled substance or by estimating that weight after dimensional measurement of the total suspected controlled substance.

(d) The chief of the law enforcement agency has determined that it is not reasonably possible to preserve the suspected controlled substance in place, or to remove the suspected controlled substance to another location. In making this determination, the difficulty of transporting and storing the suspected controlled substance to another site and the storage facilities may be taken into consideration.

Subsequent to any destruction of a suspected controlled substance pursuant to this section, an affidavit shall be filed within 30 days in the court that has jurisdiction over any pending criminal proceedings pertaining to that suspected controlled substance, reciting the applicable information required by subdivisions (a), (b), (c), and (d) together with information establishing the location of the suspected controlled substance, and specifying the date and time of the destruction. In the event that there are no criminal proceedings pending that pertain to that suspected controlled substance, the affidavit may be filed in any court within the county that would have jurisdiction over a person against whom those criminal charges might be filed.

In the instant case, the destruction failed to comply with multiple provisions of *Health & Safety Code §11479*.

First, *§11479* requires the Prosecution to take five representative samples. In the instant case, the Prosecution appears to have taken five samples from one group of live plants but failed to take five random samples of items that were seized from other locations, including other groups of live plants as well as alleged extracts, edibles, rubs, and joints.

Second, *§11479* requires the Prosecution to preserve the greater of two pounds of growing cannabis or "the amount of cannabis a medicinal cannabis patient or designated caregiver is authorized to possess…" The Prosecution neither preserved two pounds nor made any effort to determine which patients were served by the facility and the amount of cannabis they were allowed to possess.

Third, "Photographs and videos [were not] taken that reasonably and accurately demonstrate the total amount of the suspected controlled substance to be destroyed." (*§11479*, see also *People v. O'Hearn* (1983) 142 Cal.App.3rd 566). The Prosecution failed to comply with this section of the statute by failing to take video recordings. The statute clearly states, "Photographs and videos," not "Photographs or videos."

The word "and" in the statute requires a conjunctive construction of the two requirements: both photographs and videos are required. (*Kobzoff v. Los Angeles County Harbor/UCLA Medical Center* (1998) 19 Cal.4th 851, 861; *Rodriguez v. Blue Cross of California* (2008) 162 Cal.App.4th 330). Conversely, the conjunction "or" would allow compliance by the taking of either photographs or videos because "the conjunction 'or' separates two distinct alternatives" (*People v. Spaccia* (2017) 12 Cal.App.5th 1278).

When enacting *Health & Safety Code §11479*, the legislature specifically contemplated the use of the conjunction "and" to require both photographs and videos. The California Committee Report to *2015 California Senate Bill No. 303*, California 2015-2016 Regular Session notes that "Existing law provides that law enforcement may, without a court order, destroy seized controlled substances in excess of 10 pounds, where the following circumstances are present:… 3)Photographs of the material to be destroyed must be taken…. This bill:… 3)Requires the law enforcement agency, before destroying a specified amount of a seized controlled substance, to photograph and video the controlled substance so as to reasonably demonstrate how much of the substance was seized and destroyed."

Thus, the legislature conscientiously used the conjunction "and" to require both photographs and video recordings before destruction. The legislature even considered the possible additional cost of requiring video recordings, "According to the Assembly Appropriations Committee: Minor additional costs to local law enforcement agencies to videotape the evidence, offset by significant savings associated with reducing by almost 80 percent the amount of marijuana that is stored as evidence in criminal proceedings." (California Committee Report to *S.B.303*)

Fourth, the photographs are insufficient in that they do not "reasonably and accurately demonstrate the total amount of the suspected controlled substance to be destroyed" and are not complete and accurate representations of the items seized.

As an example, the description of the destruction indicates that the alleged contraband occupied a "ten foot by three foot trench" but no depth is listed, and it is unclear whether the trench was used to destroy live plants or all of the contraband.

Had the Prosecution taken proper photographs and video recordings as required by §11479, defendants would have been able to demonstrate, at a minimum, that seized items were possessed by other persons and/or were not items prohibited by law.

Fifth, the statute only allows for destruction of controlled substances, not exculpatory evidence, such as video recordings made during the search by cameras operated by MJ Madness, or items that are innocuous, such as mailing boxes, jars, office supplies, and other items that were seized.

Sixth, the "gross weight of the suspected controlled substance has [not] been determined." As discussed above, photographs indicate that officers seized and destroyed multiple items. Had the prosecution team members properly determined the weight of the suspected contraband, the defense could argue that the amount came within the Compassionate Use Act or other acts authorizing the cultivation and use of marijuana.

Seventh, There is no indication that "The chief of the law enforcement agency [or anyone else] has determined that it is not reasonably possible to preserve the suspected controlled substance in place, or to remove the suspected controlled substance to another location." The items were simply destroyed immediately after being seized.

Eighth, §11479 requires that "an affidavit shall be filed within 30 days in the court that has jurisdiction over any pending criminal proceedings pertaining to that suspected controlled substance, reciting the applicable information required by subdivisions (a), (b), (c), and (d) together with information establishing the location of the suspected controlled substance, and specifying the date and time of the destruction." Such an affidavit has not been provided to the defense, nor can one be prepared because the Prosecution failed to comply with §11479 subdivisions (a), (b), (c), or (d) as described above.

Destruction of Evidence Requires Dismissal

"Since section 11479 is essentially a legislative declaration of the required 'rigorous and systematic procedure' designed to preserve evidence of a controlled substance, nothing less than strict compliance with its provisions will satisfy the dictates of due process." (*People v. Wilson* (1987) 191 Cal.App.3rd 161)

In *People v. Hitch* (1974) 12 Cal.3rd 641 at pages 652-653, the California Supreme Court ruled that sanctions are inappropriate when evidence is intentionally destroyed in good faith only if "the governmental agencies involved have established, enforced and attempted in good faith to adhere to rigorous and systematic procedures designed to preserve the [evidence]." As indicated above, the prosecution failed to "adhere to rigorous and systematic procedures designed to preserve" evidence. (*California v. Trombetta* (1984) 467 U.S. 479 and *Arizona v. Youngblood* (1988) 488 U.S. 51, 58 limited the holding in *Hitch*).

"Whatever duty the Constitution imposes on the States to preserve evidence, that duty must be limited to evidence that might be expected to play a significant role in the suspect's defense. To meet this standard of constitutional materiality [citation], evidence must both possess an exculpatory value that was apparent before the evidence was destroyed, and be of such a nature that the defendant would be unable to obtain comparable evidence by other reasonably available means." (*Trombetta*, supra at pp. 488-489, fn. omitted.) In *Youngblood*, the court recognized that if evidence is merely potentially useful, bad faith destruction must also be established. (*Youngblood*, supra at p. 58.)

Bad faith can be demonstrated in the instant case by the officers' failure to take photographs and videos of the labels on the seedlings, failure to take photographs of the non-cannabis items at the scene of the seizure, failure to take photographs or bottle labels that would have helped establish that the bottles contained non-cannabis items, and failure to retain or take samples from items alleged to be live plants, extracts, edibles, rubs, and joints. It was only by sheer luck that these items spilled to the ground and were visible in a photograph taken of their destruction.

The destruction of evidence in the instant case is similar to *People v. O'Hearn* (1983) 142 Cal.App.3rd 566. The court in *O'Hearn* noted that "at the time the [alleged marijuana] plants were in effect destroyed by commingling them with the others in the state truck, the statute was ignored in the following particulars: (1) no photographs were taken which reasonably depicted the total amount of the defendants' plants, (2) the chief of the law enforcement agency did not determine it was not reasonably possible to remove and store the plants and (3) the gross weight of the suspected controlled substance of defendants was not determined either by actually weighing it or by estimating its weight after dimensional measurements were taken. We conclude that the People may not justify the destruction of evidence herein at issue by reliance upon Health and Safety Code section 11479 in the absence of strict compliance therewith [citation], and that evidence concerning the destroyed plants must be suppressed."

O'Hearn was decided prior to *§11479* being amended to require video recordings, and the instant case suffers from additional errors as discussed above, such as the destruction of items that are not controlled substances and the lack of an affidavit as required by the statute.

Conclusion

The Prosecution's destruction of evidence in violation of statute has deprived defendants of the ability to properly prepare for trial. Nonetheless, once the Defense establishes that the destroyed evidence was exculpatory, the burden is on the Prosecution to "show that the governmental agencies involved have established, enforced and attempted in good faith to adhere to rigorous and systematic procedures designed to preserve the" evidence (*Wilson, supra*).

f. Motion to Dismiss for Lost Witness

ROGER LAMPKIN
SB#113786
1234 L Street
Bakersfield, CA 93301
Tel: (661)633-1234
Fax: (661)863-6741
Attorney for Doug Donenabbed

IN THE SUPERIOR COURT OF THE STATE OF CALIFORNIA,

IN AND FOR THE COUNTY OF KERN

People of the State of California,	CASE NO. 123456
Plaintiffs,	DEFENDANT DOUG DONENABBED'S MOTION FOR SANCTIONS [Prosecution Interference with Witnesses]
- v. -	
Doug Donenabbed,	
Defendant	

TO THE COURT AND THE DISTRICT ATTORNEY OF KERN COUNTY: PLEASE TAKE NOTICE that Defendant moves the Court an order dismissing the charging document in this matter because of the loss of significant exculpatory witnesses.

This motion is made on the ground that the prosecution caused exculpatory witnesses to be unavailable to the defense.

The motion will be based on this Notice of Motion, on the attached memorandum of points and authorities and filed herewith and such supplemental memorandum of points and authorities that may be hereafter filed with the court or stated orally at the conclusion of the hearing, on all papers and records on file in this action and on such oral and documentary evidence as may be presented at the time of the motion.

Dated: _____

                            By   Roger Lampkin,
                                Attorney for Doug Donenabbed

POINTS, AUTHORITIES, AND ARGUMENT

The Sixth Amendment Compulsory Process Clause safeguards a criminal defendant's "right to offer the testimony of witnesses, and to compel their testimony, if necessary," as part of "the right to present a defense." (*Washington v. Texas* (1967) 388 U.S. 14, 19). By its text, "the Sixth Amendment does not by its terms grant to a criminal defendant the right to secure the attendance and testimony of any and all witnesses: it guarantees him 'compulsory process for obtaining witnesses in his favor.' " (*United States v. Valenzuela-Bernal* (1982) 458 U.S. 858, 867, quoting U.S. Const. Amend. VI).

In discussing the Sixth Amendment, the Supreme Court has stated that "[f]ew rights are more fundamental than that of an accused to present witnesses in his own defense." (Chambers v. Mississippi (1973) 410 U.S. 284, 302). "The right to offer the testimony of witnesses, and to compel their attendance, if necessary, is in plain terms the right to present a defense, the right to present the defendant's version of the facts as well as the prosecution's to the [factfinder] so it may decide where the truth lies.... This right is a fundamental element of due process of law." (Washington v. Texas (1976) 388 U.S. 14, 19; see also *Ponte v. Real* (1985) 471 U.S. 491, 510).

"A defendant in a criminal action is not entitled to a dismissal merely because he is unable to produce witnesses assertedly necessary to his defense (*People v. Kirkpatrick* (1973) 7 Cal. 3rd 480, 486). If, however, state action has made a material witness unavailable, dismissal is mandated by due process and a defendant's constitutional right to a fair trial." (*People v. Mejia* (1976) 57 Cal App 3rd 574)

In general, federal standards must be applied whenever suppression of evidence is invoked as a sanction in a criminal prosecution. (Cal. Const., art. I, § 28(d); *In re Lance W.* (1985) 37 Cal. 3rd 873, 896; *People v. Epps* (1986) 182 Cal.App.3rd 1102, 1115.) To establish materiality under the federal standard, the defendant must make a "plausible showing that the testimony of the deported witnesses would have been material and favorable to his defense, in ways not merely cumulative to the testimony of available witnesses." (*United States v. Valenzuela-Bernal* (1982) 458 U.S. 858, 873).

In addition to deporting a witness as contemplated by *Valenzuela-Bernal*, supra, the Supreme Court has recognized that other government interference with a defense witness's free and unhampered choice to testify may amount to a violation of due process. Such conduct may include intimidating a witness into not testifying (*Webb v. Texas* (1972) 409 U.S. 95, 97–98; *Earp v. Ornoski* (9th Cir.2005) 431 F.3rd 1158, 1167–1168) or prohibiting co-participants in same crime from testifying for each other (*Washington v. Texas* (1967) 388 U.S. 14, 19).

In the instant case, the following witnesses were material to the defense:
1. Juanita Juarez
2. Wally Witt
3. Nancy Newt

The witnesses are now unavailable because of the following government conduct:
1. On June 1, 2020, Defendant gave the Prosecution notice that Juanita Juarez was a material witness in this matter. She was deported on August 1, 2020.
2. Wally Witt gave an exculpatory statement to the Defense investigator, which was turned over to the Prosecution on July 1, 2020. The Prosecution interviewed Mr. Witt and "cautioned him" that his statement was incriminating. Mr. Witt then indicated that he would be invoking his right against self-incrimination unless given immunity, which the Prosecution has withheld.
3. The defense investigator attempted to interview Nancy Newt by phone and arrange to serve her a subpoena, but Ms. Newt informed the defense investigator that "Officer Johnson told me I should not let the defense know where I am or talk to the defense because they will just try to make it look like I am lying."

By these actions, the Prosecution has denied Defendant the right to compulsory process. The proper remedy is, therefore, dismissal.

5. Third Party Requests

a. Removal Order

A Removal Order is used to remove an inmate from prison or jail and bring the inmate to court to take part in the proceedings. Depending on the distance from the prison to the court, it may take three weeks or more to have an inmate brought to court. The sample request includes language for a forced cell extraction; however, inmates who are brought to court by force are generally not good witnesses.

Some counties have their own Removal Order forms and procedures, so it is best to talk to the clerks in the local court before submitting a Request for Removal Order.

ROGER LAMPKIN
SB#113786
1234 L Street
Bakersfield, CA 93301
Tel: (661)633-1234
Fax: (661)863-6741
Attorney for Doug Donenabbed

IN THE SUPERIOR COURT OF THE STATE OF CALIFORNIA, IN AND FOR THE COUNTY OF KERN

People of the State of California,	CASE NO. 123456
Plaintiffs,	REQUEST FOR REMOVAL OF CDCR INMATE
- v. -	DATE: May 4, 2022
Doug Donenabbed,	TIME: 8:30 a.m.
	DEPT: 1
Defendant	

I, Roger Lampkin, declare:

I am the attorney representing the defendant in this action.

Mark Mendoza, who is confined in the Correctional Training Facility (CTF) under CDCR# P12345 is a witness in the above-entitled case.

Therefore, I respectfully request the court for an order directing Shawn Hatton, Acting Warden of CTF, to remove this inmate from the prison, and to deliver the inmate into custody of the sheriff of this county.

Further, that the sheriff of this county be ordered to deliver this inmate to Department One of the above-entitled court on May 4, 2022, at the hour of 8:30 a.m., and at such times thereafter until the inmate's testimony is concluded, and thereafter to return said prisoner to custody of Shawn Hatton, Acting Warden of CTF.

Mark Mendoza's testimony is material and necessary because he witnessed the alleged inmate altercation.

In the event the prisoner is uncooperative, the undersigned also requests the court authorize the use of reasonable force and/or forcible cell extraction to ensure the defendant's appearance for the above-described proceedings and for any future court hearings related to this case.
Dated:

_____
By   Roger Lampkin,
Attorney for Doug Donenabbed

ROGER LAMPKIN
SB#113786
1234 L Street
Bakersfield, CA 93301
Tel: (661)633-1234
Fax: (661)863-6741
Attorney for Doug Donenabbed

IN THE SUPERIOR COURT OF THE STATE OF CALIFORNIA,

IN AND FOR THE COUNTY OF KERN

People of the State of California,	CASE NO. 123456
Plaintiffs,	ORDER FOR REMOVAL OF CDCR INMATE
- v. -	DATE: May 4, 2022
Doug Donenabbed,	TIME: 8:30 a.m.
Defendant	DEPT: 1

To: Shawn Hatton, Acting Warden of CTF:

An order having been made this day by me, that Mark Mendoza, who is confined in the Correctional Training Facility (CTF) under CDCR# P12345 be produced in this court to appear as a witness, you are commanded to deliver Mark Mendoza into the custody of Donny Youngblood, Sheriff of Kern County.

Use of reasonable force is / is not authorized.
Forced cell extraction is/ is not authorized.

Dated:

_____
By   Judge of the Superior Court

b. Motion to Discover Officer Personnel Records (Pitchess)

A Pitchess motion is a request for discovery of information regarding complaints about a peace officer. It has special notice requirements, including that it must be served on the police agency and the police agency's attorney of record. Technically, service on one or the other should be legally adequate, but agencies have been known to object when duplicate service is not made.

ROGER LAMPKIN
SB#113786
1234 L Street
Bakersfield, CA 93301
Tel: (661)633-1234
Fax: (661)863-6741
Attorney for Doug Donenabbed

IN THE SUPERIOR COURT OF THE STATE OF CALIFORNIA,
IN AND FOR THE COUNTY OF KERN

People of the State of California,	CASE NO. 123456
Plaintiffs,	MOTION FOR DISCOVERY OF PEACE OFFICER PERSONNEL RECORDS (*Pitchess*)
- v. -	
Doug Donenabbed,	DATE: October 16, 2019
Defendant	TIME: 8:30 a.m.
	DEPT: CC
	Trial date: October 31, 2019
	Readiness date: October 30, 2019

TO THE COURT AND THE DISTRICT ATTORNEY:

PLEASE TAKE NOTICE that at the date and time indicated above, or as soon thereafter as the matter can be heard in the above-entitled court, the defendant will move the Court for an order permitting discovery and disclosure of the personnel records of the following peace officers pursuant to *Evidence Code §1043*, or alternatively an in camera review by the court of said documents and release of discoverable documents:

1. Deputy Dogg, Badge 1234
2. Deputy Danny, Badge 4567

The Agency or Agencies having custody and control of the records sought are:
1. The Kern County Sheriff's Department

The motion will be based on this notice of motion, all attached documents, the records on file in this action, and on such matters as may be presented at the hearing.

Dated:

_____

By   Roger Lampkin,
Attorney for Doug Donenabbed

SCHEDULE OF ITEMS SOUGHT

Public Records

1. All records related to any incident involving the discharge of a firearm at a person by a named officer.
2. All records related to any incident in which the use of force by a named officer resulted in death or great bodily injury.
3. All records related to any incident in which a sustained finding was made by any law enforcement agency or oversight agency that a named officer engaged in sexual assault involving a member of the public.
4. All records related to any incident in which a sustained finding was made by any law enforcement agency or oversight agency of dishonesty by a named officer directly relating to the reporting, investigation, or prosecution of a crime, or directly relating to the reporting of, or investigation of misconduct by, another peace officer or custodial officer, including, but not limited to, any sustained finding of perjury, false statements, filing false reports, destruction, falsifying, or concealing of evidence.

Confidential Records

1. All records in any way related to complaints and/or investigations of:
   a. Falsifying information;
   b. Illegal search and seizure;

    c.   Excessive force;

    d.   Omissions of information in reporting investigations;

    e.   Dishonesty as the reporting of investigations; and

    f.   Conduct unbecoming of a peace officer.

For each of the named officers. This request includes complaints of misconduct. The disclosed information should include names, addresses and phone numbers of people who have filed complaints against any of the named officers pursuant to *Evidence Code § 1045* (a) and *1043(b)*. (*Pitchess v. Superior Court* (1974) 11 Cal 3rd 531; *People v. Wheeler* (1992) 4 Cal 4th 284; California Constitution article I, section 28(d); *Chambers v. Superior Court* (2007) 42 Cal. 4th 673, 679; *Warrick v. Superior Court* (2005) 35 Cal. 4th 1011, 1019; *People v. Gaines* (2009) 46 Cal.4th 172, 179).

POINTS, AUTHORITIES, AND ARGUMENT

Evidence Code § 832.7(a) states the general proposition that law enforcement officer personnel records are confidential; however, subsection (b)(1) provides exceptions to the general rule:

    "[T]he following peace officer or custodial officer personnel records and records maintained by any state or local agency shall not be confidential and shall be made available for public inspection pursuant to the California Public Records Act (Chapter 3.5 (commencing with Section 6250) of Division 7 of Title 1 of the Government Code):

    (A) A record relating to the report, investigation, or findings of any of the following:

        (i) An incident involving the discharge of a firearm at a person by a peace officer or custodial officer.

        (ii) An incident in which the use of force by a peace officer or custodial officer against a person resulted in death, or in great bodily injury.

    (B)(i) Any record relating to an incident in which a sustained finding was made by any law enforcement agency or oversight agency that a peace officer or custodial officer engaged in sexual assault involving a member of the public...

    (C) Any record relating to an incident in which a sustained finding was made by any law enforcement agency or oversight agency of dishonesty by a peace officer or custodial officer directly relating to the reporting, investigation, or prosecution of a crime, or directly relating to the reporting of, or investigation of misconduct by, another peace officer or custodial officer, including, but not limited to, any sustained finding of perjury, false statements, filing false reports, destruction, falsifying, or concealing of evidence.

(2) Records that shall be released pursuant to this subdivision include all investigative reports; photographic, audio, and video evidence; transcripts or recordings of interviews; autopsy reports; all materials compiled and presented for review to the district attorney or to any person or body charged with determining whether to file criminal charges against an officer in connection with an incident, or whether the officer's action was consistent with law and agency policy for purposes of discipline or administrative action, or what discipline to impose or corrective action to take; documents setting forth findings or recommended findings; and copies of disciplinary records relating to the incident, including any letters of intent to impose discipline, any documents reflecting modifications of discipline due to the Skelly or grievance process, and letters indicating final imposition of discipline or other documentation reflecting implementation of corrective action."

These non-confidential records should be disclosed without need of any showing.

Turning to confidential records, law enforcement agency records maintained pursuant to *Penal Code §§832.5, 832.7 and 832.8(e)* are discoverable under *Evidence Code §1043 and 1045.*

Evidence Code §1045(a) provides:

Nothing in this article shall be construed to affect the right of access to records of complaints, or investigations of complaints, or discipline imposed as a result of such investigations, concerning an event or transaction in which the peace officer participated, or which he perceived, and pertaining to the manner in which he performed his duties, provided that such information is relevant to the subject matter involved in the pending litigation.

A defendant is entitled to discovery of information relating to an officer's personnel records where the accused shows the materiality of the subject matter of the pending case and a reasonable belief that that agency possesses the requested information. (*City of Santa Cruz v. Municipal Court* (1989) 49 Cal. 3rd 74, 84.) Evidence of a law enforcement officer's tendency to be dishonest in support of Defendant's theory in this case is relevant and admissible under *Evidence Code §1103.* (*People v. Memro* (1985) 38 Cal. 3rd 658; *Pitchess v. Superior Court* (1974) 11 Cal. 3rd 531, 537; *City of Santa Cruz v.*

Municipal Court (1989) 49 Cal. 3rd 74, 84.) Likewise, evidence of an officer's excessive use of force/violence in the pending matter is relevant where the defendant is accused of resisting and delaying a peace officer.

Further, the only showing necessary is that the defense provide a plausible theory as how the discovery would be admissible for the court to grant the disclosure. (*Warwick v. Superior Court* (2005) 35 Cal. 4th 1011, 1026)

DECLARATION IN SUPPORT OF MOTION FOR DISCOVERY

I, Roger Lampkin, Attorney for Defendant, declare:

1. Defendant is presently charged with *Penal Code §243(b)* (Battery on a Peace Officer) and *Penal Code §148(a)(1)* (Resisting Arrest);
2. According to witness reports (attached), the named officers entered Defendant's residence without consent, handcuffed Defendant, then pepper sprayed him in the face.
3. Law enforcement reports (attached) differ from witness reports but confirm that Defendant was pepper sprayed.
4. I am informed and believe that during this investigation Defendant did not give consent for officers to enter his home as alleged in police reports. Defendant did not resist arrest as alleged, and officers used excessive force against Defendant in violation of department policy.
5. The officer records are relevant and material because a substantial issue in the trial of this case may include dishonesty/truthfulness, illegal search and seizure, and not performing duties legally by the officers involved, as well as their credibility.
6. The materials requested are necessary for the proper preparation of this case for trial so as to locate and investigate witnesses to the character, habits, and customs of the peace officer involved to show that the peace officer acted in conformity with that character at the time of this incident and to impeach the testimony of the peace officer.
7. Declarant is informed and believes and alleges that said records are presently within the custody of the agency or agencies listed above, and Defendant has no other means to secure said information.

I declare that the foregoing is true and correct to the best of my knowledge and belief.

Dated:

_____
By   Roger Lampkin,
Attorney for Doug Donenabbed

c.Motion for Lineup

Note: If a motion for lineup is appropriate in a given case, the motion should be filed as soon as possible. Otherwise, the court can deny it as untimely. There is no hardline rule, but the motion should generally be filed prior to the preliminary hearing.

ROGER LAMPKIN
SB#113786
1234 L Street
Bakersfield, CA 93301
Tel: (661)633-1234
Fax: (661)863-6741
Attorney for Doug Donenabbed

IN THE SUPERIOR COURT OF THE STATE OF CALIFORNIA,

IN AND FOR THE COUNTY OF KERN

People of the State of California,	CASE NO. 123456
Plaintiffs,	MOTION FOR LINEUP BEFORE WITNESS
- v. -	FRED FRENCH
Doug Donenabbed,	DATE: October 16, 2019 TIME: 8:30 a.m.
Defendant	DEPT: CC

TO THE COURT, THE DISTRICT ATTORNEY, THE KERN COUNTY SHERIFF, AND COUNTY COUNSEL:
   PLEASE TAKE NOTICE that at the date and time indicated above, or as soon thereafter as the matter can be heard in the above-entitled court, the Defendant in this matter will move for an order directing the District Attorney of Kern County and the Kern County Sheriff to conduct a physical lineup in which the defendant will be exhibited to a witness in this case, Fred French.

   This motion is made on the grounds that evidence of eyewitness identification is a material issue in this case and there exists a reasonable likelihood of mistaken identification, which a lineup would tend to resolve.

The motion will be based on this notice of motion, all attached documents, the records on file in this action, and on such matters as may be presented at the hearing.

Dated:

_____

By   Roger Lampkin,
      Attorney for Doug Donenabbed

DECLARATION IN SUPPORT OF MOTION

I, Roger Lampkin, declare as follows:

1. I am the attorney representing the defendant in this action.
2. Fred French allegedly witnessed someone fleeing from the scene of a murder carrying an assault rifle. Mr. French ducked into a bush as soon as he noticed the rifle. Mr. French eventually selected Defendant from a six-pack lineup, and Defendant was arrested and charged.
3. Eyewitness identification is a material issue in this case because there is no substantial evidence to establish that the Defendant was the perpetrator of the crime charged, other than eyewitness testimony.
4. There exists a reasonable likelihood of mistaken identification in this case because the eyewitness did not have a sufficient opportunity to observe the suspect, because of the nature of the offense charged and the allegation that a weapon was used. The eyewitness was subjected to pressures at the time of the incident that would affect his ability to identify a suspect.
5. Your declarant believes that a lineup should be conducted while the incident is fresh in the mind of the eyewitness. At the preliminary hearing and at trial the defendant will be seated next to me at counsel table. Before the witness is subjected to a confrontation that is inherently suggestive or will reinforce a mistaken identification in his mind, a properly conducted physical lineup may remedy this danger.
6. Research has shown that there are certain lineup conditions which can increase the fairness and reliability of a lineup, such as exhibiting the subjects of the lineup in a sequential fashion, that is, displayed one at a time, rather than all at the same time. When compared to the traditional simultaneous lineup procedure, empirical studies show that sequential lineups produce a significantly lower rate of mistaken identifications.
7. Studies have shown that a witness looking at a simultaneous lineup is likely, despite any cautions, to want to pick someone. In so doing they are likely to pick the person who most closely resembles the actual

perpetrator even if it is not the actual perpetrator.

8. This appears to be the error in the instant case in that the witness's description of the suspect significantly differs from Defendant's physique.

9. This tendency to select someone from the suspects presented is because the judgment that is made is a relative one. Sequential lineups, by contrast, encourage witnesses to make absolute judgments, that is, compare a single face in a lineup to their memory, instead of deciding which of the several faces in the lineup most resembles the memory trace.

10. The defendant is currently in custody, confined at the Kern County Jail. It is submitted that the lineup should be conducted by the Sheriff's Department at the jail where there is a pool of possible participants which will enhance the possibility for a proper lineup.

11. It is further submitted that a total of ten persons should be in the lineup to prevent the witness from falling into the mindset that the suspect is one of six, as is often shown in popular television shows. This would consist of Defendant and nine others of similar appearance.

I declare that I am informed and believe that the foregoing is true and correct.

Dated:

By   Roger Lampkin,
Attorney for Doug Donenabbed

POINTS, AUTHORITIES, AND ARGUMENT

The California Supreme Court concluded in *Evans v. Superior Court* (1974) 11 Cal. 3rd 617 (Evans) that "due process requires in an appropriate case that an accused, upon timely request therefor, be afforded a pretrial lineup in which witnesses to the alleged criminal conduct can participate. The right to a lineup arises, however, only when eyewitness identification is shown to be a material issue and there exists a reasonable likelihood of a mistaken identification which a lineup would tend to resolve." (Id. at 625)

The court also concluded that "[t]he questions whether eyewitness identification is a material issue and whether fundamental fairness requires a lineup in a particular case are inquiries which necessarily rest for determination within the broad discretion of the magistrate or trial judge." (Ibid.)

The court went on to note that the "motion should normally be made as soon after arrest or arraignment as practicable." (id. at 626)

The court recently reaffirmed these principals in *People v. Redd* (2010) 48 Cal.4th 691).

In *U.S. v. Wade* (1967) 388 U.S. 218 and *Gilbert v. California* (1967) 388 U.S. 263, the Supreme Court held that a pretrial lineup was a "critical stage" of the prosecution at which the accused was entitled to the presence of counsel. In *People v. Williams* (1971) 3 Cal. 3rd 853, 856, the California Supreme Court agreed.

A SEQUENTIAL DOUBLE BLIND LINEUP WILL ENHANCE THE POSSIBILITY OF A CORRECT IDENTIFICATION

Research has shown that there are certain lineup conditions which can increase the fairness and reliability of a lineup, such as exhibiting the subjects of the lineup in a sequential fashion, that is, displayed one at a time, rather than all at the same time. Further, the officers conducting the lineup should not know which suspect is associated with the matter under investigation (See, e.g. *United States v. Brown* (7th Cir. 2006) 471 F. 3rd 802, 804–05; *State v. Henderson* (2011) 208 N.J. 208, 248–49)

When compared to the traditional simultaneous lineup procedure, empirical studies show that sequential double-blind lineups produce a significantly lower rate of mistaken identifications.

Studies have shown that a witness looking at a simultaneous lineup is likely, despite any cautions, to want to pick someone. In so doing they are likely to pick the person who most closely resembles the actual perpetrator even if it is not the actual perpetrator. The judgment that is made is a relative one. Sequential lineups, by contrast encourage witnesses to make absolute judgments, that is, compare a single face in a lineup to their memory, instead of deciding which of the several faces in the lineup most resembles the memory trace. (See R.C.L. Lindsay & Gary L. Wells, *Improving Eyewitness Identification from Lineups: Simultaneous Versus Sequential Lineup Presentations* (1985) 70 J. Applied Psychology 556; Nancy Steblay, Jennifer Dysart, Solomon Fulero & R.C.L. Lindsay, *Eyewitness Accuracy Rates in Sequential and Simultaneous Lineup Presentations: A Meta–Analytic Comparison* (2001) 25 L. & Human Behavior 459; Jacqueline McMurtrie, *The Role of Social Sciences in Preventing Wrongful Convictions* (2005) 42 Am.Crim. L.Rev. 1271; Amy Klobuchar, Nancy K. Mehrkens Steblay & Hilary Lindell

Caliguri, *Improving Eyewitness Identifications: Hennepin County's Blind Sequential Lineup Pilot Project* (2006) 4 Cardozo Pub.L. Policy & Ethics J. 381)

To further ensure accuracy, the witness should not be told how many persons he will be viewing; rather, he should be instructed:

> In a few moments, some individuals will be shown to you one at a time. Each person will be assigned a number and will be referred to only by number. Each will be asked to do certain things, such as turn. The person who committed the crime may or may not be included. While looking at the individuals, keep in mind that the individuals may not appear exactly as they did on the date of the crime. Their hairstyles, facial hair, clothing, etc., may have changed. The investigation will continue whether or not you make any identification. The officer conducting the lineup does not know which individual is a possible suspect. After each individual, the officer will ask you "Is this a person who robbed you?" Take your time answering the question. If you answer "yes", the officer will then ask you, "Can you describe in your own words how confident you are of the identification?" Even if you identify someone, the officer will continue to show you all of the individuals. Do you understand the procedure and other instructions I have given you?

Practical Tip:

Learn Google search tricks. Sometimes the answer you need is as close as Google. Google has powerful operators to help find exactly what you are looking for. These are some of those operators:

"This and that"	Answer has the exact phrase in the quotes
Paralegal **93301**	Answer has paralegal in zip code 93301
Paralegal **or** LDA	Answer has paralegal or an LDA
Paralegal **and** LDA	Answer has paralegal and LDA
Paralegal **+**free	Answer must have the word free
Paralegal -free	Answer cannot have the word free
Site:msn.com law	Answer is limited to the site msn.com
Filetype:pdf limine	Answer is limited to pdf files
Related:msn.com	Answer is sites similar to msn.com
"Fred * Rogers"	Answer can have words in between Fred and Rogers

d. Motion for Confidential Phone Calls

ROGER LAMPKIN
SB#113786
1234 L Street
Bakersfield, CA 93301
Tel: (661)633-1234
Fax: (661)863-6741
Attorney for Doug Donenabbed

IN THE SUPERIOR COURT OF THE STATE OF CALIFORNIA, IN AND FOR THE COUNTY OF KERN

People of the State of California, Plaintiffs, - v. - Doug Donenabbed, Defendant	CASE NO. 123456 DEFENDANT DOUG DONENABBED'S MOTION FOR CONFIDENTIAL PHONE CALLS Date: August 2, 2022 Time: 8:30 a.m. Dept: CC

TO THE COURT, THE KERN COUNTY SHERIFF, AND COUNTY COUNSEL: PLEASE TAKE NOTICE that at the date and time indicated above, the defendant will move the court for an order directing the Sheriff of Kern County to remove the restrictions on the defendant's right to communicate confidentially with, and have access to, members of his defense team.

This motion will be made on the grounds that unless such private communications are guaranteed, the defendant will be deprived of the right to counsel under Article I, §15 of the California Constitution and the Sixth and Fourteenth Amendments to the United States Constitution.

The motion will be based on this notice of motion, all attached documents, the records on file in this action, and on such matters as may be presented at the hearing.

Dated: _____   _____

By   Roger Lampkin,
      Attorney for Doug Donenabbed

SUMMARY OF RELIEF SOUGHT

By this motion, Defendant requests an order that Defendant shall be allowed unpaid, unmonitored telephone calls to his attorney and other persons designated by counsel to assist in the defense, which includes calls to private investigators, paralegals, secretaries, and/or experts.

These members of the defense team are not named here because the Prosecution does not have a right to know their identity, but their phone numbers will be added to the attached Proposed Order after the granting of this motion.

MEMORANDUM OF POINTS AND AUTHORITIES

Defendant is currently housed in the Kern County jail where he is only allowed collect or prepaid calls, and those calls are monitored, even when calling a law firm or member of the defense team. Even if the calls were not monitored, Defendant is indigent as previously determined by this Court, so he does not have his own money to prepay for calls. Further, the jail phone system does not allow collect calls to the telephone services used by Defendant's attorney. This has resulted in Defendant having virtually no communication with members of his defense team.

Defense counsel has a "duty to consult with the defendant on important decisions and to keep the defendant informed of important developments in the course of the prosecution" (*Strickland v. Washington* (1984) 466 U.S. 668, 688)

The right of access to counsel is an essential component of the right of access to the courts. (*Bounds v. Smith* (1977) 430 U.S. 817). This right is possessed not only by convicted prisoners, but by pretrial detainees who are jailed pending trial. (*U.S. ex rel. George v. Lane* (7th Cir. 1981) 718 F. 2nd 226, 230; *Lock v. Jenkins* (1981) 641 F. 2nd 488, 489.

Starting "from the premise that telephone communication is essential for inmate contact with attorneys," the court in *In re Grimes* (1989) 208 Cal. App. 3rd 1175 upheld a trial court order that the local jail must provide inmates a cost-free telephone line to the public defender's office. The court reasoned that the use of a collect-calls only system "unreasonably restricts communications between inmates at the jail and their attorneys." Jail regulations restricting pretrial detainees' contact with their attorneys are unconstitutional where they "unjustifiably obstruct the availability of professional representation." (*Benjamin v. Fraser* (2nd Cir. 2001) 264 F. 3rd

175, 178).

"[P]rison administrators are in the best position to control inmates but this control cannot violate statutory or constitutional right (citation) Thus, the courts' traditional deference to administrative expertise in prison matters does not foreclose judicial intervention to remedy statutory or constitutional violations." (*In re Grimes* (1989) 208 Cal. App. 3rd 1175).

An inmate is entitled to "confidential consultation with attorneys" (*15 CCR §1068*). An in-custody defendant must be allowed "reasonable access to a telephone" (*15 CCR §1067*). Confidentiality rules apply not only to the attorney, but also to private investigators, paralegals, attorney employees, and other persons assisting in the defense (*15 CCR §3178*).

Jail procedures and regulations must be implemented so as not to invalidate a constitutional right. The standards set forth in Title 15 "constitute contemporary notions of decency and are advisory in nature," but the courts do not rely blindly on these standards as fixing constitutional minima. (*Inmates of the Riverside County Jail v. Clark* (1983) 144 Cal. App. 3rd 850, 860).

Defendant is allowed telephone calls now, so there is obviously no security or penological issue regarding Defendant's use of the telephone. Defendant has been deemed to be indigent, and he receives the services of counsel at no cost to him. Therefore, there appears to be no logical or legal reason to charge defendant for calls to the defense team or in having those calls monitored.

→••Ω••←

Practical Tip:
Start your own library. Collect sample pleadings, such as those found in this book. Whenever you draft any type of document that is new to you, keep a copy in your own personal library so you can reference it later. If you get a well-written document from another firm, add it to your library. If you are asked to write a pleading that is not already in your personal library, ask others at your firm if they have something similar to what you've been asked to prepare. Your library will help you on future projects.

It is best to have your library on the computer in pre-formatted pleadings, but pleadings you receive in paper form can be saved in a binder and typed into the computer as time permits. Retyping pleadings provided by others will help you improve your typing and formatting skills but it will also give you the opportunity to check and update the legal authorities in the pleadings, which will help you improve your legal research skills.

ROGER LAMPKIN
SB#113786
1234 L Street
Bakersfield, CA 93301
Tel: (661)633-1234
Fax: (661)863-6741
Attorney for Doug Donenabbed

IN THE SUPERIOR COURT OF THE STATE OF CALIFORNIA,

IN AND FOR THE COUNTY OF KERN

People of the State of California,	CASE NO. 123456
Plaintiffs,	[PROPOSED] CONFIDENTIAL ORDER
- v. -	
Doug Donenabbed,	
Defendant	

TO THE KERN COUNTY SHERIFF: YOU ARE HEREBY ORDERED:
To allow Doug Donenabbed free, unmonitored telephone calls to each of the following phone numbers:

_____

You may place reasonable restrictions on the time, length, and number of such calls by informing Doug Donenabbed and his attorney of any such restrictions.

You are further ordered to maintain the confidentiality of those numbers and this order so as to not allow anyone involved in the prosecution of this case to gain access to those numbers.

Dated: _____

By   Judge of the Superior Court

e. Motion for Outside Medical Care

ROGER LAMPKIN
SB#113786
1234 L Street
Bakersfield, CA 93301
Tel: (661)633-1234
Fax: (661)863-6741
Attorney for Doug Donenabbed

IN THE SUPERIOR COURT OF THE STATE OF CALIFORNIA,

IN AND FOR THE COUNTY OF KERN

People of the State of California,	CASE NO. 123456
Plaintiffs,	DEFENDANT DOUG DONENABBED'S MOTION FOR RELEASE FROM CUSTODY FOR MEDICAL CARE [Health & Safety Code §11479]
- v. -	
Doug Donenabbed,	
Defendant	Date: August 2, 2022 Time: 8:30 a.m. Dept: CC
	Readiness: August 12, 2022 Trial: August 22, 2022

TO THE COURT AND THE DISTRICT ATTORNEY OF KERN COUNTY: PLEASE TAKE NOTICE that Defendant moves the Court an order dismissing the instant action because of the loss of significant exculpatory evidence.

This motion is made on the ground that the prosecution failed to provide Defendant with exculpatory evidence in the constructive hands of the prosecuting attorney and the prosecution team destroyed evidence.

The motion will be based on this Notice of Motion, on the attached memorandum of points and authorities and filed herewith and such supplemental memorandum of points and authorities that may be hereafter filed with the court or stated orally at the conclusion of the hearing, on all papers and records on file in this action and on such oral and documentary evidence as may be presented at the time of the motion.

Dated: _____

By   Roger Lampkin,
Attorney for Doug Donenabbed

MEMORANDUM OF POINTS AND AUTHORITIES

Upon a proper showing, "that a prisoner confined in any city or county jail within the jurisdiction of the court requires medical or surgical treatment necessitating hospitalization, which treatment cannot be furnished or supplied at such city or county jail, the court in its discretion may order the removal of such person or persons from such city or county jail to the county hospital in such county" (*Penal Code §4011*). A "prisoner may decline such care or treatment and provide other care and treatment for himself at his own expense." (id.)

"In the event a prisoner elects to decline treatment by the county or city jail physician and to provide medical treatment at his own expense, the sheriff or chief of police may have him removed from the county or city jail to a privately owned and operated medical facility or hospital located in the county approved by a judge of the superior court for such treatment." (*Penal Code §4023*)

Penal Code §4011 calls for the sheriff, other official in charge of correctional facilities, or the district attorney to make the initial showing that outside medical care is needed. However, *Code of Civil Procedure §128*, which is applicable to criminal cases (see *People v. Jackson* (1996) 13 Cal.4th 1164) acknowledges the Court's broad powers, including the power "To control in furtherance of justice, the conduct of its ministerial officers, and of all other persons in any manner connected with a judicial proceeding before it, in every matter pertaining thereto." (subsection (a)(5)).

This power includes the power to order ministerial officers who are not a party to the proceedings to change their procedures (Adams v. Superior Court of San Diego County (1974) 12 Cal.3rd 55),

Therefore, the Court can exercise control over "the sheriff or other official in charge of county correctional facilities or district attorney" and require them to conform to the provisions of *Penal Code §4011* if sufficient evidence is presented to satisfy the Court that an inmate, "requires medical or surgical treatment necessitating hospitalization, which treatment cannot be furnished or supplied at such city or county jail…"

In the instant case, Defendant suffers from kidney failure and needs dialysis, which is unavailable to Defendant while in custody.

f. Public Records Act

ROGER LAMPKIN
SB#113786
1234 L Street
Bakersfield, CA 93301
Tel: (661)633-1234
Fax: (661)863-6741
Attorney for Doug Donenabbed

IN THE SUPERIOR COURT OF THE STATE OF CALIFORNIA,

IN AND FOR THE COUNTY OF KERN

People of the State of California,	CASE NO. 123456
Plaintiffs,	PUBLIC RECORDS ACT REQUEST
- v. -	
Doug Donenabbed,	
Defendant	

TO THE KERN COUNTY SHERIFF AND THE CHIEF PROBATION
OFFICER OF KERN COUNTY:

Pursuant to the California Public Records Act, I request a copy of the
records detailed below on behalf of my client, Doug Donenabbed. The
records are desired to help researching and determine what programs may
be available to my client, at what cost, and with what restrictions. To that
end, I request the following records:

1. Electronic Monitoring Program Policies:

All policies and guidelines for the county's administration of electronic
monitoring programs. This includes but is not limited to information
relating to program entry, medical or other restrictions on entry,
supervision standards, guidelines for issuing and responding to
violations, guidelines for damaged or malfunctioning equipment, and
program completion standards.

2. Work Release Program Policies:

   All policies and guidelines for the county's administration of any work release programs. This includes but is not limited to information relating to program entry, medical or other restrictions on entry, supervision standards, guidelines for issuing and responding to violations, guidelines for damaged or malfunctioning equipment, and program completion standards.

3. Community Service Program Policies:

   All policies and guidelines for the county's administration of any community service or volunteer programs. This includes but is not limited to information relating to program entry, medical or other restrictions on entry, supervision standards, guidelines for issuing and responding to violations, guidelines for damaged or malfunctioning equipment, and program completion standards.

4. Parole Program Policies:

   All policies and guidelines for the county's administration of any Sheriff's Parole or other early release program. This includes but is not limited to information relating to program entry, medical or other restrictions on entry, supervision standards, guidelines for issuing and responding to violations, guidelines for damaged or malfunctioning equipment, and program completion standards.

5. Inmate Labor Program Policies:

   All policies and guidelines for the county's administration of any inmate labor or other program allowing or requiring inmates to perform work while in custody. This includes but is not limited to information relating to program entry, medical or other restrictions on entry, supervision standards, guidelines for issuing and responding to violations, guidelines for damaged or malfunctioning equipment, and program completion standards.

6. Statistical Information:

   Statistical information related to all persons currently participating in any of the programs described above, including, but not limited to age, sex, and race of participants in the programs or equivalent data that can be used for statistical purposes, such as a complete list of participants along with age, sex, and race, or periodic summaries of such data for any given month this year.

Please note that the Public Records Act allows a member of the public to request records by describing their content, rather than asking for specific documents by name; an agency that receives such a request must "search for records based on criteria set forth in the search request." (*California First Amendment Coalition v. Superior Court*, 67 Cal.App.4th 159, 165-66 (1998)) This request applies to all records in your agencies' possession, including documents created by a member of another government agency or a member of the public (*California State University v. Superior Court*, 90 Cal. App. 4th 810, 824-25 (1999)) If specific portions of any documents are exempt from disclosure, please provide the non-exempt portions. (*Government Code § 6253(a)*).

Please provide entire documents, even if only parts of them are responsive to this request. If you maintain records or data in electronic format, please provide them in that same format (locked versions are acceptable) to avoid copying costs (*Government Code §6253.9*)

If you are unable to reproduce electronic records in electronic form, please provide a reason for doing so.

I request that you waive copying fees, if any, because the court has determined that Doug Donenabbed is indigent and this case was assigned to me through the county's Indigent Defense Program, so any charges made by the county for these records would be paid by the county. If you are unable to waive the copying fees, and you anticipate that these costs will exceed $50, or that the time needed to copy the records will delay their release, please contact my office so that I can arrange to inspect the document or decide which documents we wish to have copied.

Otherwise, please copy and send them as soon as possible.

Please respond to this request within ten days, either by providing all the requested records or by providing a written response setting forth the legal authority for withholding or redacting any document and stating when the documents will be made available. (*Government Code §§ 6253(c), 6255*). If you require any clarification in identifying responsive documents or focusing this request, (*Government Code §§ 6253(c), 6255*), please contact my office at the number again.

Please send all records responsive to this request to the address listed above.

Thank you for your time and attention to this matter.

Dated: _____

By   Roger Lampkin,
     Attorney for Doug Donenabbed

g. Defendant's Motion to Quash Protective Order

ROGER LAMPKIN
SB#113786
1234 L Street
Bakersfield, CA 93301
Tel: (661)633-1234
Fax: (661)863-6741
Attorney for Doug Donenabbed

IN THE SUPERIOR COURT OF THE STATE OF CALIFORNIA,

IN AND FOR THE COUNTY OF KERN

People of the State of California,	CASE NO. 123456
Plaintiffs,	DOUG DONENABBED'S MOTION TO QUASH PROTECTIVE ORDER
- v. -	
Doug Donenabbed,	Date: August 2, 2022 Time: 8:30 a.m.
Defendant	Dept: CC
	Readiness: August 12, 2022 Trial: August 22, 2022

TO THE COURT AND THE DISTRICT ATTORNEY: PLEASE TAKE NOTICE that at the date and time indicated above, or as soon thereafter as the matter can be heard, Defendant will move the Court for an order quashing the protective order issued in this case in favor of Mary Moore.

This motion shall be based on this Notice of Motion, all papers and pleadings on file with the court and such oral and documentary evidence as may be presented at the hearing.

Dated: _____

_____

By   Roger Lampkin,
Attorney for Doug Donenabbed

POINTS, AUTHORITIES, AND ARGUMENT

Penal Code §136.2 allows the Court to issue and maintain protective orders in domestic violence cases for good cause shown. There is no longer good cause in the instant case in that the alleged victim, Mary Moore, has requested removal of the order.

DECLARATION OF MARY MOORE

I, Mary Moore, declare:

I am the wife of Doug Donenabbed, Defendant herein.

I did not request the protective order issued in this case, and I did not ask for charges to be filed. I do not want a protective order, and I ask the court to lift it.

I declare under penalty of perjury that the foregoing is true and correct, and that this declaration was executed in Bakersfield, California on July 2, 2022.

Dated: _____

_____

By   Mary Moore

→••Ω••←

Practical Tip:
Tell the client twice and write it down.

Judges don't like it when a defendant misses court, but some defendants don't appear to take their court dates seriously. A paralegal should help clients understand the importance of going to court on time. Tell clients when they have court, write down the date, time, and location, and then tell them again. It is also helpful to show clients how to look up case information on the court's computer system because this will sometime prevent repeated phone calls from clients who forget dates.

h. Motion by Alleged Victim to Quash Protective Order

Mary Moore
1234 Main Street
Bakersfield, CA 93309
Tel: (661)555-1212

IN THE SUPERIOR COURT OF THE STATE OF CALIFORNIA,

IN AND FOR THE COUNTY OF KERN

People of the State of California,	CASE NO. 123456
Plaintiffs,	MARY MOORE'S MOTION TO QUASH PROTECTIVE ORDER
- v. -	Date: August 2, 2022 Time: 8:30 a.m.
Doug Donenabbed,	Dept: CC
Defendant	

TO THE COURT AND THE DISTRICT ATTORNEY: PLEASE TAKE NOTICE that at the date and time indicated above, or as soon thereafter as the matter can be heard, the alleged victim in this matter, Mary Moore, will move the Court for an order quashing the protective order in her favor.

This motion shall be based on this Notice of Motion, all papers and pleadings on file with the court and such oral and documentary evidence as may be presented at the hearing.

Dated: _____   _____

By   Mary Moore

POINTS, AUTHORITIES, AND ARGUMENT

Penal Code §136.2 allows the Court to issue and maintain protective orders in domestic violence cases for good cause shown. There is no longer good cause in the instant case in that the alleged victim, Mary Moore, has requested removal of the order.

DECLARATION OF MARY MOORE

I, Mary Moore, declare:

I am the wife of Doug Donenabbed, Defendant herein.

I did not request the protective order issued in this case, and I did not ask for charges to be filed. I do not want a protective order, and I ask the court to lift it.

I declare under penalty of perjury that the foregoing is true and correct, and that this declaration was executed in Bakersfield, California on July 2, 2022.

Dated: _____

By   Mary Moore

i. Motion for Conditional Examination

ROGER LAMPKIN
SB#113786
1234 L Street
Bakersfield, CA 93301
Tel: (661)633-1234
Fax: (661)863-6741
Attorney for Doug Donenabbed

IN THE SUPERIOR COURT OF THE STATE OF CALIFORNIA,

IN AND FOR THE COUNTY OF KERN

People of the State of California,	CASE NO. 123456
Plaintiffs,	DEFENDANT DOUG DONENABBED'S MOTION FOR CONDITIONAL EXAMINATION
- v. -	
Doug Donenabbed,	Date: August 2, 2022
Defendant	Time: 8:30 a.m.
	Dept: CC
	Readiness: August 12, 2022
	Trial: August 22, 2022

TO THE COURT AND THE DISTRICT ATTORNEY OF KERN COUNTY: PLEASE TAKE NOTICE that Defendant moves the Court an order for conditional examination of John Jones, a material witness in this matter, pursuant to *Penal Code §1335* et seq., such conditional examination to take place at a date, time, and place to be determined by the Court at the hearing on this motion.

The motion will be based on this Notice of Motion, on the attached memorandum of points and authorities and filed herewith and such supplemental memorandum of points and authorities that may be hereafter filed with the court or stated orally at the conclusion of the hearing, on all papers and records on file in this action and on such oral and documentary evidence as may be presented at the time of the motion.

Dated: _____

By   Roger Lampkin,
      Attorney for Doug Donenabbed

MEMORANDUM OF POINTS AND AUTHORITIES

Penal Code §1336(a) specifies that, "When a material witness for the defendant, or for the people, is about to leave the state, or is so sick or infirm as to afford reasonable grounds for apprehension that he or she will be unable to attend the trial, or is a person 65 years of age or older, or a dependent adult, the defendant or the people may apply for an order that the witness be examined conditionally."

"The defendant has the right to be present in person and with counsel at such examination...." (*Penal Code §1340*)

"The deposition ... may be read in evidence, or if the examination was video-recorded, ... shown by either party at the trial if the court finds that the witness is unavailable as a witness within the meaning of Section 240 of the Evidence Code." (*Penal Code §1345*)

The court has broad discretion to grant a defendant's request for a conditional examination of a witness. (*People v. Jurado* (2006) 38 Cal.4th 72, 114, *People v. Williams* (2016) 1 Cal. 5th 1166)

DECLARATION OF COUNSEL

I, Roger Lampkin, declare:

1. I am an attorney at law and am the attorney for the defendant in this case.

2. I am informed and believe that John Jones is a material witness in this case who will testify as follows: Mr. Jones was with Defendant on the day of the incident leading to his arrest. The two of them were at Lake Isabella, nearly sixty miles from the alleged crime scene. Defendant, therefore, could not have committed the charged offense.

3. I have reasonable grounds for apprehension that this witness will be unable to attend the trial based on the following: Mr. Jones is 72 years old and suffers from high blood pressure, diabetes, and cancer.

I declare that I am informed and believe that the foregoing is true and correct.

Dated: _____

       By   Roger Lampkin,
            Attorney for Doug Donenabbed

→••Ω••←

Practical Tip:

If the prosecution has an expert, find a corresponding expert for the defense, and let the attorney decide whether the expert can be used. Glen "Ace" Pierce, gave a good example of the importance of experts:

"I was appointed on a gang case where everyone appeared to agree that the defendant was an associate of a gang – even I opined that he was a gang associate. However, that's not the end of the inquiry. The crime alleged also has to be committed for the benefit of a gang. Our guy possessed meth and he had a gun, but the meth was a small quantity, so he was only charged with possession while armed - not drug sales. I, therefore, gave the opinion that possession of drugs for personal use could in no way benefit the gang. Even the prosecution experts agreed, so our guy was convicted of possession while armed, but he avoided the long prison sentence associated with the gang charges. Without evidence from an expert, he was a goner."

Glen "Ace" Pierce, Gang Expert and Private Investigator (661)633-4039

j. Motion to Release Mental Health Records

ROGER LAMPKIN
SB#113786
1234 L Street
Bakersfield, CA 93301
Tel: (661)633-1234
Fax: (661)863-6741
Attorney for Doug Donenabbed

IN THE SUPERIOR COURT OF THE STATE OF CALIFORNIA,

IN AND FOR THE COUNTY OF KERN

People of the State of California,	CASE NO. 123456
Plaintiffs,	DEFENDANT DOUG DONENABBED'S MOTION FOR RELEASE OF MENTAL HEALTH RECORDS
- v. -	
Doug Donenabbed,	Date: August 2, 2022
Defendant	Time: 8:30 a.m. Dept: CC
	Readiness: August 12, 2022 Trial: August 22, 2022

TO THE COURT, DR. ED SHRINK, VICKY VICK, AND THE DISTRICT ATTORNEY OF KERN COUNTY: PLEASE TAKE NOTICE that at the date and time indicated above, or as soon thereafter as the matter can be heard in the above-entitled court, the defendant will move for an order requiring Dr. Ed Shrink to disclose mental health records related to Vicky Vick.

The motion will be based on the grounds the records contain exculpatory evidence and are material to the defense.

The motion will be based on this Notice of Motion, on the attached memorandum of points and authorities and filed herewith and such supplemental memorandum of points and authorities that may be hereafter filed with the court or stated orally at the conclusion of the hearing, on all papers and records on file in this action and on such oral and documentary

evidence as may be presented at the time of the motion.
Dated: _____

By   Roger Lampkin,
     Attorney for Doug Donenabbed

MEMORANDUM OF POINTS AND AUTHORITIES

"In California, as in all other states, statements made by a patient to a
psychotherapist during therapy are generally treated as confidential and
enjoy the protection of a psychotherapist-patient privilege." (*People v.
Gonzales* (2013) 56 Cal.4th 353, 371). This privilege has been protected by
Evidence Code §1014, which recognizes a patient's "privilege to refuse to
disclose, and to prevent another from disclosing, a confidential
communication between patient and psychotherapist."

However, "There is no privilege under this article if the services of the
psychotherapist were sought or obtained to enable or aid anyone to commit
or plan to commit a crime or a tort or to escape detection or apprehension
after the commission of a crime or a tort" (*Evidence Code §1018*), and "There
is no privilege under this article if the psychotherapist has reasonable cause
to believe that the patient is in such mental or emotional condition as to be
dangerous to himself or to the person or property of another and that
disclosure of the communication is necessary to prevent the threatened
danger" (*Evidence Code §1024*); thus, if a patient intends to commit perjury
or presents a danger of unlawfully causing harm to Defendant, there is no
privilege.

In *People v. Hammon* (1997) 15 Cal. 4th 1117, 1128, the California Supreme
Court declined to "extend the defendant's Sixth Amendment rights of
confrontation and cross-examination to authorize pretrial disclosure of
privileged information." However, the court also recognized that "[w]hen a
defendant proposes to impeach a critical prosecution witness with questions
that call for privileged information, the trial court may be called upon ... to
balance the defendant's need for cross-examination and the state policies
the privilege is intended to serve. [Citation.]" (Id. at p. 1127.)

A defendant in a criminal case has a limited right under the confrontation
clause to require witnesses "to answer questions that call for information
protected by state-created evidentiary privileges." (*Hammon*, supra, at 1123-
1124, citing *Davis v. Alaska* (1974) 415 U.S. 308.)

Penal Code §1326 authorizes a defendant to issue a subpoena for
documents in accordance with *Evidence Code §1560*. *Penal Code §1326(c)*

provides in part, "When a defendant has issued a subpoena to a person or entity that is not a party for the production of books, papers, documents, or records, or copies thereof, the court may order an in camera hearing to determine whether or not the defense is entitled to receive the documents. The court may not order the documents disclosed to the prosecution except as required by Section 1054.3."

In the instant case, the defense has subpoenaed records from Ed Shrink, which have been delivered to the Court under seal. Defendant contends that the records are exculpatory in that they will show that the alleged victim, Vicky Vick, suffers from delusions and substance abuse problems.

An in camera review of the records is, therefore, requested.

6. Plea and Sentence

a. Motion to Enforce Plea Agreement

ROGER LAMPKIN
SB#113786
1234 L Street
Bakersfield, CA 93301
Tel: (661)633-1234
Fax: (661)863-6741
Attorney for Doug Donenabbed

IN THE SUPERIOR COURT OF THE STATE OF CALIFORNIA,
IN AND FOR THE COUNTY OF KERN

People of the State of California,	CASE NO. 123456
Plaintiffs,	MOTION TO ENFORCE PLEA AGREEMENT
- v. -	Date: August 2, 2022
Doug Donenabbed,	Time: 8:30 a.m.
Defendant	Dept: CC

TO THE COURT AND THE DISTRICT ATTORNEY: PLEASE TAKE NOTICE that at the date and time indicated above, or as soon thereafter as the matter can be heard in the above-entitled court, the defendant will move for an order to enforce the plea agreement.

The motion will be made on the ground that Defendant entered a negotiated plea, a term of which included that he would serve a sentence of no more than five years in custody.

The motion will be based on this notice of motion, all attached documents, the records on file in this action, and on such matters as may be presented at the hearing.

Dated:

_____
By   Roger Lampkin,
      Attorney for Doug Donenabbed

STATEMENT OF THE CASE

Defendant entered a negotiated plea with the provision that he serves no more than five years in custody. The probation department calculated the amount of time required for the counts and enhancements in the plea agreement and arrived at a minimum sentence of seven years.

Defendant requests that the Court sentence Defendant to the agreed upon term and suggests that this can be accomplished by striking the two-year *Penal Code §12022.1* "on-bail enhancement."

POINTS, AUTHORITIES, & ARGUMENT

"When a guilty plea is entered in exchange for specified benefits such as the dismissal of other counts or an agreed maximum punishment, both parties, including the state, must abide by the terms of the agreement. The punishment may not significantly exceed that which the parties agreed upon." (*People v. Walker* (1991) 54 Cal. 3rd 1013, 1024). When a plea rests in any significant degree on a prosecutor's promise or agreement, so that it is part of the inducement or consideration, the promise must be fulfilled. (*Santobello v. New York* (1971) 404 U.S. 257, 262); *Walker*, supra, at 1024.)

The requirements of due process attach to the plea bargain itself. (id.)

A negotiated plea agreement is in the nature of a contract and is interpreted according to general contract principles. The trial court's approval of the agreement binds the court to the terms of the bargain and the defendant's sentence must be within the negotiated terms of the agreement. (*People v. Martin* (2010) 51 Cal.4th 75, 79).

An implied term of a plea agreement is that a defendant will not be adversely affected by the underlying facts solely pertaining to a dismissed count. (*Martin*, supra, 81; *People v. Harvey* (1979) 25 Cal. 3rd 754, 758.)

b. Motion for Misdemeanor Diversion

ROGER LAMPKIN
SB#113786
1234 L Street
Bakersfield, CA 93301
Tel: (661)633-1234
Fax: (661)863-6741
Attorney for Doug Donenabbed

IN THE SUPERIOR COURT OF THE STATE OF CALIFORNIA,
IN AND FOR THE COUNTY OF KERN

People of the State of California,	CASE NO. 123456
Plaintiffs,	DOUG DONENABBED'S MOTION FOR DIVERSION [Penal Code §§1001, 1001.50, et seq]
- v. -	
Doug Donenabbed,	Date: August 2, 2022 Time: 8:30 a.m.
Defendant	Dept: CC

TO THE COURT AND THE DISTRICT ATTORNEY: PLEASE TAKE NOTICE that at the date and time indicated above, Defendant will move the Court for an order for pretrial diversion.

This motion shall be based on this Notice of Motion, all papers and pleadings on file with the court and such oral and documentary evidence as may be presented at the hearing.

Dated:

_____

By   Roger Lampkin,
     Attorney for Doug Donenabbed

POINTS, AUTHORITIES, AND ARGUMENT

With limited exceptions, such as DUI cases, *Penal Code §§1001, 1001.50* et. seq. allows the Court to defer prosecution for misdemeanor defendants when:

    (1) The defendant's record does not indicate that probation or parole has ever been revoked without thereafter being completed.

    (2) The defendant's record does not indicate that he has been diverted pursuant to this chapter within five years prior to the filing of the accusatory pleading which charges the divertible offense. [and]

    (3) The defendant has never been convicted of a felony, and has not been convicted of a misdemeanor within five years prior to the filing of the accusatory pleading which charges the divertible offense.

(Penal Code §1001.51)

The district attorney of each county has authority to approve diversion programs, "and no program shall continue without the approval of the district attorney," but "Nothing in this subdivision shall authorize the prosecutor to determine whether a particular defendant shall be diverted." (*Penal Code §1001.50*). In other words, the Prosecution is vested with authority to establish diversion programs, but the Court is vested with sole discretion to divert individual misdemeanor defendants. The Prosecution's presence at diversion hearings is not even required (*75 Ops. Cal. Atty. Gen. 51*)

"At no time shall a defendant be required to make an admission of guilt as a prerequisite for placement in a pretrial diversion program." (*Penal Code §1001.3*)

"If the divertee has performed satisfactorily during the period of diversion, the criminal charges shall be dismissed at the end of the period of diversion." (*Penal Code §1001.7*)

In the instant case, Doug Donenabbed should be diverted for multiple reasons.

First, Mr. Donenabbed has never before been accused of a crime. He has lived the first fifty-two years of his life crime-free.

Second, the alleged victim, his wife, has requested that he not be prosecuted.

Third, prosecution would create a hardship and undue expense to Mr. Donenabbed, his wife, and his children in that he would have to spend time away from them during trial and any jail sentence.

Fourth, Mr. Donenabbed has already expressed remorse and voluntarily enrolled in domestic violence counseling and parenting classes.

c. Motion for Pre-Plea Probation Report

ROGER LAMPKIN
SB#113786
1234 L Street
Bakersfield, CA 93301
Tel: (661)633-1234
Fax: (661)863-6741
Attorney for Doug Donenabbed

IN THE SUPERIOR COURT OF THE STATE OF CALIFORNIA,
IN AND FOR THE COUNTY OF KERN

People of the State of California,	CASE NO. 123456
Plaintiffs,	MOTION FOR PRE-PLEA PROBATION REPORT [Penal Code §1203.7]
- v. -	
Doug Donenabbed,	Date: August 2, 2022 Time: 8:30 a.m.
Defendant	Dept: CC
	Readiness: August 12, 2022 Trial: August 22, 2022

TO THE COURT AND THE DISTRICT ATTORNEY OF KERN COUNTY: PLEASE TAKE NOTICE that Defendant moves the Court an order directing the Probation Department to prepare a pre-plea probation report pursuant to *Penal Code §1203.7*.

This motion will be made on the ground that such a report will provide the Court, Prosecution, and Defense with information that will aid in plea negotiations.

The motion will be based on this notice and attached papers, on all papers and records on file in this action and on such oral and documentary evidence as may be presented at the time of the motion.

Dated: _____

                By   Roger Lampkin,
                Attorney for Doug Donenabbed

MEMORANDUM OF POINTS AND AUTHORITIES

Penal Code §1203.10 calls for preparation of a probation report "At the time of the plea or verdict of guilty of any person over 18 years of age…" However, *Penal Code §1203.7(a)* allows for preparation of a probation report any time following arrest:

> Either at the time of the arrest for a crime of any person over 16 years of age, or at the time of the plea or verdict of guilty, the probation officer of the county of the jurisdiction of the crime shall, when so directed by the court, inquire into the antecedents, character, history, family environment and offense of that person. The probation officer shall report that information to the court and file a written report in the records of the court. The report shall contain his or her recommendation for or against the release of the person on probation.

"Although the court is not required to give reasons for requesting the pre-plea report, it is usually ordered when the parties and the court agree that it would help plea negotiations." (Rutter Group, *California Criminal Procedure*, 2020, §14:17). The defense believes a probation report could assist in plea negotiations and result in settlement of this matter.

Practical Tip:

Provide clients with regular status updates about their case as time permits. This does not mean calling or writing the client about every little detail, but frequent communication with clients helps reassure them that their legal team is interested in and working on their case. Let clients know when motions are filed in their case, when investigators and other expert witnesses are assigned to help on the case, when new discovery comes in, and when there are new developments in the case. Two or three updates a month can make a drastic impact on a client's faith in the defense team.

d. Request to Indicate Sentence

ROGER LAMPKIN
SB#113786
1234 L Street
Bakersfield, CA 93301
Tel: (661)633-1234
Fax: (661)863-6741
Attorney for Doug Donenabbed

IN THE SUPERIOR COURT OF THE STATE OF CALIFORNIA,
IN AND FOR THE COUNTY OF KERN

People of the State of California,	CASE NO. 123456
Plaintiffs,	DEFENDANT DOUG DONENABBED'S REQUEST FOR INDICATED SENTENCE
- v. -	
Doug Donenabbed,	Date: August 2, 2022 Time: 8:30 a.m.
Defendant	Dept: CC
	Readiness: August 12, 2022 Trial: August 22, 2022

TO THE COURT AND THE DISTRICT ATTORNEY OF KERN COUNTY: PLEASE TAKE NOTICE that at the date and time indicated above, or as soon thereafter as the matter can be heard in the above-entitled court, the defendant will request an indicated sentence from the Court.

The request will be based on this notice and the attached papers, on all papers and records on file in this action and on such oral and documentary evidence as may be presented at the time of the request.

Dated:

_____
By   Roger Lampkin,
      Attorney for Doug Donenabbed

ALLEGATIONS

Defendant is charged with felony domestic violence stemming from what appears to be mutual combat when both Mr. Donenabbed and his wife were intoxicated.

Ms. Donenabbed is only alleged to have suffered scrapes and bruises, and she did not receive medical care. Mr. Donenabbed has never before been accused of a crime, and the alleged victim has requested that he not be prosecuted.

Defendant is gainfully employed and is the primary source of support for his family, including his aging parents.

A prison sentence would create an extreme hardship to Mr. Donenabbed, his wife, and his children, and his parents.

Mr. Donenabbed has already expressed remorse and voluntarily entered a rehab facility and enrolled in domestic violence counseling.

MEMORANDUM OF POINTS AND AUTHORITIES

"Sentencing is a judicial function; and when the court seeks information in order to indicate a sentence, that is a judicial, not an executive, act. The executive branch, as we will conclude, may refuse to bargain in the sense of rejecting any reduction of the charge or objecting to any proposed sentence; but it usually has no right to interfere in the process of extending an indicated sentence to a defendant willing to plead guilty to all or part of an information or indictment." (*Bryce v. Superior Court* (1988) 205 Cal.App.3rd 671, fn. 2)

The imposition of a sentence "... constitutes an exercise of judicial authority within the meaning of the constitutional doctrine of separation of powers." (*People v. Superior Court* (1974) 11 Cal. 3rd 59, 68)

When giving an "indicated sentence," the trial court simply informs a defendant "what sentence he will impose if a given set of facts is confirmed, irrespective of whether guilt is adjudicated at trial or admitted by plea." (*People v. Superior Court* (1978) 82 Cal. App. 3rd 909, 915-916; *People v. Vergara* (1991) 230 Cal.App.3rd 1564, 1567-1568.)

e. Motion to Withdraw Plea

ROGER LAMPKIN
SB#113786
1234 L Street
Bakersfield, CA 93301
Tel: (661)633-1234
Fax: (661)863-6741
Attorney for Doug Donenabbed

IN THE SUPERIOR COURT OF THE STATE OF CALIFORNIA,
IN AND FOR THE COUNTY OF KERN

People of the State of California,	CASE NO. 123456
Plaintiffs,	DEFENDANT DOUG DONENABBED'S MOTION TO
- v. -	WITHDRAW PLEA
Doug Donenabbed,	Date: August 2, 2022 Time: 8:30 a.m.
Defendant	Dept: CC

TO THE COURT AND THE DISTRICT ATTORNEY: PLEASE TAKE NOTICE that on the date and time indicated above, the defendant will move for an order to withdrawing his no contest plea and enter a new and different plea.

The motion will be made on the ground that Defendant's plea was not knowing and voluntary.

The motion will be based on this Notice of Motion, on the attached memorandum of points and authorities and filed herewith and such supplemental memorandum of points and authorities that may be hereafter filed with the court or stated orally at the conclusion of the hearing, on all papers and records on file in this action and on such oral and documentary evidence as may be presented at the time of the motion.

Dated:

_____
By   Roger Lampkin,
     Attorney for Doug Donenabbed

DECLARATION OF COUNSEL

I, Roger Lampkin, declare:

1. I am an attorney at law and am the attorney for the defendant in this case.
2. I am informed and believe that Defendant will testify as follows:
   a. Defendant appeared in Division G of this court for arraignment. The Court instructed Defendant to speak to the man at the center table when his name was called, and Defendant did so, believing that the man was his public defender.
   b. The person Defendant actually spoke to was a probation officer who convinced Defendant to take a plea.
   c. Defendant would not have taken the plea had he been informed of his possible defenses.
3. Defendant's plea was, therefore, not knowing and voluntary.

I declare that the foregoing is true and correct.

Dated:

_____

By   Roger Lampkin,
     Attorney for Doug Donenabbed

MEMORANDUM OF POINTS AND AUTHORITIES

A defendant may move to withdraw a plea of guilty or no contest at any time before judgment upon a showing of good cause. *Penal Code §1018* provides in part:

> On application of the defendant at any time before judgment the court may, . . . for a good cause shown, permit the plea of guilty to be withdrawn and a plea of not guilty substituted.

"It has long been established that guilty pleas obtained through 'coercion, terror, inducements, subtle or blatant threats' are involuntary and violative of due process. [Citation.]" (*In re Ibarra* (1983) 34 Cal. 3rd 277, 287)

Such coercion is a particular danger in the package-deal plea bargain context. In *Ibarra*, the California Supreme Court discussed the coercive nature of "package-deal" plea bargains:

> " 'Package-deal' plea bargains ... may approach the line of unreasonableness. Extraneous factors not related to the case or

the prosecutor's business may be brought into play. For example, a defendant may fear that his wife will be prosecuted and convicted if he does not plead guilty; or, a defendant may fear, as alleged in this case, that his codefendant will attack him if he does not plead guilty. Because such considerations do not bear any direct relation to whether the defendant himself is guilty, special scrutiny must be employed to ensure a voluntary plea. '[P]lea bargaining of adverse or lenient treatment for some person other than the accused ... might pose a greater danger of inducing a false guilty plea....' [Citation.]"

(*Ibarra*, supra, at 287)

When determining the voluntariness of a plea entered pursuant to a package deal, "the nature and degree of coerciveness should be carefully examined." (*Ibarra*, supra, at 289)

The Ibarra court explained that a trial court should carefully scrutinize pleas in which the defendant shares a special relationship with a person who has been promised a benefit contingent on the defendant pleading guilty and those cases in which a third party has threatened the defendant:

"Psychological pressures sufficient to indicate an involuntary plea might be present if the third party promised leniency is a close friend or family member whom the defendant feels compelled to help. '[T]he voluntariness of a plea bargain which contemplates special concessions to another—especially a sibling or a loved one—bears particular scrutiny by a trial or reviewing court conscious of the psychological pressures upon an accused such a situation creates.' [Citation.] If the defendant bears no special relationship to the third party promised leniency, he may nevertheless feel compelled to plead guilty due to physical threat. For example, if the third party had made a specific threat against defendant if he refused to plead guilty, the plea is likely to be involuntary." (id.)

"[A] plea of guilty, entered under a misapprehension of some such material fact, but for which it would not have been made, cannot be considered a free and voluntary admission of guilt and a waiver of all defenses." (*Parker v. Johnston* (N.D. Ca. 1939) 29 F.Supp. 829)

Good cause to withdraw a plea is shown if a defendant did not exercise free judgment in entering into a plea, such as entering a plea when defense counsel is obviously not prepared to proceed. (*In re Vargas* (2000) 83 Cal. App. 4th 1125) or when counsel misleads the defendant as to the sentence to be imposed (*People v. Ribero* (1971) 4 Cal. 3rd 55)

f. Statement in Mitigation

ROGER LAMPKIN
SB#113786
1234 L Street
Bakersfield, CA 93301
Tel: (661)633-1234
Fax: (661)863-6741
Attorney for Doug Donenabbed

IN THE SUPERIOR COURT OF THE STATE OF CALIFORNIA,
IN AND FOR THE COUNTY OF KERN

People of the State of California, Plaintiffs, - v. - Doug Donenabbed, Defendant	CASE NO. 123456 DEFENDANT DOUG DONENABBED'S STATEMENT IN MITIGATION Date: August 2, 2022 Time: 8:30 a.m. Dept: CC

STATEMENT OF THE CASE

Defendant is charged with felony domestic violence stemming from what appears to be mutual combat when both Mr. Donenabbed and his wife were intoxicated. Ms. Donenabbed is only alleged to have suffered scrapes and bruises, and she did not receive medical care. She has also requested that he not be prosecuted. Mr. Donenabbed entered a plea for a one-year maximum jail sentence as part of probation. It is respectfully suggested that any term of commitment be served as home confinement.

MITIGATING FACTORS

The following mitigating factors under *Rule 4.423* are presented to this court for its consideration in imposing sentence, mindful that the existence of one single mitigating factor can justify the imposition of a lesser sentence.

"(a)(1) The defendant was a passive participant or played a minor role in the crime." As noted above, both Defendant and his wife were intoxicated at the time of the offense, and she was the initial aggressor.

"(a)(2) The victim was an initiator of, willing participant in, or aggressor or provoker of the incident."   See (a)(1)

"(a)(3) The crime was committed because of an unusual circumstance, such as great provocation, that is unlikely to recur."

"(a)(4) The defendant participated in the crime under circumstances of coercion or duress, or the criminal conduct was partially excusable for some other reason not amounting to a defense." See (a)(1)

"(a)(5) The defendant, with no apparent predisposition to do so, was induced by others to participate in the crime."

"(a)(6) The defendant exercised caution to avoid harm to persons or damage to property, or the amounts of money or property taken were deliberately small, or no harm was done or threatened against the victim."

"(a)(7) The defendant believed that he or she had a claim or right to the property taken, or for other reasons mistakenly believed that the conduct was legal."

"(a)(8) The defendant was motivated by a desire to provide necessities for his or her family or self."

Dated:

_____

By   Roger Lampkin,
      Attorney for Doug Donenabbed

Practical Tip:

Start preparing for mitigation as soon as the case comes in. Ask the client's family and friends for letters of recommendation; get information about the client's family history, work history, education, military service, volunteer work, and other factors that can be used in mitigation. The evidence you collect for mitigation can be used during bail hearings and during plea negotiations.

g. Motion to Strike Prior Conviction (Romero)

ROGER LAMPKIN
SB#113786
1234 L Street
Bakersfield, CA 93301
Tel: (661)633-1234
Fax: (661)863-6741
Attorney for Doug Donenabbed

IN THE SUPERIOR COURT OF THE STATE OF CALIFORNIA, IN AND FOR THE COUNTY OF KERN

People of the State of California,	CASE NO. 123456
Plaintiffs,	DEFENDANT DOUG DONENABBED'S MOTION TO STRIKE PRIOR CONVICTION [Romero]
- v. -	
Doug Donenabbed,	Date: August 2, 2022
Defendant	Time: 8:30 a.m.
	Dept: CC

TO THE COURT AND THE PROSECUTION: PLEASE TAKE NOTICE that on the date and time indicated above, the Defendant will move for an order striking the following prior conviction for purposes of sentencing:

Penal Code §460.1 (First Degree Burglary), March 9, 1992, Case # SC123456A

The motion will be based on this notice of motion, on the memorandum of points and authorities served and filed herewith, on the records on file in this action, and on such oral and documentary evidence as may be presented at the hearing on the motion.

Dated:

_____

By   Roger Lampkin,
       Attorney for Doug Donenabbed

STATEMENT OF THE CASE

Defendant was in an altercation with his neighbor, which included throwing a tree branch at the neighbor, which hit and damaged a car. Defendant pled to one count of Assault With a Deadly Weapon, namely, the tree branch.

POINTS AND AUTHORITIES

Penal Code §1385 gives trial courts discretion to dismiss enhancements, or the punishment for an enhancement, including prior convictions, in the interests of justice. *People v. Superior Court (Romero)* (1996) 13 Cal. 4th 497; *People v. Fritz* (1985) 40 Cal. 3rd 227; *People v. Tenorio* (1970) 3 Cal. 3rd 89).

The court also has the inherent power to strike the additional punishment for prior convictions if there are mitigating circumstances and it states on the record the reasons for striking the punishment. (*Penal Code §1385; CRC, Rule 4.406(b)(7); People v. Meloney* (2003) 30 Cal. 4th 1145).

Priors may be stricken even for a defendant with a lengthy criminal record.

In *People vs. Bishop*, 56 Cal.App. 4th 1245, the defendant was charged with stealing video cassettes from a drug store. He had served prison terms for eight prior convictions and three prior convictions within the meaning of three strikes, but the trial court found it proper to strike two prior "strikes" (See also *People vs. Cruff* (2001) 87 Cal.App. 4th 991).

In the instant case, we request the Court to strike a Burglary conviction because the conviction is more than twenty years old and there was no violence on the part of Defendant. The Burglary was on an empty house while the residents were on vacation.

>••Ω••←

Why? Why do some pleadings have Readiness and Trial dates and others do not?

If a trial date has been set, a noticed motion or an ex parte pleading should contain that date, but if no trial date has been set, such as prior to the preliminary examination, the pleadings will not list the date. Motions in limine do not need to have the trial date because they are generally given to the prosecutor and the judge on the first day of trial; however, some judges require that motions in limine be filed a certain number of days before trial.

h. Motion to Strike Invalid Prior Conviction

ROGER LAMPKIN
SB#113786
1234 L Street
Bakersfield, CA 93301
Tel: (661)633-1234
Fax: (661)863-6741
Attorney for Doug Donenabbed

IN THE SUPERIOR COURT OF THE STATE OF CALIFORNIA,
IN AND FOR THE COUNTY OF KERN

People of the State of California,	CASE NO. 123456
Plaintiffs,	DEFENDANT DOUG DONENABBED'S MOTION TO STRIKE PRIOR CONVICTION
- v. -	
Doug Donenabbed,	Date: August 2, 2022
	Time: 8:30 a.m.
Defendant	Dept: CC

TO THE COURT AND THE PROSECUTION: PLEASE TAKE NOTICE that on the date and time indicated above, the Defendant will move for an order Striking the following prior conviction as being Constitutionally invalid:

Penal Code §460.1 (First Degree Burglary), March 9, 1992, Case # SC123456A

The motion will be based on this notice of motion, on the memorandum of points and authorities served and filed herewith, on the records on file in this action, and on such oral and documentary evidence as may be presented at the hearing on the motion.

Dated:

_____
By   Roger Lampkin,
      Attorney for Doug Donenabbed

MEMORANDUM OF POINTS AND AUTHORITIES

In *Boykin v. Alabama* (1969) 395 U.S. 238, 243 and fn. 5, the United States Supreme Court explained that a defendant seeking to plead guilty is denied due process under the federal Constitution unless the plea is voluntary and knowing. "Several federal constitutional rights are involved in a waiver that takes place when a plea of guilty is entered in a state criminal trial. First, is the privilege against compulsory self-incrimination.... [Citations.] Second, is the right to trial by jury. [Citation.] Third, is the right to confront one's accusers." (id. at 243). In *In re Tahl* (1969) 1 Cal. 3rd 122, the California Supreme Court held that "each of the three rights mentioned—self-incrimination, confrontation, and jury trial—must be specifically and expressly enumerated for the benefit of and waived by the accused prior to acceptance of his guilty plea." (id. at 132). In *In re Yurko* (1974) 10 Cal. 3rd 857, 863, the California Supreme Court adopted as a judicial rule of criminal procedure the requirement that the three Boykin–Tahl admonitions must also be given "before a court accepts an accused's admission that he has suffered prior felony convictions." (id. at 863).

A criminal defendant may collaterally "challenge the validity, in his present trial, of a prior felony conviction on Boykin–Tahl grounds." (*People v. Allen* (1999) 21 Cal.4th 424, 435, citing and quoting *People v. Coffey* (1967) 67 Cal.2nd 204).

"[I]t is clearly in the interest of efficient judicial administration that attacks upon the constitutional basis of prior convictions be disposed of at the earliest possible opportunity, and we are therefore of the view that, if the issue is properly raised at or prior to trial, it must be determined by the trial court." (*People v. Sumstine* (1984) 36 Cal.3rd 909

For purposes of such collateral attack on a conviction, a court must generally presume that "final judgments are valid, that official duty was performed, and that proceedings were regular." (*Allen*, supra at 449–450, 87; see also Evidence Code §§ 664, 666, *Curl v. Superior Court* (1990) 51 Cal.3rd 1292, 1303). "Application of these rules means we must assume, until the contrary appears, that court proceedings were conducted in compliance with applicable rules, including those set forth in Tahl." (*Allen*, supra, at 449–450)

"When a defendant makes sufficient allegations that his conviction, by plea, in the prior felony proceedings was obtained in violation of his constitutional Boykin–Tahl rights, the trial court must hold an evidentiary hearing. At the hearing, the prosecution bears the initial burden of producing evidence that the defendant did indeed suffer the conviction. The defendant must then produce evidence to demonstrate his Boykin–Tahl rights were infringed. The prosecution then has the right to rebuttal, at which point reliance on a silent record will not be sufficient. [Citations.]" (id. at 435).

The trial court must make findings based on the evidence, and it must strike from the charging document any prior conviction found to be constitutionally invalid. (See *Coffey*, supra at 217–218) In a collateral attack on a presumptively final conviction, "[e]ven if the defendant can prove he did not waive his constitutional rights before pleading guilty, he must also plead and prove he was actually unaware of his rights, and that he would not have pleaded guilty had he known his rights." (*Allen*, supra, at 436, fn. 3). "[A] collateral attack via a motion to strike has always required a showing of prejudice. [Citations.]" (id. at 440, fn. 5)

In the instant case, the record of Defendant's prior conviction and the attached declaration establish that his plea was not knowing and voluntary. Based on the foregoing, Defendant respectfully requests the court to strike the alleged prior convictions in this case.

i. Motion to Strike Invalid DUI Conviction

ROGER LAMPKIN
SB#113786
1234 L Street
Bakersfield, CA 93301
Tel: (661)633-1234
Fax: (661)863-6741
Attorney for Doug Donenabbed

IN THE SUPERIOR COURT OF THE STATE OF CALIFORNIA,
IN AND FOR THE COUNTY OF KERN

People of the State of California,	CASE NO. 123456
Plaintiffs,	DEFENDANT DOUG DONENABBED'S MOTION TO STRIKE PRIOR DUI CONVICTION
- v. -	
Doug Donenabbed,	Date: August 2, 2022
Defendant	Time: 8:30 a.m.
	Dept: CC

TO THE COURT AND THE PROSECUTION: PLEASE TAKE NOTICE that on the date and time indicated above, the Defendant will move for an order Striking the following prior conviction as being Constitutionally invalid:

> Vehicle Code §23152 (Driving Under the Influence), May 9, 1992, Case #BM123456A

The motion will be based on this notice of motion, on the memorandum of points and authorities served and filed herewith, on the records on file in this action, and on such oral and documentary evidence as may be presented at the hearing on the motion.

Dated:

_____

By   Roger Lampkin,
      Attorney for Doug Donenabbed

DECLARATION IN SUPPORT OF MOTION STRIKE PRIOR

I, Roger Lampkin, declare:

I am attorney of record for Doug Donenabbed, the defendant in this action.

I am informed and believe that if defendant were called to testify in this matter, he would testify as follows:

1. Defendant appeared in Division G of the above-entitled court without counsel.
2. Defendant was instructed to speak with a person present in the courtroom, a probation officer, who told Defendant that a deal had been worked out where the defendant would enter a plea in exchange for fines, probation, and classes but no jail time.
3. Defendant believed the person to be his attorney who was acting in his best interests, so the defendant entered a plea.

Defendant was, thereby, deprived of counsel and his plea was not knowing and voluntary.

Dated:

_____

By Roger Lampkin,
    Attorney for Doug Donenabbed

MEMORANDUM OF POINTS AND AUTHORITIES

In *Boykin v. Alabama* (1969) 395 U.S. 238, 243 and fn. 5, the United States Supreme Court explained that a defendant seeking to plead guilty is denied due process under the federal Constitution unless the plea is voluntary and knowing. "Several federal constitutional rights are involved in a waiver that takes place when a plea of guilty is entered in a state criminal trial. First, is the privilege against compulsory self-incrimination.... [Citations.] Second, is the right to trial by jury. [Citation.] Third, is the right to confront one's accusers." (id. at 243). In *In re Tahl* (1969) 1 Cal. 3rd 122, the California Supreme Court held that "each of the three rights mentioned—self-incrimination, confrontation, and jury trial—must be specifically and expressly enumerated for the benefit of and waived by the accused prior to acceptance of his guilty plea." (id. at 132). In *In re Yurko* (1974) 10 Cal. 3rd 857, 863, the California Supreme Court adopted as a judicial rule of criminal procedure the requirement that the three Boykin–Tahl admonitions must also be given "before a court accepts an accused's admission that he has suffered prior felony convictions." (id. at 863).

A criminal defendant may collaterally "challenge the validity, in his present trial, of a prior felony conviction on Boykin–Tahl grounds." (*People v. Allen* (1999) 21 Cal.4th 424, 435, citing and quoting *People v. Coffey* (1967) 67 Cal.2nd 204).

"[I]t is clearly in the interest of efficient judicial administration that attacks upon the constitutional basis of prior convictions be disposed of at the earliest possible opportunity, and we are therefore of the view that, if the issue is properly raised at or prior to trial, it must be determined by the trial court." (*People v. Sumstine* (1984) 36 Cal.3rd 909

For purposes of such collateral attack on a conviction, a court must generally presume that "final judgments are valid, that official duty was performed, and that proceedings were regular." (*Allen*, supra at 449–450, 87; see also *Evidence Code §§664, 666, Curl v. Superior Court* (1990) 51 Cal.3rd 1292, 1303). "Application of these rules means we must assume, until the contrary appears, that court proceedings were conducted in compliance with applicable rules, including those set forth in Tahl." (*Allen*, supra, at 449–450)

"When a defendant makes sufficient allegations that his conviction, by plea, in the prior felony proceedings was obtained in violation of his constitutional Boykin–Tahl rights, the trial court must hold an evidentiary hearing. At the hearing, the prosecution bears the initial burden of producing evidence that the defendant did indeed suffer the conviction. The defendant must then produce evidence to demonstrate his Boykin–Tahl rights were infringed. The prosecution then has the right to rebuttal, at which point reliance on a silent record will not be sufficient. [Citations.]" (id. at 435).

The trial court must make findings based on the evidence, and it must strike from the charging document any prior conviction found to be constitutionally invalid. (See *Coffey*, supra at 217–218)

In a collateral attack on a presumptively final conviction, "[e]ven if the defendant can prove he did not waive his constitutional rights before pleading guilty, he must also plead and prove he was actually unaware of his rights, and that he would not have pleaded guilty had he known his rights." (*Allen*, supra, at 436, fn. 3).

"[A] collateral attack via a motion to strike has always required a showing of prejudice. [Citations.]" (id. at 440, fn. 5)

In addition to the foregoing authority, *Vehicle Code §41403* sets forth additional protections in DUI cases and does not limit Constitutional challenges to *Boykin–Tahl* errors; rather, *§41403* requires the court to "hold a hearing, outside of the presence of the jury, in order to determine the constitutional validity of the charged separate conviction issue."

In *People v. Superior Court (Almaraz)* (2001) 89 Cal.App.4th 1353 the court considered a *§41403* challenge to the use of a non-certified interpreter in criminal proceedings. The court accepted §41403 as a proper avenue for making such a constitutional challenge but noted that "Improper procedures in the use of an interpreter do not rise to the level of a constitutional violation unless they result in prejudice demonstrating defendant was denied his right to a fair trial."

However, it has been held that *§41403* authorized challenges to a prior conviction based on Gideon error (denial of right to counsel) but does not allow a challenge based on ineffective assistance of counsel, which should be brought by petition for writ of habeas corpus (*People v. Bechtol* (2017) 10 Cal.App.5th 950)

In the instant case, the record of Defendant's prior conviction and the attached declaration establish that his plea was not knowing and voluntary.

Based on the foregoing, Defendant respectfully requests the court to strike the alleged prior convictions in this case.

→••Ω••←

Say This Instead of That
- Say, "I'll try to find that out for you," instead of, "I don't know."
- Say, "Thank you for your patience," instead of, "sorry about the long wait."
- Say, "Your case is important to Ms. Smith, but she was detained," instead of, "Ms. Smith is in a murder trial and doesn't have time."
- Say, "Let me try to get you to the right person for that," instead of, "that's not my job."
- Say, "She gets a lot of good results for her clients," instead of, "she wins most of her cases."
- Say, "Mr. Lee wants to stay on your case, so let me get you in to see the bookkeeper," instead of, "If you don't pay, Mr. Lee will get out of your case."

j. Motion to Modify Probation

ROGER LAMPKIN
SB#113786
1234 L Street
Bakersfield, CA 93301
Tel: (661)633-1234
Fax: (661)863-6741
Attorney for Doug Donenabbed

IN THE SUPERIOR COURT OF THE STATE OF CALIFORNIA,
IN AND FOR THE COUNTY OF KERN

People of the State of California,	CASE NO. 123456
Plaintiffs,	DEFENDANT DOUG DONENABBED'S MOTION TO MODIFY PROBATION
- v. -	
Doug Donenabbed,	Date: August 2, 2022 Time: 8:30 a.m.
Defendant	Dept: CC

TO THE COURT AND THE PROSECUTION: PLEASE TAKE NOTICE that at the date and time indicated above, Defendant will move the court for an order modifying probation in the above-entitled case.

This motion will be made on the grounds that Defendant has completed more than half of his probationary sentence and a modification is needed to allow him to continue to be gainfully employed.

This motion will be based on the attached documents, on all the papers and records on file in this action, and on such oral and documentary evidence as may be presented at the hearing of the motion.

Dated:

_____

By   Roger Lampkin,
    Attorney for Doug Donenabbed

STATEMENT OF THE CASE

Defendant was given a probationary sentence with the requirement that he submit to random drug testing and attend weekly Narcotics Anonymous meetings. Defendant has had no failed or missed tests, and he has attended meetings as ordered (see attached); however, his work hours have changed, and he is not able to attend meetings as currently scheduled. Defendant, therefore, requests to be relieved from the obligation to attend further NA meetings.

POINTS, AUTHORITIES, AND ARGUMENT

Penal Code §1203.3 provides in pertinent part: "(a) The court shall have authority at any time during the term of probation to revoke, modify, or change its order of suspension of imposition or execution of sentence."

k. Motion to Reduce to Misdemeanor

ROGER LAMPKIN
SB#113786
1234 L Street
Bakersfield, CA 93301
Tel: (661)633-1234
Fax: (661)863-6741
Attorney for Doug Donenabbed

IN THE SUPERIOR COURT OF THE STATE OF CALIFORNIA, IN AND FOR THE COUNTY OF KERN

People of the State of California, Plaintiffs, - v. - Doug Donenabbed, Defendant	NOTICE OF MOTION TO REDUCE FELONY TO MISDEMEANOR [*Penal Code §17(b)(3)*] Date: August 2, 2022 Time: 8:30 a.m. Dept: CC

TO THE COURT AND THE PROSECUTION: PLEASE TAKE NOTICE that on the date and time indicated above, the Defendant will move for an order reducing his conviction of violating *Penal Code §496*

(Receiving Stolen Property) from a felony to a misdemeanor.

The motion will be based on this notice of motion, on the memorandum of points and authorities served and filed herewith, on the records on file in this action, and on such oral and documentary evidence as may be presented at the hearing on the motion.

Dated:

_____

By   Roger Lampkin,
       Attorney for Doug Donenabbed

POINTS AND AUTHORITIES

"The Legislature has classified most crimes as either a felony or a misdemeanor, by explicitly labeling the crime as such, or by the punishment prescribed." (*People v. Park* (2013) 56 Cal.4th 782, 789). However, there is a special category of crimes that is punishable as either a felony or a misdemeanor, depending on the severity of the facts surrounding its commission. (*People v. Superior Court (Perez)* (1995) 38 Cal.App.4th 347, 360, fn. 17; *Penal Code §17*)

These crimes, commonly referred to as "wobblers," are "punishable either by a term in state prison or by imprisonment in county jail and/or by a fine." (*Park*, supra at 789)

The conduct underlying these offenses can vary widely in its level of seriousness. Accordingly, the Legislature has empowered the courts to decide, in each individual case, whether the crime should be classified as a felony or a misdemeanor. In making that determination, the court considers the facts surrounding the offense and the characteristics of the offender. (*People v. Superior Court (Alvarez)* (1997) 14 Cal.4th 968, 978).

" 'A wobbler offense charged as a felony is regarded as a felony for all purposes until imposition of sentence or judgment. [Citations.] If state prison is imposed, the offense remains a felony; if a misdemeanor sentence is imposed, the offense is thereafter deemed a misdemeanor. [Citations.]' " (*People v. Upsher* (2007) 155 Cal.App.4th 1311, 1320). The trial court has discretion to "reduce a wobbler to a misdemeanor either by declaring the crime a misdemeanor at the time probation is granted or at a later time— for example when the defendant has successfully completed probation." (*Park*, supra, at 793).

This authority is set forth in *Penal Code §17(b)*, which holds in part, "When a crime is punishable, in the discretion of the court, either by imprisonment in the state prison or imprisonment in a county jail… it is a misdemeanor for all purposes under the following circumstances:… When the court grants probation to a defendant and at the time of granting probation, or on application of the defendant or probation officer thereafter, the court declares the offense to be a misdemeanor."

The reduction of a wobbler to a misdemeanor is not based on the notion that a wobbler offense is "conceptually a misdemeanor." (*Necochea v. Superior Court* (1972) 23 Cal.App.3rd 1012, 1016). Rather, it is "intended to extend misdemeanant treatment to a potential felon" and "extend more lenient treatment to an offender." (Ibid.) "When the court properly exercises its discretion to reduce a wobbler to a misdemeanor, it has found that felony punishment, and its consequences, are not appropriate for that particular defendant. [Citation.] Such a defendant is not blameless. But by virtue of the court's proper exercise of discretion, neither is such defendant a member of the class of criminals" convicted of an offense the Legislature intended to be subject to felony punishment. (*Park*, supra, at 801–802).

In the instant case, a misdemeanor disposition is appropriate because this is Defendant's first offense, he has fully paid restitution, and he was given a probationary sentence.

7. Defense Funding

The prosecution team, led by a prosecuting attorney, may consist of law enforcement officers, drug recognition experts, gang experts, laboratory workers, ballistics experts, investigators, and or any number of other experts. The defense team is also entitled to experts as an essential element of effective assistance of counsel, and the state is required to pay the necessary cost of experts, including paralegals and investigators, for an indigent defendant.

The state is also required to pay the necessary expenses of trial for an indigent defendant, such as the cost of transcripts, the cost of trial clothes, and the cost of transportation for witnesses.

The types of expert witnesses needed in a case are heavily dependent on the facts of the case, but common defense experts include investigators, paralegals, gang experts, cell phone experts, computer experts, mental health professionals, medical doctors, and toxicologists.

If the attorney has been appointed by the court, the client's indigency has already been determined, and the court will probably be more liberal in its appointment of defense team members. Public defender offices and alternate defender panels often have their own preapproved investigators and paralegals, and some may have preapproved gang experts and drug recognition experts. The attorney may also have a fixed budget for paralegals, investigation, transcripts, copy fees, and support staff, but the attorney may request that the court pay all or part of the fees and expenses of the defense, even if the attorney was retained by the defendant or the defendant's family and friends.

The following are samples of pleadings that may be used to make such requests to the court. These pleadings are ex parte – they are not served on the District Attorney – and they are confidential when filed.

a. Transcript of Prior Proceedings

ROGER LAMPKIN
SB#113786
1234 L Street
Bakersfield, CA 93301
Tel: (661)633-1234
Fax: (661)863-6741
Attorney for Doug Donenabbed

IN THE SUPERIOR COURT OF THE STATE OF CALIFORNIA,

IN AND FOR THE COUNTY OF KERN

People of the State of California,	CASE NO. BF123456A
Plaintiffs,	EX PARTE REQUEST FOR ORDER FOR REPORTER
- v. -	TRANSCRIPT AT COUNTY EXPENSE
Doug Donenabbed,	(Penal Code §987 et. seq.;
Defendant	Evidence Code §§730, 952)

COMES NOW DEFENDANT, THROUGH COUNSEL, who respectfully moves the Court for an order that a transcript of the prior trial proceedings in this matter be furnished to the defendant without cost. This motion is made on the ground that Defendant is indigent, as previously determined by the court, and the transcripts are needed to prepare for post-trial proceedings.

The motion is based on this notice of motion and attached papers, on all the papers and records on file in this action, and on such oral and documentary evidence as may be presented at any hearing of the motion.

Dated: _____

By   Roger Lampkin,
     Attorney for Doug Donenabbed

TRANSCRIPTS REQUESTED

Transcript of the trial and sentencing in the instant case, *People v. Doug Donenabbed*, BF123456A, including opening and closing statements, jury instructions, and 402 proceedings.

The transcripts are needed to prepare appropriate post-conviction pleadings, including a motion for new trial. This request should result in minimal, if any additional expenses because the transcripts will need to be prepared for matters in the Court of Appeals should Defendant be sentenced in this Court.

MEMORANDUM OF POINTS AND AUTHORITIES

A STATE HAS AN OBLIGATION TO PROVIDE AN INDIGENT DEFENDANT WITH TRANSCRIPTS OF PRIOR PROCEEDINGS

As explained by the United States Supreme Court in *Britt v. North Carolina* (1971) 404 U.S. 226, 227, an indigent defendant has a constitutional right to be provided with a transcript of a prior proceeding and other tools necessary to prepare a defense:

"Griffin v. Illinois, 351 U.S. 12, 76 S. Ct. 585, 100 L. Ed. 891 (1956)) and its progeny establish the principle that the State must, as a matter of equal protection, provide indigent prisoners with the basic tools of an adequate defense or appeal, when those tools are available for a price to other prisoners. While the outer limits of that principle are not clear, there can be no doubt that the State must provide an indigent defendant with a transcript of prior proceedings when that transcript is needed for an effective defense or appeal."

In *People v. Hosner* (1975)15 Cal. 3rd 60, 66, the California Supreme Court held that the need for a complete transcript of a prior proceeding is presumed:

"[A]n indigent defendant in a criminal trial is presumed to have a particularized need for a transcript of prior proceedings, just as he is *presumed*, if he needs a transcript at all, to need nothing less than a complete transcript." [Emphasis in original.]

An indigent defendant is "presumptively entitled to a transcript of his or her first trial. A denial of a timely request, based on a showing of the necessity for the transcript to effectively cross-examine witnesses, requires automatic reversal." (*People v. Tarver* (1991) 228 Cal.App. 3rd 954, 957 [internal quotations omitted]).

ROGER LAMPKIN
SB#113786
1234 L Street
Bakersfield, CA 93301
Tel: (661)633-1234
Fax: (661)863-6741
Attorney for Doug Donenabbed

IN THE SUPERIOR COURT OF THE STATE OF CALIFORNIA,
IN AND FOR THE COUNTY OF KERN

People of the State of California,	CASE NO. BF123456A
Plaintiffs,	ORDER FOR REPORTER TRANSCRIPT AT COUNTY EXPENSE
- v. -	
Doug Donenabbed,	
Defendant	

Pursuant to Defendant's Ex Parte application, IT IS HEREBY
ORDERED that a reporter's transcript of the trial and sentencing in the
instant case, including opening and closing statements, jury instructions,
and 402 proceedings, shall be provided to Defendant at County expense.

Dated: _____

By   Roger Lampkin,
Attorney for Doug Donenabbed

→••Ω••←

Practical Tip:
Learn to do legal research by doing legal research. It isn't enough to be able
to look up a specific case; you should learn to find cases that support your
client's position. An easy place to start is by searching for "legal research"
videos on YouTube. There you will find multiple videos on the use of
Lexis, Westlaw, and other platforms. But watching videos is not enough.
Get on the computer and start researching, even if you don't have a current
case that needs research. See what you can learn by picking a random
topics and searching for cases, such as: "under what circumstances can a
cell phone be searched without a warrant?" and "when can a juvenile be
tried in adult court?"

b. Appoint Paralegal – Indigent Defendant

ROGER LAMPKIN
SB#113786
1234 L Street
Bakersfield, CA 93301
Tel: (661)633-1234
Fax: (661)863-6741
Attorney for Doug Donenabbed

IN THE SUPERIOR COURT OF THE STATE OF CALIFORNIA,

IN AND FOR THE COUNTY OF KERN

People of the State of California, Plaintiffs, - v. - Doug Donenabbed, Defendant	CASE NO. BF123456A CONFIDENTIAL EX PARTE APPLICATION FOR ORDER APPOINTING PARALEGAL VICTOR VEVEA [Indigent Defendant] (Penal Code §987.9)

TO THE ABOVE-ENTITLED COURT:

Defendant, Doug Donenabbed, requests an order appointing Victor VeVea at the expense of the county to assist the defendant and counsel on a confidential basis and for such other orders as may seem just and proper to the court.

This request is made on the grounds that the assistance of a paralegal is necessary to the preparation of the defense of this action and this appointment should result in significant savings to the County.

This request is based on the attached declaration, on the memorandum of points and authorities served and filed herewith, on such supplemental declarations, affidavits, or memorandum of points and authorities as may hereafter be filed with the court, on all the papers and records on file in this action, and on such further oral and documentary evidence as may be presented at the hearing of this request.

Dated: _____

               By Roger Lampkin,
                    Attorney for Doug Donenabbed

DECLARATION IN SUPPORT OF EX PARTE
APPLICATION FOR APPOINTMENT

I, Roger Lampkin, declare:
1. I am the attorney of record for Defendant Doug Donenabbed.
2. I am informed and believe that Defendant is indigent in that this assignment came to me through the Indigent Defense Program and Defendant is currently in custody.
3. I specifically need this paralegal, who in addition to being a skilled paralegal and computer expert is a skilled researcher and writer, to complete the following tasks:
   a. listen to the audio files
   b. view the video files
   c. review Facebook and other social media discovery
4. For me to personally review all of this evidence, much of which I expect to be mundane or wholly irrelevant, would consume many, many hours (at a billing rate nearly double that requested by this expert) and would divert my attention from more important tasks, such as reviewing the relevant evidence, conducting legal research, supervising experts, and otherwise preparing this case for trial. On many cases in the past, I have used this expert to sift through voluminous evidence, both personally and with the use of computer databases and search tools, and bring relevant evidence to my attention. This has been both efficient and economical on past cases, and I expect the same result on this case.
5. I request the appointment of Victor VeVea to accomplish the tasks described herein. Mr. VeVea has been appointed by this and other courts as a Paralegal and/or technical expert on multiple cases in the past, including multiple death penalty cases. His work is always with good result.
6. His resume is attached, which also demonstrates his qualifications.

Based on the foregoing, I am asking for an initial authorization of 60 hours at $80 per hour for a total of $4,800.

Dated: _____

By   Roger Lampkin,
Attorney for Doug Donenabbed

POINTS AND AUTHORITIES

A. PARALEGAL SERVICES ARE REASONABLY NECESSARY

"In the modern world of legal practice, the delegation of repetitive legal tasks to paralegals has become a necessary fixture. Such delegation has become an integral part of the struggle to keep down the costs of legal representation. Moreover, the delegation of such tasks to specialized, well-educated non-lawyers may well ensure greater accuracy…" (*Pincay v. Andrews* (2004) 389 F. 3rd 853).

It is well settled that "secretarial and paralegal services" are "necessary support services for attorneys" (*Salton Bay Marina, Inc. v. Imperial Irrigation Dist.* (1985) 172 Cal. App. 3rd 914; see also *Missouri v. Jenkins 491 U.S. 274; Trustees of Const. v. Redland Ins. Co.* (9th Cir. 2006) 460 F. 3rd 1253; *Otay Ranch, L.P. v. County of San Diego* (2014) 230 Cal. App. 4th 60; *No Toxic Air, Inc. v. Lehigh Southwest Cement Company* (2016) 1 Cal. App. 5th 1136).

It appears to be without dispute that paralegals result in a net cost savings. It may even be improper for an attorney to complete tasks that would better be assigned to a paralegal. For example, in *Carver v. Chevron U.S.A., Inc.* (2002) 97 Cal. App. 4th 132, the trial court properly reduced payment to the attorney because the court found "that some charges could have been reduced had a paralegal performed the tasks…"

B. THE DUE PROCESS OF EFFECTIVE COUNSEL INCLUDE THE RIGHT TO THE ANCILLARY SERVICES FOR THE PREPARATION OF THE DEFENSE

"In any case in which a person…desires but is unable to employ counsel and in which counsel is assigned in the Superior Court, Municipal Court, or Justice Court to represent the person in a criminal trial, proceeding or appeal, the assigned counsel…shall receive a reasonable sum for compensation and for necessary expenses…" *Penal Code §987.2*

Supreme Court decisions mandate that effective assistance of counsel "…requires, when necessary, the allowance of investigative expenses or appointment of investigative assistance for indigent defendants in order to insure effective preparation of their defense by their attorneys." (*Mason v. State of Arizona* (9th Cir. 1974) 504 F. 2nd 1345, 1351).

The due process right of effective counsel includes the right to the ancillary services necessary in the preparation of a defense. [Citations omitted.] The right is codified in Penal Code [Section 987.2] which provides that counsel appointed for an indigent defendant shall not only be compensated by a reasonable fee but also shall be reimbursed for his necessary expense." (*People v. Faxel,* (1979) 91 Cal App 3rd 327, 330).

"The Sixth Amendment right to counsel is a meaningless gesture if counsel for an indigent is denied the use of working tools essential to the establishment of what would appear to be a tenable or possible defense." (*People v. Gunnerson* (1977) 74 Cal App 3rd 370, 379).

It cannot be doubted that the right to counsel guaranteed by both the federal and state Constitutions includes, and indeed presumes, the right to effective counsel, and "the right to effective counsel also includes the right to ancillary services necessary in the preparation of a defense." (*Keenan v Superior Court* (1982) 31 Cal 3rd 424, 428) "A fundamental part of the constitutional right of an accused to be represented by counsel is that his attorney…is obviously entitled to the aid of such expert assistance as he may need…in preparing the defense." (*Re Ketchel* (1968) 68 Cal 2nd 397, 399-400)

C. THE RIGHT TO SUCH COURT-ORDERED SERVICES IS SUPPORTED BY STATUTE

Evidence Code §730 explicitly provides for court-appointed expert witnesses:

> "When it appears to the court, at any time before or during the trial of an action, that expert evidence is or may be required by the court or by any party to the action, the court on its own motion or on motion of any party may appoint one or more experts to investigate, to render a report as may be ordered by the court, and to testify as an expert at the trial of the action relative to the fact or matter as to which such expert evidence is or may be required. The court may fix the compensation for such services, if any, rendered by any person appointed under this section, in addition to any services as a witness, at such amount as seems reasonable to the court." *Evidence Code §731(a)* and *Government Code §29603* clearly state that the county must pay those court-ordered expenses.

While these statutes, of course, do not enumerate the type of experts to be appointed, the Supreme Court has held that "the right to such services is to be inferred from at least two statutes respecting an indigent defendant's right to legal assistance." (*Corenevsky v Superior Court* (1984) 36 Cal 3rd 307, 319)

D. A DEFENSE MOTION FOR THE APPOINTMENT OF AN EXPERT MAY BE HEARD IN CAMERA

The Supreme Court has observed that a defense motion for the appointment of an expert "was entitled to have been heard in camera, and would therefore not normally be subject to disclosure...." (*Corenevsky v Superior Court* (1984) 36 Cal 3rd 307, 321)

ROGER LAMPKIN
SB#113786
1234 L Street
Bakersfield, CA 93301
Tel: (661)633-1234
Fax: (661)863-6741
Attorney for Doug Donenabbed

IN THE SUPERIOR COURT OF THE STATE OF CALIFORNIA,

IN AND FOR THE COUNTY OF KERN

People of the State of California,	CASE NO. BF123456A
Plaintiffs,	ORDER APPOINTING PARALEGAL VICTOR VEVEA
- v. -	[Indigent Defendant] (Penal Code §987.9)
Doug Donenabbed,	
Defendant	

Pursuant to Defendant's Ex Parte application, IT IS HEREBY ORDERED that Victor VeVea is appointed to assist the Defense as a paralegal and that a maximum of $4,800 be authorized for Victor VeVea for work to be performed at a rate of $80 per hour.

Dated: _____

                By   Roger Lampkin,
                     Attorney for Doug Donenabbed

c.Appoint Technical Expert – Indigent Defendant

ROGER LAMPKIN
SB#113786
1234 L Street
Bakersfield, CA 93301
Tel: (661)633-1234
Fax: (661)863-6741
Attorney for Doug Donenabbed

IN THE SUPERIOR COURT OF THE STATE OF CALIFORNIA,

IN AND FOR THE COUNTY OF KERN

People of the State of California,	CASE NO. BF123456A
Plaintiffs,	CONFIDENTIAL EX PARTE APPLICATION FOR ORDER APPOINTING ADVANCED MICRO RESOURCE DIGITAL FORENSICS
- v. -	
Doug Donenabbed,	
Defendant	[Indigent Defendant] (Penal Code §987.9)

TO THE ABOVE-ENTITLED COURT:

Defendant, Doug Donenabbed, requests an order appointing Computer Forensics Experts at the expense of the county to assist the defendant and counsel on a confidential basis and for such other orders as may seem just and proper to the court.

This request is made on the grounds that the assistance of a Computer Forensics Experts is necessary to the preparation of the defense of this action.

This request is based on the attached declaration, on the memorandum of points and authorities served and filed herewith, on such supplemental declarations, affidavits, or memorandum of points and authorities as may hereafter be filed with the court, on all the papers and records on file in this action, and on such further oral and documentary evidence as may be presented at the hearing of this request.

Dated: _____

By   Roger Lampkin,
    Attorney for Doug Donenabbed

DECLARATION IN SUPPORT OF EX PARTE
APPLICATION FOR APPOINTMENT

I, Roger Lampkin, declare:

1. I am the attorney of record for Defendant Doug Donenabbed.
2. I am informed and believe that Defendant is indigent in that this assignment came to me through the Indigent Defense Program and Defendant is currently in custody.
3. Defendant is charged with, inter alia, Murder, and he is facing a life sentence.
4. The Prosecution seized several cell phones and computers, which are being examined by Prosecution forensic experts.
5. The Defense, therefore, needs their own Computer Forensics Experts to impeach the Prosecution experts and to find evidence available on other electronic sources that may have been overlooked by the Prosecution.
6. Advanced Micro Resource Digital Forensics are Computer Forensics Experts well known to this Court, who are properly trained in the use of Cellebrite cell phone software, social media, and computer forensics, and these experts have been previously appointed by this Court.
7. Their firm summary is attached as is the resume of their CEO.
8. I have used these experts with good results many times in the past, and their reputation in the community is outstanding.
9. After discussion with experts from Advanced Micro Resource, I estimate that the examiners will need an initial authorization of 24 hours at $250 per hour for the examination and report.
10. The total cost cannot be estimated at this time because it is impossible to know the extent of the discovery that will produced and found, but we know that, at a minimum, the Prosecution is examining two cell phones and one computer.

I, therefore, request an authorization for twenty-four hours at $250 per hour for a total of $6,000.

Dated: _____

            By   Roger Lampkin,
                 Attorney for Doug Donenabbed

POINTS AND AUTHORITIES

A. THE DUE PROCESS OF EFFECTIVE COUNSEL INCLUDE THE RIGHT TO THE ANCILLARY SERVICES FOR THE PREPARATION OF THE DEFENSE

"In any case in which a person...desires but is unable to employ counsel and in which counsel is assigned in the Superior Court, Municipal Court, or Justice Court to represent the person in a criminal trial, proceeding or appeal, the assigned counsel...shall receive a reasonable sum for compensation and for necessary expenses..." *Penal Code §987.2*

Supreme Court decisions mandate that effective assistance of counsel "... requires, when necessary, the allowance of investigative expenses or appointment of investigative assistance for indigent defendants in order to insure effective preparation of their defense by their attorneys." (*Mason v. State of Arizona* (9th Cir. 1974) 504 F. 2nd 1345, 1351).

The due process right of effective counsel includes the right to the ancillary services necessary in the preparation of a defense. [Citations omitted.] The right is codified in Penal Code [Section 987.2] which provides that counsel appointed for an indigent defendant shall not only be compensated by a reasonable fee but also shall be reimbursed for his necessary expense." (*People v. Faxel* (1979) 91 Cal App 3rd 327, 330).

"The Sixth Amendment right to counsel is a meaningless gesture if counsel for an indigent is denied the use of working tools essential to the establishment of what would appear to be a tenable or possible defense." (*People v. Gunnerson* (1977)74 Cal App 3rd 370, 379).

It cannot be doubted that the right to counsel guaranteed by both the federal and state Constitutions includes, and indeed presumes, the right to effective counsel, and "the right to effective counsel also includes the right to ancillary services necessary in the preparation of a defense." (*Keenan v Superior Court* (1982) 31 Cal 3rd 424, 428) "A fundamental part of the constitutional right of an accused to be represented by counsel is that his attorney...is obviously entitled to the aid of such expert assistance as he may need...in preparing the defense." (*Re Ketchel* (1968) 68 Cal 2nd 397, 399-400)

B. THE RIGHT TO SUCH COURT-ORDERED SERVICES IS SUPPORTED BY STATUTE

Evidence Code §730 explicitly provides for court-appointed expert witnesses:

> "When it appears to the court, at any time before or during the trial of an action, that expert evidence is or may be required by the court or by any party to the action, the court on its own motion or on motion of any party may appoint one or more experts to investigate, to render a report as may be ordered by the court, and to testify as an expert at the trial of the action relative to the fact or matter as to which such expert evidence is or may be required. The court may fix the compensation for such services, if any, rendered by any person appointed under this section, in addition to any services as a witness, at such amount as seems reasonable to the court." *Evidence Code §731(a)* and *Government Code §29603* clearly state that the county must pay those court-ordered expenses.

While these statutes, of course, do not enumerate the type of experts to be appointed, the Supreme Court has held that "the right to such services is to be inferred from at least two statutes respecting an indigent defendant's right to legal assistance." (*Corenevsky v Superior Court* (1984) 36 Cal 3rd 307, 319)

C. A DEFENSE MOTION FOR THE APPOINTMENT OF AN EXPERT MAY BE HEARD IN CAMERA

The Supreme Court has observed that a defense motion for the appointment of an expert "was entitled to have been heard in camera, and would therefore not normally be subject to disclosure...." (*Corenevsky v Superior Court* (1984) 36 Cal 3rd 307, 321)

ROGER LAMPKIN
SB#113786
1234 L Street
Bakersfield, CA 93301
Tel: (661)633-1234
Fax: (661)863-6741
Attorney for Doug Donenabbed

IN THE SUPERIOR COURT OF THE STATE OF CALIFORNIA,

IN AND FOR THE COUNTY OF KERN

People of the State of California,	CASE NO. BF123456A
Plaintiffs,	ORDER APPOINTING ADVANCED MICRO
- v. -	RESOURCE DIGITAL FORENSICS
Doug Donenabbed,	[Indigent Defendant] (Penal Code §987.9)
Defendant	

Pursuant to Defendant's Ex Parte application, IT IS HEREBY
ORDERED that Advanced Micro Resource Digital Forensics is appointed
to assist the Defense and that twenty-four hours at the rate of $250 per
hour is authorized for all necessary work to be performed, not to exceed
$6,000 total.

Dated: _____

       By Roger Lampkin,
           Attorney for Doug Donenabbed

→••Ω••←

Practical Tip:

A Criminal Defense Paralegal should have a basic understanding of digital
evidence and how it can be used in court. It is not necessary to be an
expert, but a paralegal should be able to recognize different types of digital
evidence and prepare orders to appoint appropriate experts. If a case
involves any of the following, ask the attorney if an expert should be
appointed:

- Law enforcement seized cell phones

- Law enforcement seized social media records
- The client has a cell phone, smart watch, GPS, or other personal electronics but claims he wasn't at the crime scene.
- Law enforcement seized any computer equipment
- Law enforcement seized crime scene videos
- Other electronic media is in any way involved in the case

The cell tower expert I found traced the defendant's phone to a convenience store. The investigator I found got the video from the store. The video forensics expert I found extracted frames that showed the defendant was no where near the crime scene. So, I got a BIG bonus. It was a great case.

Oh, I almost forgot. The defendant was found not guilty.

d. Appoint Investigator – Retained Case

ROGER LAMPKIN
SB#113786
1234 L Street
Bakersfield, CA 93301
Tel: (661)633-1234
Fax: (661)863-6741
Attorney for Doug Donenabbed

IN THE SUPERIOR COURT OF THE STATE OF CALIFORNIA,
IN AND FOR THE COUNTY OF KERN

People of the State of California,	CASE NO. BF123456A
Plaintiffs,	EX PARTE MOTION BY RETAINED COUNSEL TO APPOINT PRIVATE INVESTIGATOR JOE SERRANO
- v. -	
Doug Donenabbed,	
Defendant	(Penal Code §987 et. seq.; Evidence Code §§730, 952)

TO THE ABOVE-ENTITLED COURT:

Defendant requests an order appointing a Private Investigator at the expense of the county to advise the defendant on a confidential basis and testify on the defendant's behalf, to seal this request and any orders of the court based on this request, and for such other orders as may seem just and proper to the court.

This request is made on the grounds that the services of a Private Investigator are necessary to the preparation of the defense of this action.

This request is based on the attached declaration, on the memorandum of points and authorities served and filed herewith, on such supplemental declarations, affidavits, or memorandum of points and authorities as may hereafter be filed with the court, on all the papers and records on file in this action, and on such further oral and documentary evidence as may be presented at the hearing of this request.

Dated: _____

By   Roger Lampkin,
Attorney for Doug Donenabbed

DECLARATION IN SUPPORT OF EX PARTE
APPLICATION FOR APPOINTMENT

I, Roger Lampkin , declare:

I am attorney for the Defendant, having been privately retained.

As shown by the attached financial documents, Defendant is indigent.

I have not yet been fully paid for my services, and the money I did receive came from a third party. Defendant has indicated that he does not have the funds to pay any part of the fee for a private investigator.

The assistance of a Private Investigator is necessary in this case to complete the following tasks:

1. Interview three known witnesses and attempt to locate and interview additional witnesses.
2. Attempt to obtain video of the incident.
3. View and photograph alleged crime scene

I have spoken with Private Investigator Joe Serrano regarding this, and he has indicated his availability. This investigator is on the Indigent Defense Panel of investigators and has previously been appointed by this court as a Private Investigator.

It is anticipated that the investigator's services will not take more than 20 hours, at the rate of $100 per hour, so I am requesting an authorization not to exceed $2,000 total.

I declare under penalty of perjury that I am informed and believe that the foregoing is true and correct.

Dated: _____

      By   Roger Lampkin,
           Attorney for Doug Donenabbed

MEMORANDUM OF POINTS AND AUTHORITIES

AN INDIGENT DEFENDANT REPRESENTED BY PRIVATE COUNSEL IS CONSTITUTIONALLY ENTITLED TO THE APPOINTMENT, AT COUNTY EXPENSE, OF AN EXPERT WHO IS NECESSARY TO THE PREPARATION OF A DEFENSE

"May a trial court appoint experts at county expense for an indigent defendant represented by private counsel? Although no statutory authority exists in California for such appointment, we have concluded that the Constitution compels such appointment in a proper case and that the trial court has inherent power to do so.... The test of entitlement to county assistance in defense preparation must be indigency. A test based upon the status of defense counsel would be constitutionally infirm. If a criminal defendant requires the services of investigators or scientific or medical experts to assist him in preparation of his defense, that assistance must be provided. Whether it is paid for by the government or by the defendant depends solely on the defendant's economic status." (*People v. Worthy* (1980) 109 Cal. App. 3rd 514, 518-520, citations and extra punctuation omitted).

THE RIGHT TO COUNSEL INCLUDES THE RIGHT TO HAVE ANY COMMUNICATION MADE TO EXPERTS REMAIN CONFIDENTIAL

It is established that the right to counsel guaranteed by the Sixth Amendment to the United States Constitution "also includes the right to have any communications made to experts remain confidential." (*Torres v. Municipal Court* (1975) 50 Cal. App. 3rd 778, 784).

AN INDIGENT DEFENDANT REPRESENTED BY PRIVATE COUNSEL MAY NOT BE REQUIRED TO ACCEPT THE SERVICES OF THE PUBLIC DEFENDER IN ORDER TO OBTAIN AN EXPERT AT PUBLIC EXPENSE

The court has no authority to require an indigent defendant represented by counsel to accept the services of the public defender in order to obtain an expert at public expense. An indigent defendant is entitled to ancillary defense services without the court's interference with an existing attorney-client relationship. (*Taylor v. Superior Court* (1985) 168 Cal.App. 3rd 1217).

THE AMOUNT OF THE ATTORNEY'S FEE DOES NOT AFFECT THE INDIGENT STATUS OF THE DEFENDANT

If the defendant is personally indigent, the payment of the retainer fee by his relatives to his attorney does not alter his indigent status. (*Anderson v. Justice Court* (1979) 99 Cal. App. 3rd 398, 402-4034).

Even if the defendant's attorney was paid more by his relatives than the "ordinary and customary charges in the community," this would not change the defendant's indigent status. Only if some part of the money paid were deemed to be the defendant's or if he had transferred all his property, could he be considered not indigent. The application of an ordinary-and-customary-charges test in cases where retained counsel seeks public funds for ancillary services would interfere with the principle that, when possible, a defendant should be afforded retained counsel of choice. (*Tran v. Superior Court* (2001) 92 Cal. App. 4th 1149, 1154)

ROGER LAMPKIN
SB#113786
1234 L Street
Bakersfield, CA 93301
Tel: (661)633-1234
Fax: (661)863-6741
Attorney for Doug Donenabbed

IN THE SUPERIOR COURT OF THE STATE OF CALIFORNIA,

IN AND FOR THE COUNTY OF KERN

People of the State of California,	CASE NO. BF123456A
Plaintiffs,	ORDER APPOINTING PRIVATE INVESTIGATOR JOE SERRANO
- v. -	
Doug Donenabbed,	[Indigent Defendant] (Penal Code §987.9)
Defendant	

GOOD CAUSE HAVING BEEN SHOWN, IT IS HEREBY
ORDERED: The Court hereby appoints Private Investigator Joe Serrano
to assist the defense on a confidential basis at the expense of the County.
Joe Serrano shall be compensated at $100 per hour, not to exceed $2,000
total.

Dated: _____

By   Roger Lampkin,
Attorney for Doug Donenabbed

→••Ω••←

Practical Tip:

If you don't know, don't tell. A client asked a very nice paralegal, "how
much time do you think I'll get?" She answered that people convicted of
Driving Under the Influence rarely spent time in jail, so he would probably
get probation. Her answer was bad – very bad. The client was facing his
sixth DUI, and there was an injury accident. He was almost surely going to
prison. Further, the paralegal gave a legal opinion, which is beyond the
qualifications of a paralegal. Refer such questions to an attorney.

e. Appoint Counsel of Choice

Note: Other ex parte requests generally require an order for the judge to sign, but most courts do not require an order for appointment of counsel unless the attorney is requesting a specific dollar amount. Rather, when appointing counsel, the court will usually refer the attorney to an alternate defender panel for payment.

ROGER LAMPKIN
SB#113786
1234 L Street
Bakersfield, CA 93301
Tel: (661)633-1234
Fax: (661)863-6741
Attorney for Doug Donenabbed

IN THE SUPERIOR COURT OF THE STATE OF CALIFORNIA,

IN AND FOR THE COUNTY OF KERN

People of the State of California,	CASE NO. BF123456A
Plaintiffs,	MOTION TO APPOINT DEFENDANT'S COUNSEL OF CHOICE
- v. -	
Doug Dave,	Date: August 2, 2022
	Time: 8:30 a.m.
Defendant	Dept: CC
	Readiness: August 12, 2022
	Trial: August 22, 2022

TO THE COURT AND THE DISTRICT ATTORNEY:
PLEASE TAKE NOTICE that on the date and time indicated above, or as soon thereafter as the matter can be heard in the above-entitled court, the defendant will move for an order appointing Roger Lampkin at county expense to represent Defendant in this action.

This request is made on the grounds that Defendant is entitled to continuity of counsel; said counsel is familiar with the case and has represented Defendant for the past nine months, and this appointment is desired by the Defendant.

The motion will be based on this notice and attached papers, on all papers and records on file in this action, and on such oral and documentary evidence as may be presented at the time of the motion.

Dated: _____

       By   Roger Lampkin,
            Attorney for Doug Donenabbed

DECLARATION OF COUNSEL

I, Roger Lampkin , declare:
1. I am an attorney at law and am the attorney for the defendant in this case.
2. I have represented Defendant for approximately nine months, have reviewed discovery, and conducted investigation and trial preparation.
3. Defendant indicated that he is unwilling to waive time for new counsel to review discovery I have already reviewed, and he wishes to continue with his current defense team. However, Defendant is unable to pay for continued representation.

I declare that the foregoing is true and correct.

Dated: _____

       By   Roger Lampkin,
            Attorney for Doug Donenabbed

MEMORANDUM OF POINTS AND AUTHORITIES

THIS COURT HAS COMPELLING AUTHORITY TO APPOINT DEFENDANT'S CURRENT COUNSEL AT COUNTY EXPENSE

"The right of a criminal defendant to counsel and to present a defense are among the most sacred and sensitive of our constitutional rights." (*People v. Ortiz* (1990) 51 Cal. 3rd 975, 982)

If a defendant who desires counsel is unable to afford counsel, the court must assign counsel to represent the defendant at public expense. (*Penal Code §987.2(a)*).

Penal Code §987.2 permits the court, in its discretion, to appoint counsel who previously represented the defendant. As the California Supreme Court stated in Ortiz, supra at 989, "Section 987.2, however, offers no barrier to appointment of previously discharged counsel." In the instant case, counsel has not been discharged by the Court. Rather, Defendant is unable to pay the cost of representation.

REQUESTED COUNSEL NEED NOT BE ON THE APPROVED COURT APPOINTMENT LIST OR COVERED BY A CONTRACT

Our Supreme Court has held that it is error for the trial court to limit the appointment of counsel to only those on an approved court list. In *People v. Chavez* (1980) 26 Cal. 3rd 334, an indigent defendant requested the appointment in the superior court of the same attorney that was appointed to represent him at the preliminary hearing. The superior court declined because the attorney was not on the superior court's approved list. The Supreme Court held:

> it is clear that the superior court in the present matter improperly adhered to a fixed policy of appointing its "own" counsel in every case. The exercise of the court's discretion in the appointment of counsel should not have been restricted by an inflexible rule, but rather should have rested upon consideration of the particular facts and interests involved in the case before it.

COUNSEL MAY WITHDRAW IF NOT PROPERLY COMPENSATED

"It is generally recognized that the failure or refusal of a client to pay or secure the proper fees or expenses of the attorney after being reasonably requested to do so will furnish grounds for the attorney to withdraw from the case" (*People v. Prince* (1968) 268 Cal. App. 2nd 398, 406).

Impressment of an attorney to perform pro bono publico work without compensation violates equal protection rights (*Cunningham v. Superior Court* (1986) 177 Cal.App.3rd 336, 347)

THE COURT ABUSES ITS DISCRETION IF IT FAIL TO APPOINT DEFENDANT'S CHOICE OF COUNSEL IF THAT COUNSEL HAS EXTENSIVE KNOWLEDGE AND EXPERIENCE RELATING TO THE CASE

The court abuses its discretion by refusing to appoint counsel who has "had extensive experience and knowledge relating to the charged crime" (*People v. Daniels* (1991) 52 Cal. 3rd 815, 845; Harris v. Superior Court (1977) 19 Cal. 3rd 786, 796-799). The reason for such a limitation on the court's discretion is grounded in judicial economy, but also on Defendant's rights to effective assistance and a speedy trial. If previous counsel is not appointed, new counsel must spend the time and expense of acquainting himself with the knowledge of the case already possessed by the previous counsel. Such a waste of time and money should be avoided.

As stated by the California Supreme Court in *People v. Ortiz* (1990) 51 Cal.

3rd 975, 989:

> [F]requently, as here, it may be a more efficient use of both time and money to appoint the attorney who represented the defendant in an earlier proceeding than to begin again with a new attorney.

The Supreme Court in *Harris v. Superior Court* (1997) 19 Cal. 3rd 786, 799 created an exception to the rule that a defendant is not entitled to an attorney of his own choosing, if there is a documentary showing of "objective" criteria supporting the appointment of a particular attorney. The court held:

[W]hen that statement of preference, timely made, is supported by objective considerations of the consequence here involved, and where there are no countervailing considerations of comparable weight, it is an abuse of sound judicial discretion to deny the defendant's request to appoint the counsel of his preference.

"In exercising its discretion, the trial court should take into account not only the foregoing subjective factors, but also objective factors such as previous representation of defendant by the requested attorney in the underlying or in any other proceeding, any extended relationship between defendant and the requested attorney, the familiarity of the requested attorney with the issues and witnesses in the case, the duplication of time and expense to the county of appointing an attorney other than the requested attorney, and the timeliness of the request." (*Alexander v. Superior Court* (1994) 22 Cal. App. 4th 901, 916).

Your Honor, if you like these twelve motions in limine, I'll have my paralegal bring a dozen more.

I. SERVICE OF PROCESS

A Criminal Defense Paralegal may be called upon the serve process.

Service of process is the formal delivery of a subpoena, summons, or other legal documents in a case to a person by someone who is not a party to the case. Simply put, you may be asked to deliver documents to someone.

On TV, service of process is often portrayed as a cat-and-mouse game where the process server chases down their target or must trick them into accepting papers, but this sort of drama is usually reserved for the screen.

In criminal cases, the process server most often will serve pleadings on the district attorney before filing the papers with the court. Most district attorney offices have a date stamp used to acknowledge receipt of papers, but for others you may be required to fill out a proof of service. Some district attorney offices also accept service of process by mail, e-mail, fax, drop box, or through other methods.

A Criminal Defense Paralegal may also be asked to serve subpoenas. Subpoenas are commonly served on law enforcement agencies, laboratories, and medical facilities. These places usually have an office designated to receive subpoenas, and this person will often use a date stamp to acknowledge receipt.

It is also common to serve subpoenas on favorable witnesses, such as a defendant's family members, who may need the subpoena to get an excuse from work, school, or other obligations. For these witnesses, you should complete a proof of service every time.

It is less common for a Criminal Defense Paralegal to serve process on a witness who is uncooperative, such as an alleged crime victim, but these persons may be hostile or may attempt to avoid service.

No matter who you are attempting to serve, you should conduct yourself in a professional, courteous manner. Instead of the dramatic, "you've been served!" common to TV, it is best to simply inform the person being served what they are being served with, such as, "I have papers for you from John Smith, the attorney for Jane Doe. The papers concern your appearance in court on May 1, 2022. His phone number is on the papers, and I've also brought you one of his cards so you can call him if you have any questions."

Notice that the statement does not tell the person that they are required to appear in court on the given date. That is up to the attorney and the court. Often, the person being served will simply have to produce papers and documents for the attorney or the attorney will put a person being subpoenaed "on call" so the person can continue with their daily routine until the attorney calls and lets the person know when their appearance in court will be needed. The date indicated on a subpoena is often the date a trial or other proceeding starts, so all witnesses are subpoenaed for that date, but in a criminal trial, most witnesses will be put on call and informed of the date they are needed a day or two before their testimony is expected.

Penal Code §1328 generally holds that a "subpoena may be served by any person" other than the defendant. However, *Business and Professions Code §22350* requires that a "person who makes more than 10 services of process within this state during one calendar year" must be registered or be exempt from registration. Fortunately, one of the exemptions is for "An attorney or his or her employees, when serving process related to cases for which the attorney is providing legal services."

"Substitute service" is serving a person other than the person named in the document to be served.

Penal Code §1328(b)(1) requires substitute service on the parent of a minor, and *Penal Code §1328(c)* allows for substitute service on a peace officer if service is made at least five court days in advance. Most law enforcement agencies have a subpoena coordinator or other designated person to receive subpoenas and coordinate court appearances.

Substitute service is also the norm when serving process on doctors, attorneys, and other professionals, and most will have a person in their office designated to receive service of process. If you try to serve papers at an office, someone on staff will often inform you that they are authorized to accept service for the person you are trying to serve.

For most types of documents, substitute service may also be used after making reasonable attempts to personally serve someone. If you are unable to serve someone on the first attempt, you should generally make at least two additional attempts at different times of the day at both the person's home and place of business, if known.

If you are still unable to deliver the papers, ask the attorney if you can do substitute serves by giving the papers to another adult at the person's home or place of business.

"[A]n individual may be served by substitute service only after a good faith effort at personal service has first been made: the burden is on the plaintiff to show that the summons and complaint 'cannot with reasonable diligence be personally delivered' to the individual defendant. [Citations.] Two or three attempts to personally serve a defendant at a proper place ordinarily qualifies as " 'reasonable diligence.' " " (*American Express Centurion Bank v. Zara* (2011) 199 Cal. App. 4th 383, 389.)

A person cannot actively avoid service of process by refusing to answer the door, stating that they are not accepting the documents, or running away from the process server. It is not uncommon for a person who does not want to be served to stand on the other side of a screen door and chat with a process server before saying that they will not accept the documents.

It is best not to argue; instead explain that you are just doing what you were told to do, and you will leave the documents for them in case they want to have a look. Make a note for the attorney of what happened, what was said, and where you left the documents in case service is challenged.

The court in *In re Ball* (1934) 2 Cal. App. 2nd 578, 579, found service of process proper in a related situation. The process server informed the defendant that he had " 'another one of those things for you,' " but the defendant moved away, so the process server threw a summons and complaint (the starting papers in a civil action) so that the papers fell a few feet away from the defendant. The court found that this was proper service and noted, "We take it that when men are within easy speaking distance of each other and facts occur that would convince a reasonable man that personal service of a legal document is being attempted, service cannot be avoided by denying service and moving away without consenting to take the document in hand."

In *Ludka v. Memory Magnetics International* (1972) 25 Cal. App. 3rd 316, the process server went into the defendant's offices but was denied access to the corporate officer, so the server threw the papers on a coffee table saying " 'You're served.' " and then mailed copies to the defendant. The court found service proper because the process server provided actual notice of the documents to the person who appeared to be in charge of the defendant's office and who had prevented the server from going inside the office.

"[P]re-1969 service of process statutes required strict and exact compliance. However, the provisions are now to be liberally construed to effectuate service and uphold jurisdiction if actual notice has been received by the defendant." (*Bein v. Brechtel-Jochim Group, Inc.* (1992) 6 Cal. App. 4th 1387, 1392)

However, anytime you serve someone who tries to avoid service, be sure to prepare a note or memo for the attorney. In civil actions, such as *Ball* and *Ludka*, the remedy against someone avoiding process may be to take a default judgement, but in a criminal case, there may be no reasonable remedy. The person served may face contempt charges or monetary sanctions, but your client, the defendant, may lose a valuable witness during trial.

→••Ω••←

J. OBJECTIONS

A Criminal Defense Paralegal should understand basic objections. Knowing types of evidence that are objectionable helps the paralegal understand motions, avoid putting objectionable material in pleadings, and prepare written objections for consideration by the attorney. Some of the more common objections include:

Relevance

> Evidence must be relevant. Evidence is relevant when it tends to prove or disprove a fact of consequence. (*Evidence Code §§210, 350, and 351.*)

352

> A trial judge may exclude relevant evidence if its probative value is substantially outweighed by its prejudicial effect. Evidence is prejudicial if it may bias the jury, confuse the jury, waste time, or unduly delay the proceeding. (*Evidence Code §352.*)

Facts Not in Evidence

> A question may not assume as true a fact that has not yet been introduced in evidence. For example, "when did you leave the crime scene?" assumes that the person was at a particular location and that a crime has been committed.

Foundation

> Closely related to Facts Not in Evidence, and sometimes interchangeable, is a foundation objection. An attorney cannot ask the witness to answer a question that lacks foundation. "What did you see the defendant do?" lacks foundation unless it is first established that the witness was present and could see something. (*Evidence Code §400, et seq.*)

Hearsay

> Hearsay is a statement made other than when the person is testifying that is offered for the truth of the matter stated. Hearsay is generally not admissible, but there are many exceptions. Also, an out of court statement that is not being offered to prove the truth of the statement

is not hearsay. (*Evidence Code §1200*; see further discussion of hearsay in the chapter entitled, *Select Legal Authorities*).

Example: Fred testifies that Wilma told him she saw defendant kill the victim. Fred's testimony is not admissible because it is being offered to prove that Wilma saw the defendant kill the victim.

Personal Knowledge

A witness may not testify to facts unless he personally observed the facts in some way. (*Evidence Code §403.*)

Narrative

Questions should be closed-ended and call for short answers on only one subject. A question that calls for a long explanation permits the witness to narrate and is impermissible.

Compound

A question with two subjects is compound and improper. "Did you go to the store and buy a soda?" is compound in that it is asking the witness whether he went to the store and whether he bought a soda.

Speculation

A question that invites the witness to speculate or guess the answer, such as "What was he thinking?" or "What did he do after you left?" The witness cannot know the answer to either of these questions, but can make a logical guess. Such guesses are not allowed, no matter how logical.

Beyond the Scope

A witness first faces direct examination by the party who called the witness to testify. When the other party cross-examines the witness, questions are limited to the topic raised by the first party and matters that would tend to impeach the witness.

Calls for a Conclusion

Witnesses must testify to facts, not their opinion as to the facts. It is the duty of the jury or the judge to form conclusions based on the facts as presented. It is, therefore, wrong for a witness to state a conclusion, such as "the defendant murdered that man" or "the defendant was driving drunk."

Best Evidence

A party trying to prove the contents of a writing can do so by producing the original document or by producing some secondary evidence of the document. However, this secondary evidence cannot be used if "A genuine dispute exists concerning material terms of the writing and justice requires the exclusion" or "Admission of the secondary evidence would be unfair." A Best Evidence objection is claiming that the secondary evidence is inadmissible for one of these two reasons.

In Limine

Objection indicating that a party is violating the court's previous rulings made during hearing of motions in limine.

Vouching

Objection indicating that an attorney is personally vouching for the credibility of a witness.

Unresponsive

The witness's answer is nor responsive to the question asked.

→••Ω••←

Practical Tip: Ask how to do it instead of doing it wrong.

It may be difficult to admit you do not know how to do a task, especially if it is something you have done in the past. Your employer may get a bit upset if you ask how to do a task that you have already been trained to do, but she will probably be a lot more upset if you do it wrong.

Take for example, Mark. Mark was asked to file an ex parte request for appointment of expert that had been prepared by another paralegal. To complete the task, he just needed to make copies, put them in an envelope, and deliver them to the ex parte clerk, but Mark forgot the procedure.

Instead of asking how to do it, he processed the ex parte as a regular motion, served the Prosecution, and filed the motion in the felony department. This gave the prosecution advanced knowledge of the defense expert and strategy, and it caused the ex parte to be returned unsigned.

K. SAMPLE LETTERS

1. Notice of representation

Roger Lampkin
1234 L Street
Bakersfield, CA 93301
(661)633-1234

Pollak County District Attorney
5678 Court Street
Pollak, CA 91111

Attn: Deputy District Attorney John Jones

Dear Mr. Johnson,

Please, take notice that this office represents David Davis in the matter of People v. Davis, BF123456A. I request that discovery materials and all further communications regarding this matter be directed to my attention.

Thank you for your assistance in this matter.

Sincerely,

Roger Lampkin

2. Request for discovery

Roger Lampkin
1234 L Street
Bakersfield, CA 93301
(661)6331234

Pollak County District Attorney
5678 Court Street
Pollak, CA 91111

Attn: Deputy District Attorney John Jones
Re: People v. Davis, BF123456A.

Dear Mr. Johnson,

On behalf of Defendant David Davis, I request that, not later than fifteen days from the date of this informal request, you disclose to the defense all discovery required by *Penal Code §1054.1*, included, but not limited to:

1. Prosecution trial witnesses

The name and address of every person the prosecution reasonably anticipates they are likely to call as a witness at trial.

2. Statements of all defendants

Every oral, written, or recorded statement of each defendant, whether that statement is exculpatory, inculpatory, or neutral.

3. Statements of all witnesses

Every written or recorded statement of each person the prosecution reasonably anticipates they are likely to call as a witness at trial.

4. Real evidence

All real evidence seized or obtained as a part of the investigation of the offenses charged.

5. Prosecution trial exhibits

An opportunity to examine all real evidence, including charts, diagrams and other exhibits, whether obtained as part of the investigation of the offenses charged or not, that the Prosecution intends to display to the jury in any way.

6. Felony convictions

The existence of each felony conviction of every defendant and every witness, including every defense witness whose identity is disclosed to the Prosecution.

7. Prosecution expert witness reports

Every oral, written, or recorded report or statement made in conjunction with this case by any Prosecution expert.

8. Prosecution examinations and tests

The results of any physical or mental examinations, scientific tests, experiments or comparisons conducted by any member of the Prosecution team.

9. Social media evidence

If the Prosecution has examined or collected any social media evidence, all documents used for production of items, including but not limited to search warrants, description of items sought, affidavits for procurement, and copies of all items seized including but not limited to statements, certificates, or affidavits of persons from social media companies including but not limited to custodian(s) of records who in any way vouched for the authenticity of any item produced. The defendant further demands all metadata related to any photos or other postings.

10. Exculpatory evidence

Any and all exculpatory evidence within the meaning of *Brady v. Maryland* (1963) 373 U.S. 83, including but not limited to the following:
    A. Any evidence that directly counters the defendant's guilt.
    B. Any evidence of third-party culpability for a charged offense.
    C. Any evidence that may tend to affect the credibility of a material prosecution witness, including:
        a. Conflicting statements of a prosecution witness.
        b. Pending criminal charges against a prosecution witness.
        c. Explicit or implied promises, offers, or inducements to a prosecution witness.
        d. The parole or probation status of a prosecution witness.
        e. Misconduct of a prosecution witness involving moral turpitude, whether resulting in a conviction or not.
        f. Prior false reports to law enforcement by a prosecution witness.
        g. Prior false or inaccurate statements or reports by a prosecution witness.
        h. Any evidence contradicting a prosecution witness statement or report.
    D. Evidence that supports the expected defense testimony as disclosed to you through reciprocal discovery under *Penal Code §1054.3.*
    E. Evidence that would mitigate the Defendant's punishment if convicted.

11. 911 calls

Any and all 911 recording and all logs related to such recordings.

12. DNA testing results and raw data

All reports and evidence related to DNA analysis including but not limited to photographs, reports on quality variance, reports on findings, bench notes, and raw DNA files.

13. Dispatch records

All records of law enforcement communications including recordings and logs related to those communications.

14. Photographs

All photographs related to this case in any way.

15. Warrants

All arrest and search warrants in any way related to the investigation or preparation of this case, and all supporting documents and orders related thereto.

16. Gang evidence

Any and all evidence tending to indicate that Defendant is a gang member or has any connection to any gang member, including, but not limited to street checks, gang packets, gang files, cases in which Defendant has been used as part of a predicate, PowerPoint or other presentations that include or refer to Defendant, any list of documented gang members (however maintained) alleging that Defendant was a gang member on or before the date of the crime charged herein, a list of all persons alleged to be in a gang with Defendant, and any photograph of Defendant maintained by law enforcement as part of a group of photographs interrelated to gang activity.

Thank you for your assistance in this matter.

Sincerely,

Roger Lampkin

3. Transmittal of discovery

Note: The attorney does not have to give a defendant all the discovery in a case. There are some items that the attorney, and consequently the paralegal as a member of the defense team, cannot physically give a defendant because of custody status, such as CDs. There are some items the attorney cannot legally give the defendant, such as witness identifying information. For other discovery, it is generally discretionary whether the attorney gives it to the defendant or not. Use this letter as a sample to transmit discovery to a defendant. Read the section in this book labeled "Discovery" prior to providing discovery to anyone other than members of the defense team.

Roger Lampkin
1234 L Street
Bakersfield, CA 93301
(661)633-1234

John Jones
5678 Main Street
Bakersfield, CA 93301

Re: People v. Jones, BF123456A discovery

Dear Mr. Jones,

Enclosed are the following documents related to your case.

1.   Photographs of the alleged crime scene
2.   Photographs of each item of evidence seized.
3.   Reports from the Bakersfield Police Department

You will notice that pages in the reports are numbered 1 of 23, 2 of 23, 3 of 23, etc. but not all 23 pages have been provided, and you will notice that some matters have been blacked out. These omissions and redactions are required by state and federal law.

Sincerely,

Paralegal Paula

4. Notice of team member

Roger Lampkin
1234 L Street
Bakersfield, CA 93301
(661)633-1234

John Jones
5678 Main Street
Bakersfield, CA 93301

Re: People v. Jones, BF123456A team members

Dear Mr. Jones,

Mr. Lampkin has secured the services of Private Investigator Thomas Magnum to assist with your case. He is a member of the defense team, so your communications with him are confidential.

Please, remember Mr. Lampkin's instruction to not discuss your case with anyone except the members of your defense team.

Sincerely,

Paralegal Paula

L. SELECT LEGAL AUTHORITIES

Evidence Code §350

No evidence is admissible except relevant evidence.

Evidence Code §351

Except as otherwise provided by statute, all relevant evidence is admissible.

Evidence Code §352

The court in its discretion may exclude evidence if its probative value is substantially outweighed by the probability that its admission will
(a) necessitate undue consumption of time or
(b) create substantial danger of undue prejudice, of confusing the

issues, or of misleading the jury.

Evidence Code §402

(a) When the existence of a preliminary fact is disputed, its existence or nonexistence shall be determined as provided in this article.
(b) The court may hear and determine the question of the admissibility of evidence out of the presence or hearing of the jury; but in a criminal action, the court shall hear and determine the question of the admissibility of a confession or admission of the defendant out of the presence and hearing of the jury if any party so requests.
(c) A ruling on the admissibility of evidence implies whatever finding of fact is prerequisite thereto; a separate or formal finding is unnecessary unless required by statute.

Evidence Code §1200

(a) "Hearsay evidence" is evidence of a statement that was made other than by a witness while testifying at the hearing and that is offered to prove the truth of the matter stated.
(b) Except as provided by law, hearsay evidence is inadmissible.
(c) This section shall be known and may be cited as the hearsay rule.

There are many exceptions to the hearsay rule that allow hearsay statements to be introduced into evidence. Some of the more common exceptions include:

- *Evidence Code §1220* - Admission of party, such as a defendant's statements
- *Evidence Code §1230* – Declaration against interest, such as a confession or claim of gang membership.
- *Evidence Code §1235* – Inconsistent statements. A witness's prior statement that contradicts his current testimony can be used against him.
- *Evidence Code §1236* – Prior consistent statements. If a witness's credibility is attacked by showing inconsistencies in his testimony, evidence may be presented to show that the witness previously gave the same version of events.
- *Evidence Code §1237* – Past recollection recorded, such as a report written at the time of an incident that contains details of the incident the witness no longer recalls.
- *Evidence Code §1238* – Prior eye witness identification.
- *Evidence Code §1240* – Spontaneous statement, such as "he shot her!"

- *Evidence Code §1241* – Statement made by declarant explaining his conduct, such as, "I'm going to the store."
- *Evidence Code §1242* – Dying declaration. Statements from a person who believes they are dying regarding the cause of death.
- *Evidence Code §§1250, 1251* – Statement of the speaker's state of mind, such as "I'm tired" or "my leg hurts."
- *Evidence Code §1253* – Statements to medical professionals.
- *Evidence Code §§1271, 1280* – Business records, such as a hotel receipt or a birth certificate.
- *Evidence Code §1291* – Former testimony, such as statements made during a preliminary hearing.
- *Evidence Code §1320, 1324* – The general reputation of a person.
- *Evidence Code §1350* – Statements from a witness made unavailable by the defendant. If a defendant makes a witness unavailable, the witness's prior statements may be used against the defendant.

Penal Code §977

(a)(1) In all cases in which the accused is charged with a misdemeanor only, he or she may appear by counsel only, except as provided in paragraphs (2) and (3). If the accused agrees, the initial court appearance, arraignment, and plea may be by video, as provided by subdivision (c).

(2) If the accused is charged with a misdemeanor offense involving domestic violence, as defined in Section 6211 of the Family Code , or a misdemeanor violation of Section 273.6 , the accused shall be present for arraignment and sentencing, and at any time during the proceedings when ordered by the court for the purpose of being informed of the conditions of a protective order issued pursuant to Section 136.2 .

(3) If the accused is charged with a misdemeanor offense involving driving under the influence, in an appropriate case, the court may order a defendant to be present for arraignment, at the time of plea, or at sentencing. For purposes of this paragraph, a misdemeanor offense involving driving under the influence shall include a misdemeanor violation of any of the following:
(A) Subdivision (b) of Section 191.5 .
(B) Section 23103 as specified in Section 23103.5 of the Vehicle Code.
(C) Section 23152 of the Vehicle Code.
(D) Section 23153 of the Vehicle Code.

(b)(1) Except as provided in subdivision (c), in all cases in which a felony is charged, the accused shall be personally present at the arraignment, at the time of plea, during the preliminary hearing, during those portions of the trial when evidence is taken before the trier of fact, and at the time of the imposition of sentence. The accused shall be personally present at all other proceedings unless he or she shall, with leave of court, execute in open court, a written waiver of his or her right to be personally present, as provided by paragraph (2). If the accused agrees, the initial court appearance, arraignment, and plea may be by video, as provided by subdivision (c).

(2) The accused may execute a written waiver of his or her right to be personally present, approved by his or her counsel, and the waiver shall be filed with the court. However, the court may specifically direct the defendant to be personally present at any particular proceeding or portion thereof. The waiver shall be substantially in the following form:

"Waiver of Defendant's Personal Presence"

"The undersigned defendant, having been advised of his or her right to be present at all stages of the proceedings, including, but not limited to, presentation of and arguments on questions of fact and law, and to be confronted by and cross-examine all witnesses, hereby waives the right to be present at the hearing of any motion or other proceeding in this cause. The undersigned defendant hereby requests the court to proceed during every absence of the defendant that the court may permit pursuant to this waiver, and hereby agrees that his or her interest is represented at all times by the presence of his or her attorney the same as if the defendant were personally present in court, and further agrees that notice to his or her attorney that his or her presence in court on a particular day at a particular time is required is notice to the defendant of the requirement of his or her appearance at that time and place."

(c)(1) The court may permit the initial court appearance and arraignment of defendants held in any state, county, or local facility within the county on felony or misdemeanor charges, except for those defendants who were indicted by a grand jury, to be conducted by two-way electronic audiovideo communication between the defendant and the courtroom in lieu of the physical presence of the defendant in the courtroom. If the defendant is represented by counsel, the attorney shall be present with the defendant at the initial court appearance and arraignment, and may enter a plea during the arraignment. However, if the defendant is represented by counsel at an arraignment on an information in a felony case, and if the defendant does not plead guilty or nolo contendere to any charge, the attorney shall be present with the defendant or if the attorney is not present with the defendant, the attorney shall be present in court during the hearing. The defendant shall have the right to make his or her plea while physically present in the courtroom if he or she so requests. If the defendant decides not to exercise the right to be physically present in the courtroom, he or she shall execute a written waiver of that right. A judge may order a defendant's personal appearance in court for the initial court appearance and arraignment. In a misdemeanor case, a judge may, pursuant to this subdivision, accept a plea of guilty or no contest from a defendant who is not physically in the courtroom. In a felony case, a judge may, pursuant to this subdivision, accept a plea of guilty or no contest from a defendant who is not physically in the courtroom if the parties stipulate thereto.

(2)(A) A defendant who does not wish to be personally present for noncritical portions of the trial when no testimonial evidence is taken may make an oral waiver in open court prior to the proceeding or may submit a written request to the court, which the court may grant in its discretion. The court may, when a defendant has waived the right to be personally present, require a defendant held in any state, county, or local facility within the county on felony or misdemeanor charges to be present for noncritical portions of the trial when no testimonial evidence is taken, including, but not limited to, confirmation of the preliminary hearing, status conferences, trial readiness conferences, discovery motions, receipt of records, the setting of the trial date, a motion to vacate the trial date, and motions in limine, by two-way electronic audiovideo communication between the defendant and the courtroom in lieu of the physical presence of the defendant in the courtroom. If the defendant is represented by counsel, the attorney shall not be required to be personally present with the defendant for noncritical portions of the trial, if the audiovideo conferencing system or other technology allows for private communication between the defendant and the attorney prior to and during the noncritical portion of trial. Any private communication shall be confidential and privileged pursuant to Section 952 of the Evidence Code .

(B) This paragraph does not expand or limit the right of a defendant to be personally present with his or her counsel at a particular proceeding as required by Section 15 of Article 1 of the California Constitution .

Penal Code §995

...the indictment or information shall be set aside by the court in which the defendant is arraigned, upon his or her motion [if] the defendant had been committed without reasonable or probable cause.

Penal Code §1054.1

The prosecuting attorney shall disclose to the defendant or his or her attorney all of the following materials and information, if it is in the possession of the prosecuting attorney or if the prosecuting attorney knows it to be in the possession of the investigating agencies:
(a) The names and addresses of persons the prosecutor intends to call as witnesses at trial.
(b) Statements of all defendants.
(c) All relevant real evidence seized or obtained as a part of the investigation of the offenses charged.
(d) The existence of a felony conviction of any material witness whose credibility is likely to be critical to the outcome of the trial.
(e) Any exculpatory evidence.
(f) Relevant written or recorded statements of witnesses or reports of the statements of witnesses whom the prosecutor intends to call at the trial, including any reports or statements of experts made in conjunction with the case, including the results of physical or mental examinations, scientific tests, experiments, or comparisons which the prosecutor intends to offer in evidence at the trial.

Penal Code §1054.2

(a) (1) Except as provided in paragraph (2), no attorney may disclose or permit to be disclosed to a defendant, members of the defendant's family, or anyone else, the address or telephone number of a victim or witness whose name is disclosed to the attorney pursuant to subdivision (a) of Section 1054.1, unless specifically permitted to do so by the court after a hearing and a showing of good cause.
(2) Notwithstanding paragraph (1), an attorney may disclose or permit to be disclosed the address or telephone number of a victim or witness to persons employed by the attorney or to persons appointed by the court to assist in the preparation of a defendant's case if that disclosure is required for that preparation.

Persons provided this information by an attorney shall be
informed by the attorney that further dissemination of the
information, except as provided by this section, is prohibited.
(3) Willful violation of this subdivision by an attorney, persons
employed by the attorney, or persons appointed by the court is a
misdemeanor.

(b) If the defendant is acting as his or her own attorney, the court
shall endeavor to protect the address and telephone number of a
victim or witness by providing for contact only through a private
investigator licensed by the Department of Consumer Affairs and
appointed by the court or by imposing other reasonable
restrictions, absent a showing of good cause as determined by the
court.

Penal Code §1054.3

(a) The defendant and his or her attorney shall disclose to the
prosecuting attorney:
(1) The names and addresses of persons, other than the defendant,
he or she intends to call as witnesses at trial, together with any
relevant written or recorded statements of those persons, or
reports of the statements of those persons, including any reports or
statements of experts made in connection with the case, and
including the results of physical or mental examinations, scientific
tests, experiments, or comparisons which the defendant intends to
offer in evidence at the trial.
(2) Any real evidence which the defendant intends to offer in
evidence at the trial...

Penal Code §1382

(a) The court, unless good cause to the contrary is shown, shall order
the action to be dismissed in the following cases:
(1) When a person has been held to answer for a public offense
and an information is not filed against that person within 15
days.
(2) In a felony case, when a defendant is not brought to trial
within 60 days of the defendant's arraignment on an
indictment or information... However, an action shall not be
dismissed under this paragraph if either of the following
circumstances exists:
(A) The defendant enters a general waiver of the 60-day trial
requirement...

    (B) The defendant requests or consents to the setting of a
        trial date beyond the 60-day period…

  (3) Regardless of when the complaint is filed, when a defendant
      in a misdemeanor or infraction case is not brought to trial
      within 30 days after he or she is arraigned or enters his or her
      plea, whichever occurs later, if the defendant is in custody at
      the time of arraignment or plea, whichever occurs later, or in
      all other cases, within 45 days after the defendant's
      arraignment or entry of the plea, whichever occurs later…
      [unless the defendant waives time as noted above]…

Penal Code §1473

(a) A person unlawfully imprisoned or restrained of his or her liberty,
    under any pretense, may prosecute a writ of habeas corpus to
    inquire into the cause of his or her imprisonment or restraint.

(b) A writ of habeas corpus may be prosecuted for, but not limited to,
    the following reasons:

  (1) False evidence that is substantially material or probative on the
      issue of guilt or punishment was introduced against a person at
      a hearing or trial relating to his or her incarceration.

  (2) False physical evidence, believed by a person to be factual,
      probative, or material on the issue of guilt, which was known
      by the person at the time of entering a plea of guilty, which
      was a material factor directly related to the plea of guilty by the
      person.

  (3)

      (A)New evidence exists that is credible, material, presented
      without substantial delay, and of such decisive force and value
      that it would have more likely than not changed the outcome
      at trial.

      (B) For purposes of this section, "new evidence" means
      evidence that has been discovered after trial, that could not
      have been discovered prior to trial by the exercise of due
      diligence, and is admissible and not merely cumulative,
      corroborative, collateral, or impeaching.

(c) Any allegation that the prosecution knew or should have known of
    the false nature of the evidence referred to in paragraphs (1) and
    (2) of subdivision (b) is immaterial to the prosecution of a writ of
    habeas corpus brought pursuant to paragraph (1) or (2) of
    subdivision (b).

(d) This section does not limit the grounds for which a writ of habeas
    corpus may be prosecuted or preclude the use of any other

remedies.

(e)

(1) For purposes of this section, "false evidence" includes opinions of experts that have either been repudiated by the expert who originally provided the opinion at a hearing or trial or that have been undermined by later scientific research or technological advances.

(2) This section does not create additional liabilities, beyond those already recognized, for an expert who repudiates his or her original opinion provided at a hearing or trial or whose opinion has been undermined by later scientific research or technological advancements.

Note that a habeas corpus petition can be used to challenge the validity of a conviction or the conditions of confinement at the jail. *Penal Code §1473* is included in this book because there are so many inquire about it, but a habeas corpus petition is almost always the wrong thing to file prior to a defendant being convicted and appealing the conviction.

Penal Code §1538.5

(a) (1) A defendant may move for the return of property or to suppress as evidence any tangible or intangible thing obtained as a result of a search or seizure on either of the following grounds:

(A) The search or seizure without a warrant was unreasonable.

(B) The search or seizure with a warrant was unreasonable because any of the following apply:

(i) The warrant is insufficient on its face.

(ii) The property or evidence obtained is not that described in the warrant.

(iii) There was not probable cause for the issuance of the warrant.

(iv) The method of execution of the warrant violated federal or state constitutional standards.

(v) There was any other violation of federal or state constitutional standards...

M. ABOUT BAKERSFIELD PARALEGAL

Bakersfield Paralegal assists litigants who represent themselves by employing Licensed Document Assistants to prepare pleadings in family law, unlawful detainer, guardianship, probate, and other types of cases.

In addition, Bakersfield Paralegal conducts legal research and prepares pleadings for attorneys in criminal cases, including motions, petitions, writs, and appeals. They also assist with criminal trial preparation, including organizing and reviewing discovery, coordinating and assisting with lay and expert witnesses, and case management.

Bakersfield Paralegal has clients in Bakersfield and throughout the state.

N. ABOUT THE COMMENTATOR

Roger Lampkin earned his bachelor's degree from University of Texas at Austin. His Juris Doctor degree is from South Texas College of Law where he was editor of the Law Review, and where he was an adjunct professor after graduation. Mr. Lampkin became an attorney in Texas in 1973 and in California in 1984. He has published various award-winning articles. After coming to California, he was an adjunct professor in a California law school and taught a legally orientated course at California State University.

From 1973 to 1987, Mr. Lampkin was in the legal department of major oil companies supervising outside counsel in substantial litigation. He entered private practice in 1987 and has offices in Bakersfield and Taft. He is licensed to practice in Texas, California, and Federal Courts. His successful representation of thousands of clients has included extensive trial experience; where he learned the importance of pretrial motions and became highly skilled at preparing and arguing all necessary and essential motions. A trial may be won or lost at the motions stage, when the "ground rules" for the conduct of trial are set, so Mr. Lampkin brings an abundance of motions in almost every case.

Mr. Lampkin is an author of three editions of *California Criminal Defense Motions in Limine* and one edition of *Handbook for the Accused*. He is a contributor to several other books.

Made in the USA
Las Vegas, NV
24 February 2024

86175182R00184